BUDGETING, AUDITING, AND EVALUATION

Comparative Policy Analysis Series
Ray C. Rist, Series Editor

Program Evaluation and the Management of Government,
edited by Ray C. Rist

Budgeting, Auditing, and Evaluation,
edited by Andrew Gray, Bill Jenkins, and Bob Segsworth

BUDGETING, AUDITING, AND EVALUATION

Functions and Integration in Seven Governments

Edited by

Andrew Gray
Bill Jenkins
Bob Segsworth

With a foreword by
Ray C. Rist

Transaction Publishers
New Brunswick (U.S.A.) London (U.K.)

350.723
B927

Library of Congress Catalog Number: 92-14731
ISBN: 1-56000-071-6
Printed in the United States of America

Library of Congress Cataloging-in-Publication Data
Budgeting, auditing, and evaluation : functions and integration in seven governments / edited by Andrew Gray, Bill Jenkins, Bob Segsworth
    p. cm.
  Includes bibliographical references and index.
  ISBN 1-56000-071-6
  1. Budget. 2. Finance, Public—Auditing. I. Gray, Andrew. II. Jenkins, Bill. III. Segsworth, Bob.
HJ2043.B92   1992
350.72'32—dc20

qP   92-14731
                                                CIP

Publisher's note: All chapters have been edited to conform to standard American spelling.

Contents

Foreword

There happens, in instances that are few and far between, that the publication of a book defines a field, establishes the intellectual framework for further discussion, and brings together in a coherent picture that which heretofore has been blurred. Such is my reaction to the present volume. What we are presented with here is a thorough set of studies on the relation of budgeting, auditing and evaluation that now allow us to see the international contour in a way that we previously have been unable to do. Seven country-specific analyses are juxtaposed and the comparisons and contrasts come into sharp relief. It is to the credit of the authors that they have written with detail and clarity that provides straightforward and unambiguous descriptions of the relations of budgeting, auditing, and evaluation in each country. The individual country portraits are painted with care.

To ask the question on the relation among these three functions of government is to address a new and intriguing problem. There is no tradition in any of the seven countries to presume that the integration of these functions is to be taken for granted, or even pursued. One of the strongest messages to come from the papers is that the autonomy of these functions is both historical in nature and institutional in form. Yet it is also clear that the nature of governmental responsibilities are changing and that the status quo will no longer hold. Thus, these three key functions of central government, budgeting, auditing and evaluation, are finding themselves being pushed closer and closer together. The marriage may be arranged, and the partners may not be enamored of one another, but the societal and institutional pressures to make it work are strong. Indeed, divorce does not even seem to be an option; the pressures are building on governments to constrain public spending more effectively, manage public resources better, select the appropriate policy tools, and then implement successfully. As a result, the question is not *whether* to integrate these functions of government, but rather, *how*.

It has to be said immediately and in defense of the authors that this volume does not seek to answer the how question. Rather, it addresses the antecedent question of what now exists and how the present conditions have come to be. Their contribution, and it is no small one, is to describe what forces have shaped the present institutional arrangements in the seven countries. It is from this perspective, then, that we are able to assess the distance yet to be traveled in each country toward more integration of these functions, assuming in each instance it is important to do so. The how question is framed by Gray and Jenkins in the concluding chapter where they ask, once the horse had been led to water, how do you get it to drink. These two authors thus begin the discussion on the question of the feasibility of integration and what political and institutional forces are at work to both encourage and inhibit such movement.

The authors in this volume are not on a bandwagon of governmental integration for its own sake. They have no ideological agenda here to push governmental restructuring because of any a priori assumptions. Rather, they seem especially attuned to the historical and legal precedents for the present set of arrangements. Stated differently, the present arrangements are not seen as deficits to be corrected. Indeed, there is clear sensitivity to the structural realities that have generated current separations and even conflicts. Each of the seven countries discussed here is Western in its value systems and democratic in its forms of political expression. That Spain is a recent addition on the latter point only adds to the interest in including it here. Thus it is to expected that in the pursuit of democratic systems of governing, there would be both hesitation and suspicion in creating central governments of too much power and too much rationalization. There is, as it were, an implicit assumption among the citizens of democratic societies that the preservation of liberty and freedom necessitates some checks and balances on central governments. In each of the cases presented here such constraints exist and are not lightly dismissed.

The strength of the papers comes in the recognition of this tension between the need for structural change to respond to the political and economic forces that are sweeping the globe and the particular historical and institutional arrangements in each of our respective societies. The argument for bringing more closely together the functions of budgeting, auditing and evaluation is thus made both on the grounds of enhancing governmental responsiveness within the context of both domestic and international pressures and in the context of stressing greater accountability of present efforts to be both economically competitive and more prudent stewards of public resources. Indeed, one can argue that the pressure to consolidate and integrate these functions comes from a growing concern about perceived weaknesses in the present institutional arrangements, not from perceived strengths that need to be checked through more stringent oversight.

Some Thoughts on Methodology

As I prepared to write this foreword, I searched for comparative material on budgeting, auditing and evaluation. I was able to find material on each individually, but none on the interrelations among the three. Thus, the unique contribution of this book.

I am not sure which is the most robust of several possible explanations of present dearth of comparative material, but the following are offered. First, there are few institutional bases from which such work can be done. It is difficult to conceive of an individual academic researcher being able to conduct a comparative study of such magnitude where the collection of original data is involved. Gathering the necessary information in one country is difficult; expecting to locate it in seven (as here), let alone ten or twenty countries, is beyond the possibility of most individual researchers. Perhaps a team of researchers at one university or study center could amass the funds and time to conduct such work. But I could locate a few instances in which comparative work had been conducted on these governmental functions.

This leads to the presumption that international organizations are the groups best placed to conduct such work. Here there is the possibility of bringing together teams of researchers from different countries to address comparative questions. This strategy permits the creation of an agreed-upon framework that allows for roughly parallel contributions from all involved. Unfortunately, few do on a systematic and sustained basis. The IIAS which has sponsored this present work and the OECD are isolated examples to the contrary.

A second possible explanation focuses on the state of case study research in different countries. The case study methodology in general is not applied from a common set of assumptions across countries. Thus, in the absence of a special effort such as this present volume, it would be hard to aggregate studies that are country-specific, but beginning from different premises or methodological assumptions. Stated differently, the ability to develop a comparative evaluation synthesis or meta-summary on these central government functions, based on whatever one is fortunate to find in the research literature, is a highly unlikely probability.

Third, there is an explanation from the vantage point of the sociology of knowledge. Comparative analysis on the three government functions of interest here has not been broadly based because these are functions that heretofore have not have much need or pressure to learn from one another. So long as each country was sovereign unto itself and more or less economically independent, the need for systematically learning from others was minimized. A new era has forced a shift in perspective where questions about how other nations are conducting their budgeting, auditing and evaluation functions are now seen to be both legitimate and relevant. On a new playing field where no one has previous experience, it is well to study alternative strategies and game plans. This is a situation now facing all industrialized and developed countries. It would, from this vantage, be surprising if there was not more comparative work because of the necessary information to be gained on how others are trying to sustain current policy processes and develop new policy options. Add to this the need to become much more sophisticated in all aspects of government operations and no country can afford to say it knows all it needs to know.

A fourth (and here last) possible explanation has to do with the nature of these three fields as areas of intellectual inquiry. There are sizable numbers of persons in each of these three areas that see themselves as practitioners, as hands-on types that are more concerned with the activity itself than with the development of theoretical underpinnings for what is done. Each of these three areas are thought to be, by most of its members, applied areas where success comes from the actual conduct of the activities for which one is so trained. Spending time on research, especially comparative research that may be perceived to have little relevance to the day-to-day conduct of one's craft, is simply of little interest. Further, the disciplines provide little inducement or recognition for doing so: journals for the respective fields carry few articles describing comparative research, professional meetings devote few sessions to comparative findings, and the number of graduate level courses on comparative study are few and far between. The end result is the creation of a pragmatic, applied, and country-specific craft.

But lest I be misunderstood, none of these explanations is to be thought of as negative or derogatory. Rather, they are logical and plausible explanations for three government functions that, until recently, worked rather well in their isolation both from one another and from colleagues in the same field, but in a different country. That independence (and lack of interdependence) now appears counterproductive both within and between countries. Such is the central tenant of this present book and a key rationale for its preparation. The authors are to be commended for their efforts to begin the comparative analysis and to reframe the questions we ask. They have pried open for all of us a window on the integration of government functions that has too long been closed.

RAY C. RIST

United States General Accounting Office

The views expressed here are those of the author and no endorsement by the United States General Accounting Office is intended or should be inferred.

Acknowledgment

The contributors wish to record their appreciation of the encouragement and support of the International Institute of Administrative Sciences in the writing of this book.

1

Perspectives on Budgeting, Auditing, and Evaluation: An Introduction

Andrew Gray, Bill Jenkins, and Bob Segsworth

As governments the world over edge toward the twenty-first century, there is increased interest in the prudent use of resources to sustain public policy and to develop much-needed policy initiatives. Further, as many industrialized countries struggle to come out of recession, the need for better budgetary management and the evaluation of both past and prospective policies has been seen by many practitioners and observers as central to restore or retain economic growth. Hence, in areas as diverse as those of Scandanavia, the European Community, North America, and Australasia, governments have sought to achieve more effective control and management of public expenditure and to plan and evaluate public policy. To all this can now be added the recent dramatic events in Eastern Europe where many countries, faced with the challenge of developing and sustaining a market economy, have turned to the West for advice and assistance in reforming their public expenditure and policy planning processes.

The International Institute for Administrative Sciences (IIAS) is keenly concerned with all these matters. As an international organization devoted to the study and improvement of public administration and management, it seeks through its conferences, workshops, and sponsorship of research to improve the quality of public administration, to promote dialogue between different national groups on a variety of important issues and to act as a catalyst for organizational and institutional learning within the international political and administrative community.

1

As part of these efforts, the IIAS has sponsored a Working Group on Policy and Programme Evaluation. Over a number of years, this group has sought to study and advance the cause of policy evaluation from an international perspective. Its early work involved the study of the development of policy and program evaluation in a variety of countries. This sought to examine both the causes and consequences of individual national developments in policy evaluation and to promote comparative understanding (Rist 1990a, 1990b). Encouraged by these studies, the group extended its interests by focusing, first, on the utilization of evaluation and the connection between policy evaluation and organizational learning and, second, the relationships between budgeting, audit, and evaluation.

This book is devoted to an exploration of this second focus. For some time, individual members of the IIAS Working Group have been aware of the importance of the links between auditing and evaluation (e.g., Rist 1989). In its early work, moreover, the group noted that in many countries state audit offices played a significant role in the development of the evaluation function (Derlien 1990). This was particularly so in the development of performance or value-for-money (VFM) auditing. Thus, although auditing was frequently institutionally and functionally different from evaluation in many countries, it generated information that could affect on budget decisions. In addition, efforts to develop policy evaluation often had strong connections with national budgetary processes. However, national experiences differed and these required investigation.

It was therefore decided to explore this area in greater depth. Initially the members of the Working Group concentrated on describing the budgetary processes of their respective countries. They viewed auditing and evaluation as activities that generated information about (and thus could have an effect on) government programs and their management. In other words budgeting, auditing, and evaluation were elements of an interactive process that informed government decision making. What functions were performed by each and how interactive or integrated they had become in different countries seemed unexplored. Thus this volume brings together different national experiences of the development and linkages of budgeting, auditing, and evaluation and seeks to make some comparative statements of the consequences of these for the policy process. What follows in this introductory chapter develops the logic for this decision, identifies the major common points of interest, and, finally, details and explains the contents of the book.

Budgeting, Auditing, and Evaluation: Convergent or Divergent Processes?

The primary concern of most governments over the past three decades has been the *control* of public expenditure and the *planning* of policy. Budgeting, auditing, and evaluation have been significant instruments. Through budgets differing activities can be managed, coordinated and planned; through audit financial control and the accountability of resource use can be ensured; and through evaluation economy, efficiency and effectiveness can be promoted. Even if political cultures and environments mediate and influence different national patterns in fundamental ways, budgeting, auditing and evaluation have been used by governments to strengthen *control, planning* (and learning) and *accountability* in the policy process. These functions have been regarded as central both to the cohesion of the political system and the sustaining of economic growth.

Is any of this really new? After all, any cursory examination of political history shows that budgeting, auditing and evaluation have origins that are linked fundamentally to national political traditions. Budgeting, for example, has always been at the heart of the political process and may in fact be the expression of politics itself since it is in the budget that the questions of "who gets what, when and how" are determined. As a result, the role of finance ministries has a traditionally strategic position affecting their relationships with other departments and the processes through which these operate (Heclo & Wildavsky 1981).

Auditing, too, has its history. Indeed there may be a case for seeing the auditor as one of the oldest professionals in government, and audit as a process of deep historical significance. This is certainly true for many European countries such as Germany, where the legal tradition gives audit a role distinct from that in other countries and affects the interrelationships with budgeting and evaluation (see Ch. 4 below). In contrast, policy evaluation may not have such a long historical pedigree as a separate activity in its own right, with identifiable evaluators and a professional community. Rather, it might be seen as part of an "enlightenment" process developed in tandem with rational planning and reflecting a particular view of "good" government and "good" administration. As such its developmental path and underlying ideology may differ from the processes of budgeting and auditing already discussed.

It is important therefore to recognize that the processes of budgeting, auditing and evaluation in individual countries may reflect different patterns of political development and different political and administrative traditions. It may well be that, over the last twenty years, these processes have converged in particular national contexts. This has been justified in terms of better policy making and resource allocation. However, to prescribe specific patterns of integration for budgeting, auditing and evaluation is to deny the importance of national contexts and conditions in favor of a rationalist utopian vision that there is "one best way" of political and policy development.

In this volume we will explore the possibility of this integration and assess its effects on the policy process of different national political systems. In doing so, however, we are as interested in differences as in similarities. In particular we wish to explore how differences in political history and culture, changing political and economic environments, and in the internal politics of resource allocation and management have influenced developments. Before this can begin, however, we must address the definitional problems posed by the key concepts we are investigating and then elaborate theoretical approaches that have been and could be used to interpret them.

Budgeting, Auditing, and Evaluation: Meanings and Interpretations

Rose has argued that in comparative analysis "we need generic concepts that are not restricted in time or place" (1990). In dealing with budgeting, auditing and evaluation this may take some realizing. In any gathering of practitioners and administrators concerned with public policy and management there would be little dispute that budgeting, auditing and evaluation were important parts of political life. Whether there would be similar agreement on formal definitions, however, might be another story. Certainly the experience of the IIAS Working Group has suggested that an attempt to move from general descriptions to precise definitions of these processes immediately reveals a variety of concepts and usage. This is not surprising. If budgeting, auditing and evaluation are developed in different political cultures by different political communities, their definitions and interpretations will reflect the contexts from which they emerge. This may be true within as well as between countries and even where there have been attempts to forge professional communities with common professional languages. Audit is a good example here. The International Organisation of Supreme Audit Institutions (INTOSAI) has attempted to develop international standards for audit. It has sought to define the remit of audit tightly with specific (although to some narrow) conceptualizations of terms such as effectiveness and accountability. Audit may also be defined as an essentially legal process and thus exclude evaluation from its remit on the grounds that the setting of objectives is a political matter. But precisely because the policy process matters, it is possible to see audit as a much broader function of the accountability of public policy management.

Thus, the *meanings* and *interpretations* of concepts such as budgeting, auditing and evaluation may reflect important differences in professional and political cultures. In turn, these differences may be central to any understanding of differing patterns of development. Language and terminology are not neutral; rather, they reveal particular meanings and ideologies. The development and dominance of particular ways of looking at the world is reflected in such language and this is central to the problems this book seeks to discuss. For example, the recent strengthening of state audit in countries as varied as the United Kingdom, Finland and Canada may reflect a common attempt to strengthen public sector management in a particular way using terminology drawn from private sector practice. In contrast, the development of state audit in Germany is very different, possibly indicating the influences of political history and culture that has channeled growth down a different path. These complexities may go some way toward explaining why it would be misleading to force the concepts of budgeting, auditing and evaluation into a narrow definitional framework. However, some elucidation is necessary if only to provide the reader with a benchmark against which to characterize the usages of the following chapters

Budgeting and Budgets

Perhaps nowhere is the conceptual variation clearer than in the case of budgeting, where both practical experience and academic analysis indicate a multifunctional activity for most nation states and indeed most large organizations. Budgeting, as defined by most central finance ministries, refers to the raising and allocating of public expenditure. This is usually regarded as both historical and dynamic, i.e. it takes place over time and is influenced by changing internal and external political environments and history (Likierman 1988; Wildavsky 1975). For some, however, budgeting is solely allocatory, i.e., the process through which the annual resource cake is cut between the competing claims of departments or agencies. For others again, it is only concerned with revenue raising; in the United Kingdom, for example, the Chancellor of the Exchequer's Budget is limited to raising revenue, the decisions on expenditure having been pronounced four months earlier, a peculiarly perverse British custom!

Regardless of definition, however, the product of budgeting is a statement that sets out the results of the decision-making process. This might be taken as the simple outcome of a rational process. Yet, as a variety of academic commentators have established, not only is the budget a multipurpose document but the very process of budgeting is a multifunctional activity in a political system (Wildavsky 1975; Brown-John et al 1988). Just as budgets serve planning, coordination, control, and motivation in the management of public policy, at the most basic level the budgetary process acts as a mechanism for integrating differentiated interests into the regularities of the political process.

As a consequence budgeting is not only a process that seeks to install *economic efficiency* in the political process but also a major mechanism for ensuring *political efficiency* by acting to resolve competing interests. This book begins with the assumption that budgeting describes the process whereby government funds are distributed among competing interests. It is therefore concerned with how this system has developed, who the major actors in the process are and what criteria are used to resolve the choices the process throws up. We are also crucially interested in the links (if any) between this system and the processes of auditing and evaluation and the consequences of these relationships for the making and development of public policy.

Auditing and Audits

In some ways auditing is more easily defined than the other major terms we deal with. Caldwell (1983), for example, argues that the scope of audit may include financial matters, compliance relationships and the performance of operational controls and programs. However, we observe in common currency a somewhat wider definition going beyond the simple independent examination of the adequacy of records, information and control systems to include such other assessments as administrative adherence to prescribed rules and policies, the fairness of financial statements and performance reports and the efficiency and effectiveness of programs and operations (Knighton 1975).

A distinction may be made between *internal audit*, a quasi-independent but internally staffed service for departmental management, and *external audit*, performed by independent bodies often attached to sovereign legislatures. The latter's visibility, through such supreme audit bodies as the General Accounting Office in the United States or the Riksrevisionsverket in Sweden, has perhaps led to some underestimation of the role of internal audit. Traditionally internal audit's task, at least as spelled out by government audit manuals, is to appraise the soundness of accounting and financial controls (attest auditing), promote compliance with established policies and procedures (compliance auditing), ensure that safeguards against losses are in place, and check the integrity and reliability of financial information (Likierman 1988, Ch. 8).

Traditionally both internal and external audit have concentrated on the attest and compliance functions (Thomas 1988) on the grounds that these are "reasonably objective" and thus more likely to be regarded as legitimate (Siegal 1986). However, more recently this notion of objectivity has been challenged by a contention that auditing is essentially normative, assessing "what is against what ought to be" (Rist 1990c, p. 10; see also Chelimsky 1985). This idea has caused unease among the auditing profession especially when the scope of audit is extended from *financial* and *compliance* audits to *value-for-money* and *comprehensive* audits that may have, as part of their scope, a concern for the efficiency and effectiveness of government programs. For many, moving from a mandate that may be served by objective analysis to one in which analysis may challenge policy threatens the neutrality of the auditor (Hopwood 1984). Further, there is a fear that audit has neither the skills nor methods to operate in this field; the search for comprehensive auditing may thus be akin to that for "fool's gold" (Thomas 1988). Clearly performance and value-for-money audits involve much more than financial regularity. In dealing with efficiency, auditors may be functioning as if they were management consultants and when they deal with effectiveness, especially in terms of policy and program matters, they may be close to becoming policy analysts or indeed policy evaluators.

As we shall see in later chapters, evaluation is being used increasingly to inform budgetary allocation decisions. This implies at least an indirect integration of audit with both evaluation and budgeting. This is clearly a crucial development. As a result, in some countries audit has been obliged to make rapid changes not always to the liking of the audit profession (e.g. in UK and Canada). In others, audit has remained very much a traditional activity confined by its past and by the political and legislative climate in which it has developed. This book seeks to identify and explain the variety of roles of audit in different national contexts and its relationships with the development of evaluation and budgeting.

Policy and Program Evaluation

But if audit is changing, what of policy evaluation? In particular how has this been defined and how has the activity evolved? Evaluation cannot claim the historical pedigree of audit, nor is it such a systemized part of the political and budgetary process of most national governments. In contexts such as the United States and Canada, however, there have been attempts to professionalize evaluation both through the establishment of professional bodies and setting standards for the scope of evaluation practice (Rossi 1982). At its simplest, program evaluation may be seen as the ex-post assessment of a program's achievement against preset objectives. However, as the evaluation literature demonstrates, this simple definition has been extended to include not only ex-ante evaluations (now often labeled policy analysis) but also developmental evaluations, program monitoring and the evaluation of evaluation itself (Rossi 1982).

This development has been charted and analysed by Rist (1990c), who distinguishes between prospective (or policy) analysis and the retrospective nature of program and policy evaluation. He also notes that evaluation has become more sophisticated and potentially useful to policy makers as the type and number of methodologies used in evaluation has expanded. This leads him to the conclusion that policy evaluation has become of vital importance to decision makers, since evaluations can close the learning loop in the policy process, i.e., by feeding into the policy cycle the information obtained from evaluation studies.

This perspective is another important starting point for this book. Much of the literature has indicated a failure of incrementalism in budgetary systems to contribute to effective learning. This interpretation of incrementalism can of course be challenged (Lindblom 1979). Nevertheless, the central issue for the work of the IIAS group has been the extent to which evaluation has been incorporated into the budgetary processes of various countries, the reasons for this, and the consequences for the budgetary process of any evaluative role for audit.

In a utopian world it might be assumed that the integration of budgeting, auditing and program evaluation would lead to political system stability and effectiveness. However, this neglects potential paradoxes. It has been argued, for example, that the development of an evaluative role for audit could threaten political system stability and that the rationalizing of the budgetary process could threaten the internal coherence of political systems (Wildavsky 1975). Although these points are not addressed in detail here, they indicate that the contribution of budgeting, auditing and evaluation to political system development is problematic and that patterns of fragmentation between these activities may be as important as those of integration. Nevertheless, it remains necessary to explore the theoretical frameworks that might be useful in cross-national comparisons.

Theoretical Perspectives

From the outset the IIAS group has been concerned with the theoretical and methodological problems of mapping the patterns of development observed in individual countries and comparatively. A variety of frameworks have been considered: a traditional institutional approach, a systems or structural-functional model and a developmental model of the budgetary process. In this section we touch on the first two and consider the third in more detail.

In the first instance it may be possible to assess the differential developments of budgeting, auditing and evaluation from the perspective of traditional institutional political analysis. The countries examined in this volume include parliamentary and presidential systems (Canada and USA), unitary and federal states (UK and Germany), and strong and weak party systems (UK and Spain). There are also sharply differing historical traditions encompassing states with a strong legalistic tradition (Germany) and those distinguishing parliamentary and executive audit functions (Finland and Sweden). Such differences can form the basis of a comparative developmental analysis. How far such comparisons can explain the variety of experiences reported remains to be established as the chapters proceed.

In contrast, a more conceptual view of the political world could be adopted drawing on the systems ideas of Easton (1953) and Almond and Powell (1966). Such structural-functional models of political systems have, of course, been heavily criticized and consequently their utility as a basis for comparative political analysis may well be limited. However, the processes of budgeting, auditing and evaluation contribute to political system maintenance and growth not least by strengthening control, managerial and learning functions. However, it is also possible that certain combinations of these activities may be dysfunctional given particular sets of political circumstances. For example, a search for greater efficiency may in fact destabilize rather than stablize political system operations, especially if it is at the expense of public accountability. At this stage this point should be taken as speculative, but it has been raised for example by UK government departments seeking to minimize the influence of the supreme audit body, the National Audit Office. Greater powers for the NAO, it is argued, threaten the efficiency and legitimacy of government.

The idea that budgeting is a changing activity serving a number of essential functions in political system development has been put forward by Schick (1986, 1988, 1990). A model that emerged from his early work on budgetary behavior in the U.S. national and state systems has been extended to the international context via work on OECD countries such as the United States, Canada, United Kingdom, France, Germany and Australia. In these studies Schick seeks to explain changes in patterns of *budgeting development* over time in different national contexts and in changing economic and political circumstances. Although his principal focus is on budgets and budgeting, his cross-national work also examines the use of evaluation and the role of audit. These ideas are clearly relevant to our current investigations.

The basis of Schick's analysis is relatively simple. From his earlier work in the USA he sees budgeting as a developing process moving from what he terms an immature to a mature system. At the heart of this development is the ability of budgetary processes to contribute to three functions crucial to political system maintenance: control, management and planning.

For Schick successful *control* mechanisms are essential to basic budgetary development. These involve the establishment of line-item budgeting and strong internal accounting systems. Audit plays a central role through its focus on financial inputs. However, control does not ensure either stability or budgetary system development. Rather, there is a need to integrate activities and to ensure the efficient conduct of operations to maximize the benefits from programs and policy. Schick therefore argues that development demands the addition of a *management* function to the control function. Quoting post-World War II experience in the United States, he notes the development of mechanisms to ensure operational efficiency and cross-government integration. These drew on cost-accounting and scientific management to help transform the budgeting culture. Yet, even these changes did little to relate budgetary inputs to outputs, i.e., to examine program effectiveness or to install a feedback loop into the resource allocation system.

The third phase of Schick's model therefore involves the forging of a *planning* function within the budgetary system. Through the evolution of techniques such as Planning, Programming and Budgeting Systems (PPBS), this phase sought to rationalize both policy making and the budgetary process. It also saw the introduction of policy analysts and evaluators into the political system. This reform set the seal on what Schick terms a mature budgetary system, i.e., one in which all three functions, control, management and planning, are firmly embedded. These mature systems need no longer be reformed. Rather, they must adapt to changing circumstances.

The difficulty with Schick's analysis is that the era of mature systems appears to have been brief. Experiments such as PPB appear to have had a limited shelf life and the last decade or so has seen many national governments, especially in the OECD countries, reassert resource management and control at the expense of planning. Schick's response to this is that it has been necessary for nation states to cope with a new financial environment that emphasized fiscal restraint (1986, 1988, 1990). Mature systems have been able to adapt to this, for example via cutback mechanisms, the shortening of budgetary time horizons and the adoption of rigorous financial management strategies (1986, p. 125). Thus the 1980s and 1990s has been an era of financial management with the accompanying development of an appropriate culture within government to reflect this fiscal environment. In such a world Schick argues that planning still exists but that it differs from the heady days of PPBS and rational planning. Instead, planning now corresponds very much to the tenets of Management by Objectives (MbO) and management accounting, i.e., there is an emphasis on productivity measures, delegated budgets, targets and short-time horizons. Thus the idealistic position of the 1970s has been replaced by the more pragmatic stance of the 1990s.

Despite these qualifications, there remain good reasons for being cautious with Schick's analysis. First, it is developed from rather a narrow and ethnocentric empirical base. Thus, while his later studies inolve cross-national comparisons, his developmental model is based almost exclusively on U.S. experience. Second, and consequent on this, the model is deterministic in form and tone, leaving little room for any understanding of immature systems or budgetary systems that do not fit neatly into this categorization. Further, it tends to oversimplify the relationships between budgetary strategy and political structure. Why particular budgetary arrangements are adopted at particular times is not a knee-jerk reaction but a process that reflects particular sets of political and historic circumstances.

Yet, if these points are correct, why pursue Schick's ideas at such length in this particular context? Accepting the criticisms made above, the authors of the chapters in this volume nevertheless found diagnostic value in viewing budgeting as a system in which control, management and planning were important functions, and auditing and evaluation as processes reflecting dominant values in the political system. Such a perspective does not assume an integration of budgeting, auditing and evaluation as either likely or necessarily desirable but rather assesses why particular combinations have emerged at particular points in time. Thus, rather than looking for a mature system it assumes a plurality of systems and seeks to explain the implications of these differences.

Budgeting, Auditing, and Evaluation in Seven Governments: Suggested Themes

The foregoing discussion suggests three sets of themes that may be followed by a reading of the chapters presented in this volume. First, it is clear that there is a range of *functions* that budgeting, auditing and evaluation may perform in different countries. Specifically, we might expect a variety of *budgetary* emphases on resource planning and control. Accounts of how particular emphases come to be made will be worth noting. Similarly, *auditing* may range from a concern with accountability, thus emphasizing regularity of expenditure, to a comprehensive feedback facility in which the economy, efficiency, and effectiveness of expenditures and their programs are adjudicated. *Evaluation* may range from similarly limited ex-post concerns with checking up on the progress and appropriateness of programs to include more elaborate ex-ante assessments of program and expenditure choices. All these functions may vary between the countries portrayed here and over time.

A second theme is the *pattern of integration* of budgeting, auditing and evaluation. Our conclusion will seek to determine the extent to which in the countries studied there is logical, organizational, social and informational integration. *Logical* integration refers to the mutual consistency of the products of budgeting, auditing and evaluation; *organizational* integration is their structural and processual coming together through the allocation of authority and function and the regularities of decision making and control; *social* integration refers to the homogeneity of officials who facilitate these processes, a homogeneity achieved through common backgrounds and/or training; and *informational* integration is the sharing of data, the processes by which they are translated into information and then disseminated. The chapters might not be expected to offer observations or insights on all these equally but the developments of budgeting, auditing and evaluation seem at least to beg the question of the extent and ways in which they have become integrated in the different systems of management described here.

Finally, the functions and especially the integration of budgeting, auditing and evaluation imply the satisfaction of *preconditions for effective operation*. The group's deliberations have suggested at least four sets. There must be *technical* compatibility of skills, systems and data, *organizational* structures and processes that facilitate and promote functionality and effective linkages, *political* mechanisms for registering and resolving differentiated needs and interests, and *legal* procedures for enabling flexible responses to the changing demands on budgeting, auditing and evaluation.

Although the editors believe there is ample material in the following chapters to sustain a healthy curiosity in these themes, they offer an analytical health warning. The countries portrayed here have not been selected according to an a priori scheme. Rather, they are the products of coincidental interest among the group of auditors and academics brought together under IIAS auspices. Further, each chapter has been written primarily with the aim of describing and explaining one country's practice. The group is still, at least in the work represented here, seeking to familiarize itself with the history and practice of its member countries (although more recent work has set out to trace themes *across* countries). It has been up to the individual authors to determine the extent to which it makes sense in the context of portraying their own systems to develop explicitly the themes outlined above. As the conclusion will show, it has been up to the editors to offer the comparative observations.

The chapters begin with accounts from countries that may be seen as representing distinct governmental traditions: the United States of America, the United Kingdom and the Federal Republic of Germany. The United States represents a presidential federation, powers separated between the branches of government, weak political party discipline and a traditional emphasis on the management of government. David Mathiasen's chapter takes as its focus the budgetary process in such a disaggregated structure and links the auditing and evaluative developments to it. This suggests an important integrating function for the budget itself within the govermental system generally.

The United Kingdom, on the other hand, represents quite a different context: parliamentary and unitary with a fusion of the powers of the branches of government, supported (if that is quite the word) by strong party discipline just in case any cracks should emerge. Gray and Jenkins portray arrangements (they can hardly be said to be a system) that not only suggest a fragmentation of budgeting, auditing and evaluation but even within each of these. If the United States suggests a fragmented superstructure there is evidence of an integrating process at work, while in the United Kingdom the most integrated structure of government (at least of the countries studied here) is associated with the most fragmented processes.

The Federal Republic of Germany represents a different model again. Derlien portrays a system rooted in a tradition of public law and an evolution from an absolutist state to a parliamentary democracy. Thus, many of the provisions of budgeting and auditing are enshrined in constitutional provisions and their functions reflect historical circumstance. Evaluation has developed more recently and more pragmatically. Thus, although there are connections between budgeting and auditing on the one hand and policy making and evaluation on the other, German practice is essentially two-track.

The next four chapters, on Canada, Spain, Sweden and Finland, reflect various combinations of influences of the American, British and German models within their own unique context. Canada has inherited much of the British parliamentary practice but has fashioned a synthesis of this with the structures and processes of its southern neighbor, including a separation of auditing and comptrolling functions. Perhaps this explains why Segsworth is most able to make use of Schick's developmental model cited above. But he concludes that Canada is still an immature system and developments in budgeting, auditing and evaluation have not evolved in any logical sequence and remain unsynchronised.

For many European observers, Spain is perhaps the most fascinating case of all those dealt with here. Still only a decade and a half from its emergence from dictatorship it has experienced a cascade of reforms emphasizing the European tradition of public law but, as Zapico points out, without yet paying much attention to organizational and administrative cultures. The result is a pattern of budgeting, auditing and evaluation characterized by elaborate procedures, strong legal rationality, but little facility for organizational or program development through learning.

In the conclusion to the IIAS group's first publication, Derlien suggested that Sweden was one of the earliest countries to develop systematic policy and program evaluation but that its efforts were rather fragmented. As Sandahl shows, one of the distinguishing features of the Swedish system of government is the separation of the executive responsibility for program delivery from the policy formulating ministries. This is mirrored in a further separation of the audit function between the supreme audit function related to the legislature and the audit of agencies carried out by ministries. An intriguing experiment is under way, however, in the new three-year budgetary plan and, although he is cautious in making too early a judgment, Sandahl finds some prospect of effective integration of budgeting, auditing and evaluation therein.

This integration could be reflected in Sweden's neighbor, Finland, from which it has inherited many constitutional provisions including a system of public law. But, as Ahonen and Tammelin point out, the Finnish context is much more diverse than this would imply. Prior to independence, both Swedish and Russian influences were central, with the latter continuing to be important economically. Finland has developed a noticeable Nordic model of the welfare state but its system of public management has borrowed many Anglo-American practices. But, for Ahonen and Tammelin, this shift from the cameral tradition so evident at the beginning of the century has not been coherent. Constrained by competing traditions and influences and one of the most severe economic recessions suffered by any European country, Finnish government has "muddled through" to a set of arrangements in which budgeting is only "loosely coupled" with auditing and evaluation.

These miniature portraits of the countries discussed in this volume can offer only a glimpse at both the diversity and commonality of their experiences and practices. In the conclusion we will attempt a more systematic comparison based on the themes we have outlined here.

References

Almond, G.A., and G.B. Powell. (1966). *Comparative Politics: a Developmental Approach*. Boston: Little Brown & Co.

Brown-John, C., A. Leblond, and D. Marson. (1988). *Public Financial Management: A Canadian Text*. Scarborough: Nelson.

Caldwell, K. (1983). "Operational Auditing in State and Local Government." in R. Golembiewski and J. Rabin, eds., *Public Budgeting and Finance*. 3d Ed. New York: Marcel Dekker.

Chelimsky, E. (1985). "Comparing and Contrasting Auditing and Evaluation: Some Notes on Their Relationship." *Evaluation Review* 9(4).

Derlien, Hans-Ulrich (1990). "Genesis and Structure of Evaluation Efforts in Comparative Perspective," chap. 9 in Ray C. Rist, ed., *Program Evaluation and the Management of Government*. New Brunswick, N.J.: Transaction Publishers.

Easton, D. (1953). *The Political System*. New York: Alfred A. Knopf.

Heclo, H. and A. Wildavsky (1981). *The Private Government of Public Money*. 2d Ed. London: Macmillan.

Hopwood, A. (1984). "Accounting and the Pursuit of Efficiency," chap. 9 in A. Hopwood and C. Tomkins eds., *Issues in Public Sector Accounting*. Oxford: Philip Allan.

Knighton, L. (1975). "An Integrated Framework for Conceptualising Alternative Approaches to State Audit Programs," in R. Golembiewski and J. Rabin eds), *Public Budgeting and Finance*. New York: Marcel Dekker.

Likierman, A. (1988). *Public Expenditure: The Public Spending Process*. Harmondsworth: Penguin Books.

Lindblom, C. (1979). "Still Muddling, Not Yet Through." *Public Administration Review* 39: 517-26

Rist, R. C. (1989). "Management Accountability: The Signals Sent by Auditing and Evaluation." *Journal of Public Policy* 9(3): 355–69.

Rist, R. C. (ed) (1990a). *Program Evaluation and the Management of Government: Patterns and Prospects across Eight Nations.* New Brunswick, N.J.: Transaction Publishers.

Rist, R. C. (ed) (1990b). *Policy and Program Evaluation: Perspectives on Design and Utilisation.* International Institute of Administrative Sciences (IIAS).

Rist, R. C. (1990c). "Managing of Evaluations or Managing by Evaluations: Choices and Consequences," chap. 1 in R. C. Rist ed., *Program Evaluation and the Management of Government.* New Brunswick, N.J.: Transaction Publishers.

Rose, R. (1990). *Prospective Evaluation Through Comparative Analysis: Youth Training in a Time-Space Perspective.* Studies in Public Policy No. 182, University of Strathclyde.

Rossi, P. (ed) (1982). *Standards for Evaluation Practice.* San Fransisco: Evaluation Research Society and Jossey Bass.

Schick, A. (1986). "Micro-budgetary Adaptation to Fiscal Stress in Industrialised Democracies." *Public Administration Review* 46(2): 124–34.

Schick, A. (1988). "Micro-budgetary Adaptation to Fiscal Stress in Industrialised Democracies." *Public Administration Review* 48(5): 523–33.

Schick, A. (1990). "Budgeting for Results: Recent Developments in Five Industrialised Countries." *Public Administration Review* 50(1): 26–34.

Siegal, D. (1986). *Value for Money Audit: Two Perspectives.* mimeo.

Thomas, P. (1988). "Effectiveness Reporting and Auditing: A Search for Fool's Gold?." *IPAC Bulletin* 11(6).

Wildavsky, A. (1988). *Budgeting: A Comparative Theory of the Budgetary Process.* 2d ed. Boston: Little Brown.

2

The Separation of Powers and Political Choice: Budgeting, Auditing, and Evaluation in the United States

David Mathiasen

In the United States, budgeting, auditing and evaluation grew out of different traditions. Now, however, they seem to be converging, not into a neat rational pattern, but in a politically driven way. Auditing is associated with the institution of the General Accounting Office (GAO), even though for many years most detailed audit work has been done internally by agencies and departments themselves. It is also associated with the Office of Management and Budget (OMB) and budgeting because GAO and the Bureau of the Budget, OMB's predecessor, were created by the same law in 1921. In fact, while modern budgeting in the United States at the national level did originate with that act, auditing grew out of a much older tradition.

Evaluation is much more recent, developing from the operations research techniques of the 1960s. At its inception it was associated with the budget process. However, to an increasing extent GAO has focused its efforts on program evaluation, often couched superficially in the terminology of the auditor. Today GAO does far more evaluation work than audit work, and is more active in this area than OMB. In fact during the past decade OMB has relied more heavily on broad principles of public policy, such as the use of free market incentives or assigning roles to various levels of government under the U.S. federal structure, than on evaluation to determine budget priorities.

The linking of evaluation with the budget process implies that evaluation results will influence funding levels. There are, of course, other reasons to conduct evaluations. In fact most evaluations in the United States are probably aimed at improving program effectiveness rather than at increasing or decreasing funding levels. Budgeteers, of course, care about program effectiveness, but ultimately their role is to determine spending priorities, and if evaluations are not relevant to that process they are not going to be of great interest. As a result, in this chapter evaluation is considered as a tool to influence spending levels.

This chapter attempts to follow these trends and to draw some conclusions about how evaluation and auditing relate to the contemporary budget process.

The U.S. Budget and Audit System

The two most permanent features of the U.S. governmental system, i.e., a federal structure and a separation of powers among the executive, the legislature, and the courts, have heavily influenced the audit, evaluation and budget process. Since a modern budget and auditing process was set up by the Budget and Accounting Act of 1921, the president presents to Congress a comprehensive budget plan annually. This plan is the result of a comprehensive executive branch review of individual agency spending requests. It also reflects economic projections and policies developed jointly by the Treasury, the President's Council of Economic Advisors (CEA), and the Office of Management and Budget (OMB). The budget is assembled for the president by OMB, and he then transmits it to Congress. However, as an independent branch, Congress may alter that plan as it sees fit. In so doing it deals with a combination of permanent spending law (such as Social Security), annual appropriations (which are contained in thirteen separate bills), and some spending laws that come up for periodic, but not annual, renewal. Examples of the latter are the national highway program and agricultural commodity price supports. To become law, any single piece of legislation must be signed by the president. If he fails to do so it becomes law only if it is approved by a two-thirds majority of each house of Congress. Once the legislation is passed it is up to the executive branch to carry out the programs.

Both Congress and the Executive have strong interests in audit and evaluation, but they are different. Congress is interested in seeing that its legislated requirements are being honored and that the Executive is properly carrying out its responsibilities. The latter is interested in its employees obeying the laws and in appearing to be effective and responsible. It is also formally responsible for seeing that its actions are legally correct, since the attorney general, who is a member of the president's Cabinet, is responsible for federal law enforcement and prosecution, including the prosecution of federal employees. Both branches of government are normally interested in the effectiveness of programs, although their definition of effectiveness may differ. In some instances the executive branch may be responsible for administering a program that it believes is wasteful, low priority, or undesirable.

Many domestic programs that are either fully or partially financed with federal funds are carried out by other levels of government. This reflection of the federal system of government adds another level of complexity to issues of compliance with the laws and program effectiveness.

The audit tradition in the federal government predated the modern budget process, and indeed went back to the founding of the nation. Initially, the audit responsibility was in the Treasury, part of the executive branch. However, the same law that established the modern budget process also moved these functions to the General Accounting Office. It was viewed by some as an independent body and by others as an agent of Congress. Its head, the comptroller general, is appointed by the president and confirmed by the Senate, but is removable only by Congress. In 1986, the Supreme Court resolved the ambiguity and ruled that the GAO is a legislative branch agency.

The existence of the GAO did not eliminate executive branch audit functions. Rather, over the years executive agencies have strengthened their own audit activities. Most recently, during the 1980s, all major federal agencies were required by law to establish Offices of Inspectors General. Thus, the first line of defense against financial irregularities and program mismanagement is with federal agencies themselves, partly in order to protect themselves from criticism by the GAO. As an agency of Congress reporting to committees and members of Congress, its reports are a potential source of embarrassment. The GAO itself evolved from a voucher audit agency first, to a financial management agency in the 1950s and then to an audit and evaluation agency under Comptroller General Elmer Staats in the 1960s and 1970s (Havens 1990). The standard outline of the U.S. budget process is shown in Table 2.1. However, the above description of the development of the institutions involved makes it clear that such a textbook description of the budget and evaluation process is simplistic.

Table 2.1 Formal Budget Process

September	Agencies submit budget to OMB.
November	OMB informs agencies of allocations.
December	Final presidential decisions.
January	President submits budget to Congress.
March - October	Congress hold hearings and passes budget legislation.
October 1	Fiscal year begins. Agencies obligate funds.
September 30	Fiscal year end. Audit activity begins.

Budget decision making has become a very messy process in the United States. It often takes place well outside the boundaries of the official timetable and the form and nature of decisions may vary from year to year and may be difficult to predict.

Because of this, and because of the separation of powers between the branches of government, the evaluation and audit processes often do not fit into a regular cycle. Evaluation may be at the instigation of the OMB, of an agency, of a committee of Congress or of another unit of government. It may not fit into the annual budget cycle, not least because many program evaluations take too long to do that. Moreover, evaluations and audit results may not be treated as entirely objective. Users of evaluations may be suspicious of their sources. Administration officials, for example, may react to GAO evaluations as criticisms that are politically motivated or designed to be needlessly embarrassing to the administration. Congressional committee members may distrust administration evaluations as being self-serving or superficial. As in the case of a major education program evaluation documented below, administration officials may even distrust its *own* evaluation if it is carried out because of congressional requirements or not controlled by political officials.

Attitudes towards audits are similar. Executive branch agencies want audit functions to prevent improper actions, but the same agencies may feel the legal requirements imposed by Congress are too strict and be tempted to evade them. Certainly if there are some adverse findings they want to keep them quiet and limit political damage. The GAO normally reports adverse findings to members of Congress or its committees, which in turn will publicize them to encourage corrective action. In some instances, some members or committees of Congress may share a common interest with the executive branch in minimizing publicity of adverse fundings. (This was the case with some members of Congress in connection with the savings and loan association failures of the 1980s).

For the most part, audit and evaluation activities in executive branch agencies are seen as quite separate. The first are designed to detect poor or illegal management practices. The second are designed to determine the degree to which programs meet their objectives. In the legislative branch, the GAO tends to see these as complementary activities, based on the notion that a well-managed program (including good financial management) is clearly linked with the ability to achieve program goals.

The Origins of Evaluation

The linkage between modern evaluation and the national budget process in the United States grew out of the Planning, Programming, and Budgeting System (PPBS) installed in the Defense Department by Secretary Robert McNamara, the Ford Motor Company vice-president appointed by President Kennedy. The Defense Department was a loose and uneasy association of the three main services: the Navy, the Air Force, and the Army. It was clear (to civilian analysts at least) from the invasion of Europe and the Korean War that approaching defense strategy on a service-by-service basis was not very effective. Moreover, the new analytical challenges, i.e., guerrilla and thermonuclear warfare, did not fit neatly into the traditional land-sea-air distinctions. Under McNamara the new civilians in the department approached defense budgeting in terms of what they called major missions, combining the forces of the services in ways that were designed to optimize the role of each in contributing to that mission.

This was, of course, an exercise in the allocation of resources. These resources were provided in the form of appropriations by Congress to the individual military services.[1] The originators of PPBS, as it soon became known, contemplated restructuring the appropriations to coincide with major missions. However, they were unable to convince the congressional committees on appropriations of the merits of doing so. As a result, to this day the PPBS decision system and the allocations of resources through appropriations are structured fundamentally differently, and linking the two is a complex task.[2]

It was this PPBS approach that President Johnson ordered adopted by the civilian agencies, and with it a new government-wide emphasis on evaluation. Henceforth, agencies would have to articulate their program goals in specific, preferably quantified, results, and conduct evaluations to measure the degree to which these results were achieved.

These origins reveal much about the relationships between budget, evaluation, and audit at the inception of the government-wide evaluation movement. The clear implication of the Defense Department application of PPBS was that the "experts" (i.e., the military heads of the uniformed services) no longer had the final word on how to prepare for armed conflict. Indeed, because their expertise was linked so closely to a particular service, they could not be expected to bring objectivity and purely rational analysis to the table. Now analytically armed civilians, using tools of operations research and microeconomics, could second-guess the military on the most profound question of the peacetime military: what to buy. It was, of course, just a matter of time before microeconomists would feel quite comfortable moving into domestic areas, and, for example, telling physicians how a national health system, or even a hospital, should be run.

It is also clear that originally audit and evaluation were not linked. Indeed, in the case of defense, the fundamental difference in the accounting structure of defense missions and congressional appropriations made the audit issues irrelevant to the programming process. But there was more to it than that. Evaluation was part of a new culture in which the audit questions were not relevant. Auditors would ask, for example, whether a field trip was properly conducted; that is, were the tickets purchased according to prescribed regulations, and at the lowest price. Auditors might even ask if the trip itself was necessary. To the program evaluator the question was were the program goals achieved. The audit questions were seen as quite separate.

This was a time, of course, when government was part of the solution, not the problem. The civil service reform movement had not eliminated corruption, but at least created a rebuttable premise that the mechanics of administration were well known and could be safely left with professional administrators. The auditors belonged to that community of administrators. Their concern for the proper and efficient use of funds was tied closely to line item (or object class, as it is called in the U.S. system) budgeting. Under this approach, how much you spent for travel *did* matter. However, it was an approach that a new generation of analysts were trying to get away from. It was an era where the perceived shortage was in economists and operations research experts, not in honest and competent managers. It was a time when new efforts to improve government were cast quite seriously in terms of learning to ask the right questions.

The audit tradition was deeply rooted in the GAO. As an agency of Congress, it reflected the different cultural origins of audit and evaluation functions that were reinforced by the separation of powers doctrine central to the system of government in the United States. The constitution requires that "no money shall be drawn from the treasury, but in consequence of appropriations made by law". Thus, all expenditures must satisfy strict requirements that they are in the amounts and for the purposes laid down in statutes. This encourages auditors to ask, as their first question, not "was the program effective in achieving policy goals?" or even "was the program efficiently managed?" but rather "was the expenditure of funds in accordance with law?"

The Evolution of Evaluation 1965–1980

The development of the new methodologies of evaluation coincided with a burst of new activities for social purposes under the auspices of President Johnson's "Great Society" programs. Earlier President Franklin Roosevelt's "New Deal" had greatly expanded the scope of the federal government through new direct federal operations: the national Social Security system, the Tennessee Valley Authority (an agency that took over economic development in seven states) and a national price support system for farmers and many others. In the 1960s, Johnson's new Great Society programs took advantage of another major feature of the U.S. governmental structure: federalism. Most of the new initiatives of the 1960s, while partly or wholly funded by the central government, were administered by states, localities, or nonprofit voluntary organizations.

The amounts budgeted for these activities are shown in Table 2.2.[3] The data show that from the start-up of the new society programs in 1966 they almost tripled in real terms in five years. The rapid growth continued during the administration of President Nixon and then declined during the Reagan years (1981–1989). These data demonstrate a large and rapid growth in spending for exactly the kinds of programs for which program evaluation is designed. It was a market waiting to be served. But it was an evaluation market rather than an audit market partly because of the use of third parties as instrumentalities: the states, the localities, and nonprofit organizations. During the period 1965–1980, state and local employment, fed in part by this (and other) federal money, almost doubled, from 7.7 million in 1965 to 13.5 million in 1980. During the same period, federal civilian employment grew only slightly, from 2.5 million in 1965 to 2.8 million in 1980.

It is hard to imagine more fertile ground for a fledgling evaluation industry. First, there was the rapid increase in funds. Second, programs could be operating in as many as fifty states. While federal agencies would write regulations attempting to impose some uniformity, there were bound to be differences in program implementation, in part reflecting the diversity among the states. Finally, since these programs were *not* administered directly by federal bureaucrats, evaluation was a natural tool. As was the case with PPBS and the uniformed military services in McNamara's defense department, state program managers would not be expected to be objective about "their" (state and local) programs using "our" (federal) money. As was the case with systems analysis applied to defense, rigorous analysis of independent evaluators could substitute for expert opinion of the line administrators.

The distinctions between the growth of direct federal operations and programs operated by third parties is a matter of degree. Clearly some funds were also going to the directly administered programs that were good candidates for program evaluation. For example, although the large new medical assistance programs were administered by states or other third parties, the Veterans Administration (now the Department of Veterans Affairs) also ran the largest hospital system outside of the communist bloc. However, in general the growth of federal programs associated with the "Great Society" took place using third-party instrumentalities.

The imposition of PPBS on the domestic agencies carried with it the requirement that they set up formal evaluation programs. Clearly, the intent of the Office of Management and Budget (then called the Bureau of the Budget) was to extract evaluation studies as the price of program expansion in the president's budget request to Congress. As the federal budget process became overwhelmed by a sea of PPBS-generated paper, evaluation became a more discretionary activity. The Nixon administration instituted one of the periodic attempts to promote management to a status equal to or superior to budgeting, which further diverted attention from evaluation, although the main permanent change was a name: The Bureau of the Budget became the OMB. Moreover, "When money for new programs dried up under Vietnam War pressures in the late 1960s and less favorable economic conditions in the 1970s, so too did interest in PPBS. It was futile to analyze program options when there was no money for them" (Schick 1990, p. 35).

Table 2.2 Federal Budget Payments to States for Programs Likely to be Evaluated 1965–1989*
(in billions of constant 1982 dollars)

Fiscal Year	Amount
1965	7.0
1966	11.4
1967	15.4
1968	18.5
1969	17.7
1970	20.0
1971	22.0
1972	25.8
1973	25.0
1974	23.4
1975	27.1
1976	30.1
1977	30.2
1978	35.5
1979	35.3
1980	32.9
1981	30.2
1982	22.7
1983	21.6
1984	20.8
1985	21.3
1986	20.4
1987	19.8
1988	20.0
1989	20.2

Source: Office of Management and Budget. *Total federal grants to state and local governments excluding amounts for capital projects, payments for individual, general revenue sharing, and shared revenues.

The Carter administration installed zero-based-budgeting (ZBB) in 1977, which despite the name in practice focused on marginal increments and decrements to a baseline level. As with PPBS, the analyst was supposed to be able to judge the merit of budget issues based on a rational analysis of alternative resource levels relative to clearly defined program goals. Evaluation was encouraged anew. As a result, it appeared that evaluation might become a permanent part of the budget process regardless of changes in administration or the availability of funds. It seemed hard to oppose a budget process that included the explicit articulation of program goals and the systematic measurement of the degree to which they are achieved. Of course such a process might not be relevant to all parts of the budget, or it might be overwhelmed by political or other considerations from time to time, but as one element in the decision-making process, it seem destined to become a standard part of the repertory.

The Evolution of Audit Activities

The role of the executive branch auditor continued on a separate course. The fact that much of the program expansion was carried out by third parties reinforced this already existing separation. The separate units of government were clearly subject to their own audit standards often for the functions they undertook with federal money. Ultimately, they were also responsible to the state and local voters. Federal funds were often commingled with funds from their own sources, indeed matching federal money was often a requirement. There was constant potential for conflict between federal standards in areas such as contracting and employee safety and state and local standards. Auditors were dealing in areas of constant tension between the administrative advantages of delegating managerial functions to lower levels of government and the temptation to use federal program dollars to impose procedures or standards on those who used them. Executive branch auditors had their hands full sorting out accounting standards and coordinating financial management roles of different federal agencies without wondering whether program objectives were being effectively achieved. In contrast, the GAO was moving extensively into program auditing, which began to look more and more like evaluation (Havens 1990).

The Demise of Program Evaluation

The Reagan administration budget policies clashed with the view that program evaluation was central to the budget decision-making process. It did not do so explicitly, but the evidence became clear. The General Accounting Office, concerned with what appeared to be a lowered priority for evaluation, began to review the course of evaluation efforts by the Reagan administration. By 1988, it concluded "program evaluation and the data collection that supports it, are—with few exceptions—in a depleted state in executive agencies today. Further, case studies show that basic data are lacking on such disparate and wide-ranging issues as health care quality, the state of the environment, and the results of weapons testing" (GAO 1988).

In retrospect, the origins of this situation are evident from the outset of the new administration. The Reagan administration presented its initial budget program during a year that began on February 20, 1981, one month after taking office, and ended with the presentation of its first detailed full-scale budget early in 1982. That program consisted of tax cuts, domestic spending reductions, reductions in the regulation of economic activity, and advocacy of a monetary policy of stable growth. (Under the U.S. system the president does not have direct control of the Central Bank). It would seem that program evaluation would be an essential factor in supporting the changes in spending priorities that the administration hoped for.

For a complex set of reasons, that turned out not to be the case. As Table 2.3 demonstrates, there were many justifications that the new administration was comfortable with for reducing or eliminating programs in the budget that did not rely on rigorous and often lengthy evaluations. Federalism could justify eliminating an item from the national budget regardless of its merits. Economic efficiency and free market forces could be used as reasons for closing down subsidy programs. A "freeze" principle could justify clipping a broad range of programs across the board. Additional flexibility in the administration of grants to state and local governments could be used as a justification for lowering their amounts.

Table 2.3
Summary of Impediments to the Use of Evaluation Studies for Making Budget Policy

Issue	Rationale
Only large deficits will restrain program growth	Rejects the rational model of budget decision making. Since all decisions are political, and since political representatives benefit from program growth, only overwhelming general pressure will restrain spending.
Free market orientation	Market solutions are more efficient than administered solutions. Therefore, any market-oriented alternative can be chosen without the need for evaluation.
Fungibility of grants to states and localities	With increased use of multipurpose block grants, the link between a given budget allotment and a specific program outcome becomes tenuous.
Best decisions are made at the lowest levels of government	Citizens at the community level understand their needs. If they are given the authority to allocate funds and make program decisions the results will be positive without the need for formal evaluation.
Program decisions are inherently political; evaluations are inherently biased	The evaluation process is controlled by program advocates and bureaucrats. They have a vested interest in the outcome and cannot be expected to be objective.
Not a federal role	Whether a program is effective or not, some activities should be the responsibility of nonfederal levels of government or the private sector, so evaluation is irrelevant for purposes of national budget decisions.
Budget allocations are independent of program decision, e.g., defense "top line"	Overall allocation made on an aggregate basis (e.g., defense in the Reagan administration). Evaluation may influence program mix and systems choices, but will not have a budget impact. Implication: there are always more effective systems than there is money.

Continued on next page

Table 2.3—Continued

Issue	Rationale
Budget allocations are made on the basis of very broad categories determined by political jurisdiction	With the need for political accommodation among the executive branch and the constituent parts of Congress, enforceable budget agreements are only practical using very broad categories. Moreover, these categories often represent jurisdictional boundaries, not program alternatives. Evaluation may influence allocation within these categories, but not overall levels.
Formula budgeting	"Freeze", across-the-board cuts, and formula grants to states mean that program results are not relevant to the allocation process.
Urgency	If larger and rapid budget reductions are needed, the evaluation process is too slow to influence allocation decisions. Medicare is an example of a program so big and growing so fast it always gets cut but badly needs long-term reform.
Phony evaluations	Advocacy groups frequently contract for arguments for or against programs that are written as if they were objective policy analysis, using economic and statistical jargon and concepts. Although they do not meet professional standards, these are treated in the political arena as legitimate. Bad analysis tends to drive out (or at least discourage) good.

Moreover, it quickly became evident that the huge, and rapid, budget savings that the administration believed were necessary and which it set out to achieve were beyond anything that program evaluation could justify. During its first year the administration produced what seemed to be endless streams of complex numbers to support its budget policies. However, it is unnecessary to review them in detail; a single illustration from the "Program for Economic Recovery" makes clear how challenging its domestic budget policy was. For fiscal year 1983, the second year of the administration and, thus, one where its policies might show most of their full effect, it called for tax reductions of $100 billion and defense increases of $21 billion, which implied offsets of $121 billion in domestic spending if the deficit were to be held constant. Total baseline outlays for that year were estimated at $792 billion, so the domestic cuts implied were huge. (In any event, the recession, which began in 1981, made matters much worse.) Cuts of the magnitude called for were vastly greater than anything that could be gained from marginal reductions in less effective programs.

There is also evidence that at least some in the administration did not believe in the policy analysts' "rational" model of decision making, a model implicit in the use of evaluation to determine budget levels. For some, tax cuts and the ensuing large deficits themselves constituted a policy of restraining the size of government. New York State Senator Moynihan, a critic of this policy, has stated that it was based on the view that "it is impossible to persuade Congress that expenditures must be reduced, unless one creates deficits so large that absolutely everyone becomes convinced that no more money can be spent" (Moynihan 1988, p. 273; see also, National Economic Commission 1989, pp. 44-5). William Niskanen, a member of the original Council of Economic Advisors under President Reagan, confirms this view (Penner 1991, p.194). The administration, however, never publicly admitted to such a position, so it needed to present budgets that showed declining deficits. To do so, it badly needed domestic spending cuts immediately; both the size and the urgency precluded the application of evaluation methods.

The official rationale for the Reagan administration budget policies, first laid out during "Program for Economic Recovery", were further discussed in the fiscal year 1982 budget revisions. (Under the American system, the official 1982 budget was submitted, as called for by law, by outgoing President Carter.) However, the Reagan policy changes were the most sweeping since the end of World War II so there was not time to prepare a comprehensive set of proposals for 1982. As a result his policies were further refined and justified in the 1983 budget documents.

Examined in their totality, the budget materials prepared during this time show little use in the budget documents of program evaluation conclusions but considerable reliance on doctrine. For example, the Economic Development Administration was proposed for elimination, because while it was supposed to be targeted to depressed areas, 80 percent of U.S. communities qualified for assistance. Furthermore, the budget documents argued, overall macro policy would do more for such areas than EDA assistance, and there was "little evidence" that it was effective. In another case seven housing programs were identified for reduction or termination. The reasons cited were that costs had become uncontrollable, choice was restricted (a widely used free market rationale) and that unit costs were too high.

Mass transit subsidies were considered to be a local responsibility, and passenger railroad (Amtrak) subsidies were up to the states. Education was similarly a state role. In some cases the justification was purely a matter of funding priorities. For example, subsidies for public broadcasting were condemned simply because of the need for fiscal stringency, and student aid costs were condemned because they were growing too fast.

For some programs, particularly entitlements such as food assistance to the poor or cash aid to families with dependent children, there was at least the implication of program evaluation behind the budget recommendations. The key words that signified this was the need for "better targeting" of benefits, or the need to improve "program design". It is not the nature of budget documents to suggest uncertainty of purpose, so it is unclear the degree to which redesign was based on a formal evaluation of the existing program structure, rather than the need to lower funding levels.

The free market orientation theme had many variations. The market was expected to take care of export development, financing the District of Columbia government, substitute for public service jobs provided under the Comprehensive Education and Training Act, and make economic development grants unnecessary.

This substitution of doctrine for evaluation has not gone unnoticed. DeLeon, in his discussion of evaluation and policy terminations, recognizes the phenomenon of political ideology substituting for objective evaluation in program terminations. However, he does not explore the degree to which it pervaded budget policy through what he calls "partial termination" (budget cutbacks) (DeLeon 1987). He notes the Reagan reductions and termination were "openly based on two related ideological tenets: the decentralization of government services from the federal to local level and the relative efficiency of the private, as opposed to the public, sector in distribution of goods and services" (DeLeon 1987, p. 182). He documents the application of these principles to budget policies for education, housing, passenger rail services, farm price supports, and energy.

DeLeon also claims that the application of "value-dictated . . . criteria" can lead to superficial arguments: "Gross budget cuts are brusquely proposed without the benefit of analysis. For instance, the entire issue of privatization is extremely contentious . . . but amenable to empirical research; yet the level of discourse has rarely gone beyond the purely polemic" (ibid). The example is a good one. Claims of huge budget savings from privatization forthcoming from conservative circles often go unchallenged despite the fact that a careful reading of President Reagan's own Commission on Privatization yields little in the way of direct budget deficit reductions (Report of the President's Commission on Privatization 1988).

Value-dictated criteria did not only preclude evaluation, but could also influence very detailed and sophisticated evaluations. Such an experience is described in some detail by Birman and Kennedy (1989). The authors directed an evaluation of the programs authorized by Chapter 1 of the National Education Act. Expenditures for these programs totaled $4.3 billion in 1988 and provided services for five million school-age children. Congress directed the secretary of education to conduct a national assessment of Chapter 1 in December 1983 through "independent studies and analyses." Applying the principles of federalism and the free market cited by DeLeon (1987) above, the administration had initially decided to replace Chapter 1 programs with a block grant, and when that failed it proposed turning it into a voucher plan. It also proposed to abolish the Department of Education. The directors of the assessment found it impossible to escape from the political pressures because "decision making environments do not come with rules that protect participants. Evaluators do not enjoy the protection that, say, football referees have" (Birman and Kennedy 1989, p. 629).

The assistant secretary of education (a political appointee), who oversaw their work, essentially supports the view that doctrine dominated analysis. He later wrote about the evaluation:

> This profound clash in belief systems transcended the Chapter 1 debate and the events recounted by Birman and Kennedy, but it is impossible to understand their essay without keeping that backdrop in sight. This was much more than politics-as-usual, in which one party tries to score points on the other. It was philosophical, doctrinal, involving the basic world views, self-concepts, and missions of the participants. For depth and intensity, the best analogy I can suggest is to the clash between the

established Catholic church and the Protestant dissidents in Reformation Europe. (Finn 1989, p. 634)

Whether the voters had so momentous a view of education issues when they voted for President Reagan is, of course, a different question. From the beginning, Congress was the consumer of the assessment, since it intended to rewrite Chapter 1, not repeal it. The Counsel of the Committee on Education and Labor of the U.S. House of Representatives observed: "We must reflect on whether we want to face tense congressional executive disputes over data collection and analysis which can shape the outlines of the debate on reauthorization. But if we do not require such an assessment, either through the Department of Education *or by some other organization capable of the task*, we may be deciding the future of the national government's largest education program without a good analytical foundation" (Jennings 1989, p. 640; emphasis added).

It is not surprising that program evaluation declined. As Havens notes:

> Strong ideology - of any sort - is often the enemy of analysis. Those who fervently believe they know the "truth" find facts inconvenient. Similarly, those who have a stake in a program can feel threatened by questions about effectiveness.
> These attitudes were the foundation for what happened to program evaluation at the federal level in the 1980s. Two data points developed by the General Accounting Office (GAO) through surveys of federal agencies help describe that experience. Subsequently, the GAO reevaluated the issue as part of its Transition Series (United States General Accounting Office, 1988).
> . . . The GAO started by simply looking at the number of units performing program evaluations. In 1980, there were 180 units in non-defense agencies reporting that they were engaged in program evaluation activities. By 1984, this was down to 133. And this was not just an illusion reflecting consolidation or reorganization. The resources devoted to program evaluation were down as well. Measured in constant dollars, spending was down 37 percent and professional staff resources were down 22 percent. (Havens 1990, p. 2)

Another major factor that lessened the influence of program evaluation on budget allocations was the changing way in which budget decisions were being made in the U.S. Congress. In the beginning of the Reagan administration the 1981 recession, combined with tax cuts and a growing defense budget, produced record deficits by any measure.

The deficit peaked at 6.3 percent of GNP in 1983, two percentage points above the previous high in 1976. The economic recovery did not erase the deficit; it remained at 3 percent of GNP or above for the rest of the decade. During the 1980 decade, while Republicans controlled the presidency, Democrats controlled the House of Representatives. For six years, the Republicans also controlled the Senate, but by a narrow majority. In this political environment, budget policy would have been hard enough to work out, but large deficits and a lack of consensus on what to do about them made the process contentious. It was simply impossible to develop compromises on hundreds of individual program issues. Congress and the administration focused by necessity on very broad budgetary categories. In this context, evaluation could influence the course of a particular program, but was unlikely to affect the broad resource allocation agreements that determined budget levels (Mathiasen 1988).

In the fall of 1990, this process reached what may have been a final stage with a three to five year budget agreement between the executive and legislative branches of the government. Among other things, the agreement set forth total spending amounts for all domestic programs that are funded by annual appropriations for three fiscal years (1991–1993). (Other long range spending policies were also set forth.) Under these rules the impact of evaluation can *only* be in terms of shifting priorities *within* the prescribed limits. Therefore, program advocates will not only need to muster all available analytic justifications for growth of priorities they favor, but must also be prepared to propose cutbacks in other programs.

The Bush Administration and a New Emphasis on Auditing

During this period events were taking place that would be of major importance to the audit community. The first was that the newly deregulated savings and loan institutions were busy making billions of dollars of speculative, and in some cases corrupt, loans using deposits guaranteed by the Federal Deposit Insurance Corporation, an agency of the U.S. Government backed by its full faith and credit. The second was that the Department of Housing and Urban Development was following policies that would develop into a major political scandal.

These two events shaped the attitudes toward program evaluation in the post-Reagan era. There had been many largely ideologically based arguments as to whether government programs were effective, arguments about whether government could help to alleviate problems or, as President Reagan was proud of saying, was part of the problems. But in the aftermath of the Reagan administration the question was not effectiveness in reaching policy objectives, it was honesty and integrity in administration. Audit and financial accounting standards were no longer bit players in the policy business, but a defining part of it. Meanwhile, OMB under President Bush began to rebuild its almost discarded commitment to evaluation. By the end of the second year a small effort was under way. The 1992 budget, published in February 1991, shows the contrast between audit and evaluation concerns. The evaluation plan in the entire human resource area for 1992 was limited to two efforts, both for a minor agency, the Occupation Safety and Health Administration. Beyond 1993, the plan included five evaluations of the Department of Education programs, two in the Department of Health and Human Services, and two in the Department of Labor.

The programs involved had outlays of a little more than $8 billion. To place this in context, total 1989 outlays for human resource programs were $370 billion, *excluding* the Social Security programs. This suggested that either the administration was basically satisfied that the remaining $360 billion was being well spent, or that it did not see evaluation as a major tool in making budget allocations. It is clear, however, that the administration is *not* happy with federal programs. Elsewhere in the budget it identified 257 programs and 3,737 projects for termination, and 109 programs and 261 projects for reduced funding for the 1992 budget. There was no discussion of this in the administration's section on program evaluation, nor any indication of the degree to which these cuts were based on program evaluations.

Meanwhile, in the area of audit, the budget contained seventeen pages of detailed analysis of 117 high financial risk areas in twenty different government agencies. The identification of these high-risk areas grew out of the scandal at the Department of Housing and Urban Development. The OMB reviewed all major departments and agencies to determine areas that might be susceptible to similar problems. The areas so identified were the subject of special monitoring. The analysis in the budget statements provided considerable detail into the nature of the risks, corrective action under way, progress to date, and current status.

Conclusion

This survey is designed to assess audit and evaluation and their relation to budget decision making at the presidential level. It ignores efforts that no doubt go on all the time within agencies to improve the effectiveness of the programs they administer or finance. This is not to say that such efforts are unimportant, but merely to say that they are not the subject of this review. Nor is the OMB the only actor. Each year the GAO issues more than 1000 reports, many of which constitute major evaluations. These are done largely at the request of committees or members of Congress. They will, to varying degrees, be reflected in hearings and even legislation.

If the subject of this chapter were limited to audit and budget traditions in the United States, its content and conclusions would be straightforward and rather dull. Financial audits continue at all levels of government. At the national level, inspectors general routinely investigate and report. A new Chief Financial Officer's Act took effect in 1991 with the aim of focusing responsibility for financial management and of developing financial statements as useful tools for public sector management. The program evaluation movement continues to develop as analysts at national, state, and local levels of government persist in their quest to improve public programs and policies. The audit and evaluation communities remain separate, perhaps less so than in the past, but each still has its own trade craft and traditions.

However, adding the national budget to the equation complicates matters. As stated at the beginning of this chapter, the budgeteer's interest in these tools is practical: do they contribute to determining budget levels? At the national level the budget, with its very large deficits, has been a major focus of debate between the Republican-controlled executive branch and the Democratic party, which has controlled one or both of the Houses of Congress during this period. Indeed, with the demise of the Cold War, budget policy and the deficit is the single largest all-encompassing policy dispute facing the country.

In this context, the conclusions change radically. Audit raises such issues of scandals in the Department of Housing and Urban Development, the collapse of the savings and loan industry, which is adding tens of billions of dollars annually to the deficit, and inefficient and corrupt procurement practices affecting the huge defense budget. Evaluation may be viewed as irrelevant, self-serving, unnecessary, or merely too lengthy a process. In any case, as far as the use of major program evaluation efforts as an integral part of the budget priority setting by the executive branch is concerned, the promise that Charles Hitch brought to Washington from the Rand Corporation 30 years ago remains unfulfilled.

Notes

1. The concepts behind this approach to budgeting had been developed at the Rand Corporation, the first institution to which the label "think tank" was attached. Charles Hitch was hired by Secretary McNamara from Rand to be Assistant Secrteray of Defense, Comptroller. At that point the Rand Corporation was financed almost entirely by the Air Force (Hitch 1965).
2. Hitch later made a virture out of the necessity by stating that for programming decisions the mission categories were the most useful, while for financial management purposes the appropriations accounts made the most sense.
3. The proxy for measuring the volume of this new activity is the amounts of federal grants to state and local governments (measured in constant dollars) *excluding* transfer payments, capital grants, general revenue sharing, and shared revenues.

References

Birman, B. and M. Kennedy. (1989). "The Politics of the National Assessment of Chapter I." *Journal of Policy Analysis and Management*, 8/4

DeLeon, P. (1987). *The Politics of Program Evaluation*. Beverley Hills: Sage Publications.

Finn, C. (1989). "Comment: An Executive Branch Perspective." *Journal of Policy Analysis and Management*, 8/4

General Accounting Office (1988). *Program Evaluation Issues*. Washington D.C.: Transition Series (OCG-89-8TR).

Havens, H. (1990). "The Erosion of Federal Program Evaluation." *The American Review of Public Administration*, 20/7

Hitch, C. (1965). *Decision-Making for Defense*. Berkeley: University of California Press.

Jennings, J. (1989). "Comment: A Congressional Perspective." *Journal of Policy Analysis and Management*, 8/4

Mathiasen, D. (1988). "Evaluation of the Office of Management and Budget Under President Reagan." *Public Budgeting and Finance*, 8/3

Moynihan, D. (1988). *Came the Revolution: Argument in the Reagan Era*. San Diego: Harcourt, Brace, Jovanovich.

National Economic Commission (1989). *Minority Report*. Washington D.C.

Penner, R. (1991). *The Great Fiscal Experiment*. Washington D.C.: The Urban Institute.

President's Commission of Privatization (1988). *Privatization: Toward More Effect Government*. A Report of the President's Commission on Privatization. Washington D.C.

Schick, A. (1990). *The Capacity to Budget*. Washington D.C.: The Urban Institute.

3

Separate Developments: Budgeting, Auditing, and Evaluation in the United Kingdom

Andrew Gray and Bill Jenkins

In January 1989 Britain's Conservative government responded to criticism that the quality of health care was falling and that insufficient resources were being put into the National Health Service (NHS). In *Working for Patients* (CM 555, 1989), a "White Paper" that set out its policy, the government argued that in real terms health budgets were steadily increasing, but admitted that the service was inefficient, badly managed and in need of structural change. It proposed to remedy this by a complex set of organizational and financial reforms. The central idea was the creation of internal markets in health care: health authorities would buy services from hospitals and thus give patients greater choice and improve the quality of service. Hospitals would be allowed to become self-governing trusts (and hence achieve a great degree of independence) and family doctors with large numbers of patients would hold their own budgets.

Unsurprisingly, the White Paper plans aroused controversy, not the least within the medical profession, which saw them as a threat to clinical autonomy, and among those who viewed the proposals as a first step away from a state-financed medical care system. A particularly fierce debate ranged over the proposals to create self-governing hospitals and give family doctors their own budgets. Medical pressure groups and others argued that there was little evidence to justify such radical change and suggested that if changes were to be made this should be only after careful and controlled *evaluations*. These arguments were rejected by ministers who contended that evaluation would take place naturally as part of policy implementation. For ministers the main problem was the uncertainty that would only be prolonged by such unnecessary and unhelpful exercises.

For the government's critics the main problems with U.K. health care stemmed from a resource famine. Hence while *budgets* were squeezed by cash limits and services overloaded by demand, quality of service and outputs continued to fall. To make resources go further, the White Paper (CM 555) sought to install mechanisms for improving value for money (VFM) by improving systems of *audit*. This was to be done by extending the remit of the Audit Commission (an independent body with responsibilities to local government) to the NHS. The intention was to strengthen audit, to pursue VFM studies and to provide an independent source of advice to ministers (CM 555, paras. 2.29–2.33).

This brief account of recent developments in the health area illustrates a hitherto rare phenomenon in British government: the integration (at least in theory) of budgeting, auditing and evaluation in a major policy area. It also brings out important issues involved in such a coming together. Of central importance is the political climate in which developments take place and the economic imperatives of the central executive. This leads to a policy rhetoric through which evaluation and audit are defined, organized and legitimized in a particular fashion. While there is much talk of freedom, choice and markets these are, almost inevitably, linked to particular systems of control and inter-organizational relationships where power is rarely, if at all, yielded by the center.

It is against this background that this paper will discuss the development of, and present relationships between, budgeting, auditing and evaluation in the UK. The first section describes the budgetary system in central government and is followed by a section on auditing, accountability and evaluation. The final section focuses on the systemic nature of budgeting, auditing and evaluation; the intention is to identify what links are present (or absent from) current arrangements.

The Budgeting Process in the UK

Public Expenditure: Community and Process

To understand budgeting in any state or organization it is necessary to examine its history, identify the major actors involved and relate it to wider environmental pressures. In the United Kingdom, budgeting is, formally at least, a political activity in which executive decisions taken by the Cabinet are ratified by Parliament. Constitutionally, authorization of funds can only be made by Parliament, which also has the task of satisfying itself that such funds are used properly for the purpose they were intended (Likierman 1988, p. 141). Needless to say, this picture of the detail of parliamentary procedure has little other than symbolic value in describing the budgetary proceess. As Heclo & Wildavsky (1981) so clearly demonstrate, the realities of deciding public spending allocations involve a small and tightly knit public expenditure community. Her Majesty's Treasury plays the central coordinating role, being "administratively and indeed physically, at the centre of government decision taking" (Likierman 1988, p. 52). In particular, no proposals with expenditure implications can go to the Cabinet unless they have been first discussed with the Treasury, nor before Parliament without the support of a Treasury minister.

In the departments themselves those involved in the budgetary process are small in number, at least in terms of those who negotiate with the Treasury. Interaction between departmental finance teams and Treasury officials takes place on what is almost a continuous basis as part of the public expenditure process (PES) (see below). Ministers are rarely involved in these negotiations unless they take a specific interest in particular issues. However, in the end it is the minister who must take his budget to the Cabinet and it is the Cabinet that makes the final decision on spending allocations.

The total of public expenditure, approved by the Cabinet on an annual basis, and ratified by Parliament is therefore, in the main part, the sum of departmental bids agreed with the Treasury or arbitrated on by the Cabinet (Barnett 1982, Likierman 1988). However, not all those funds are in the direct control of the bidding departments. Many services such as housing and welfare are administered indirectly by bodies such as local authorities and executive agencies. Thus, in certain cases, there is another budgetary arena in which such organizations negotiate with departments over spending levels (both current and capital) on both a short and long term basis. In the end, however, the parent department must negotiate with the Treasury to obtain the required funds.

While the structure of the public expenditure community may have changed in minor detail over the years (e.g. with the changing departmental organization of government), its broad shape, and indeed (until recently) its norms and practices have remained relatively stable. For the Treasury, *control* (i.e., restraint) of departmental spending always had a high priority and this lay at the heart of reforms that followed the First World War. In this period Treasury officials had little hesitation in interfering in departmental policy (Hennessy 1989, Ch.2). However, at that time there was little in the way of a systematic budgetary process. Instead a diffuse and decentralized system evolved based on pragmatism and tradition. This survived through World War II and into the 1950s when it was criticized by a Parliamentary Committee as "a complex of administrative practices that had grown up like a tree over the centuries, natural rather than planned, empiric rather than theoretical" (Clarke 1978, p. 3). Criticisms such as these led to a concerted effort to reform the whole budgetary process.

However, as Heclo and Wildavsky note (1981, Ch. 8), the impetus for budgetary reform in the late 1950s came as much from the Treasury as from its critics. In a postwar political climate that favored increased public spending and paid little heed to where this might come from, the Treasury felt that the mechanisms of restraint were inadequate. In particular there seemed to be no formal link between expenditure and revenue that required policy proposals to be linked to macroeconomic policy and there was no forward planning or assessment of the consequences of current spending decisions. As a result macroeconomic policy appeared to be characterized by a stop-go cycle, which led to gross mismanagement of programs and projects at the micro level. The search for a system that would avoid such difficulties ended with the Public Expenditure Survey (PES).

PES was the brainchild of the Plowden Committee, which reported in 1961. This committee was an internal Treasury review established to assess the criticisms of budgetary arrangements and to suggest solutions. It found that the coordination and planning of policies and public expenditure required an organized budgetary system. Plowden attempted to link together planning and *financial control* and to coordinate macro and microeconomic strategies.

The details of PES and its operations have been described extensively elsewhere (e.g. Barnett 1982, Heald 1983, Heclo & Wildavsky 1981, Pliatzky 1982). PES is a planning system in which departments bid for resources and justify past performance. It is also a continuous process coordinated by the Treasury that sets out planning assumptions and issues guidelines for resource bids. This formal framework for PES has remained intact over the years even if, crucially, the ground rules have changed as the economic climate has altered.

Beneath the formal face of the process, however, lies what Heclo and Wildavsky (1981) have termed "the bargaining game", first at administrative levels between departmental officials and the Treasury and later at ministerial levels between departmental and Treasury ministers. Although the PES process aims to operate in a systemic way to draw together departmental bids, the PES Committee (the formal coordinating body) is not a bargaining forum. Rather it aggregates the bids or agreements arrived at by bilateral discussions between departmental and Treasury officials and then presents them through a Treasury minister (the Chief Secretary) to the Cabinet. If differences still exist between departments and the Treasury, ministers take up the negotiations and if necessary these come to the Cabinet. Thus it is the Cabinet that is responsible for final decisions on programs and aggregates. These are announced in the Autumn Statement and published in a series of expenditure White Papers in the following January. Meanwhile, back in the departments, the PES process moves toward its next cycle (see Fig. 3.1).

PES was intended to achieve a number of objectives: to improve public expenditure *control*, to develop a *medium term planning system*, to aid *prioritization* within and between departments and to assist the development of systematic *program evaluation* (i.e., to move beyond a consideration of inputs to an assessment of program outputs). The Treasury welcomed the introduction of this system, partially because macroeconomic policy was to set the parameters for spending decisions and departmental spending was to be planned. For the departments too PES offered advantages in the way it could resolve some of their uncertainties and move them out of the stop-go cycle.

As with many planning systems, however, the practice of PES has often been some distance from the theory that underpins it, although for Heclo and Wildavsky the early decade of PES was one of partial success. Undoubtedly there were technical difficulties, but the Survey became an integral part of the process through which government funds were allocated (1981, Ch. 5). PES evolved primarily as a planning instrument, but also embryonically as a mechanism of control. The latter, however, was weakened by the absence of an *evaluative capacity*, especially one that like Planning Programming and Budgeting (PPB) could be linked to budgeting (i.e. to PES). Treasury and even departmental arguments for such a reform were answered in 1970 with the introduction of Programme Analysis and Review (PAR).

Table 3.1: The Public Expenditure Survey (PES) Timetable

January (15)	Post mortem on previous survey
February (14)	
March (13)	Treasury issues guidelines for next survey
April (12)	Baselines agreed
May (11)	Departments submit materials on outputs, performance and value for money
June (10)	Expenditure bids from departments and Treasury analysis of them
July (9)	Chief Secretary's proposals to Cabinet for overall total, which Cabinet then decides
August (8)	
September (7)	Bilateral negotiations begin between Treasury and departments
Oct/Nov. (6/5)	Cabinet decisions on departments and publication of these in "Autumn Statement"
December (4)	Departments submit bids for Estimates to Treasury
January (3)	Publication of "Public Expenditure White Paper"
February (2)	Treasury ministers approve Estimates
March (1)	Budget day; publication of "Financial Statement and Budget Report"; Supply Estimates published
April (0)	Start of fiscal year

Source: Based on Likierman (1988), p. 40.
Notes: Numbers in ( ) indicate months before fiscal year takes effect; Chief Secretary: equivalent to deputy finance minister; Estimates: applications to Parliament for cash.

The varied history of PAR has been discussed elsewhere (Gray & Jenkins 1982). Its brief heyday and fall from grace coincided with a change in the economic climate that led to what has been termed the "collapse" of PES. This period (i.e., 1973-6) also marked a shift in emphasis in the U.K. budgetary system from what may be termed the *management of policy* to the *management of resources*, i.e., ideas of rational planning, analysis and objective setting were replaced by an emphasis on cash control and financial management.

PES in the 1970s: From the Management of Policy to the Management of Resources

We have discussed this change in the nature and form of PES in earlier papers (Gray & Jenkins 1989, 1990). These developments have also been noted by Heclo and Wildavsky (1981), Schick (1986, 1988) and Wright (1980). In the volatile economic climate of the mid-1970s public spending ran "out of control". This was blamed by politicians on external factors such as the oil crisis, which brought high inflation and recession, but to those in the Treasury and to many observers it was also clear that the PES system was incapable of dealing with the difficulties it faced. In part the problems lay with the technical basis of the system, which gave no incentive to departments to control their spending. To remedy this cash limits were introduced, i.e., a regime in which programs were to be financed by a fixed cash allocation. In such a world, control and cash management became the preoccupations and planning only acceptable within the terms set by these parameters. Since the mid-1970s (i.e., before the election of Mrs. Thatcher's government in 1979), the dominant mode of the U.K. public expenditure process as reflected in the PES system has therefore been the *management of resources*. This has been reflected in the refinement of cash limits into a cash planning system now known as the Medium Term Financial Strategy.

This evolution of cash budgeting has been a gradual process, reflecting a continued and sustained effort by the Treasury to gain more detailed control over public expenditure (Pliatzky 1982; Thain & Wright 1988). However, the speed of developments has been aided by a number of changes following the election of the Conservative government of 1979, not least a policy to curb public spending, cut civil service numbers and promote a management culture throughout the public sector. Thus during the later 1970s and the 1980s, the nature of the U.K. budgetary process changed in response to political, economic and administrative pressures. Hence, while the PES cycle itself survives, the ground rules under which it operates and the relationships between the participants have altered. Planning and evaluation have given way to *financial control* and public expenditure decisions have been driven by macroeconomic priorities that emphasise keeping the size of the public sector in check.

Reforms in the 1980s: The Financial Management Initiative and Associated Developments

The move toward strengthening the *management of resources* in U.K. central government intensified throughout the 1980s and into the 1990s, first through the Financial Management Initiative (FMI) (Gray et al. 1991) and, more recently, via what has been termed the Next Steps, through which departments are being encouraged to hive off administrative operations into freestanding agencies under chief executives and to adopt more businesslike modes of operation (Flynn et al. 1990).

These developments have great significance for budgeting. They enhance the role of management accounting in the public sector and, more importantly, attempt to change the administrative culture. In broad terms the FMI, initiated in 1982, has aimed to decentralize financial management at all levels within departments and to hold officials (now called "managers") accountable for their budgets and, increasingly, their operational targets. It has also sought to develop both top management information systems for the coordination of departmental activities and systems of performance measures and performance indicators.

PES has therefore changed in subtle ways. In the bidding process the Treasury now requires each department to demonstrate via performance indicators what it has achieved. Further, some of the more rigid elements of Treasury controls (such as annuality rules and one-year allocations) have been relaxed for departments that can demonstrate that they have a robust system of performance indicators or they can produce a sound three-year Management Plan. In practice the freedoms yielded in this area are limited but such moves may signal a slight shift in the budgetary game that allows departments to plan with a little more certainty (Thain & Wright 1990).

In a broader sense, however, the influence of the FMI has also triggered a wider concern with budgeting in departments. In 1986 an internal efficiency review of budgeting in Whitehall was published. This set out four basic principles of departmental budgeting:

1.   All managers should be involved in budgeting;

2. Budgets should be linked to government expenditure plans;

3. Budgets should include indicators of output or performance;

4. There should be clear accountability for the different aspects of the process (Treasury 1986).

Two years later progress toward achieving these objectives was assessed by a Treasury team. Of the thirty- four departments reviewed thirteen were declared to have reached a satisfactory degree of implementation on all four principles (Port 1990). But what does budgeting mean in this context? The emphasis is on decentralized budgetary control, with managers accountable for their resources (in cash terms) and performance but only as far as this relates to managerial activities. Program expenditure plans are mentioned but only as a general influence on managerial activities.

In all this there is little mention of PES as a system or of evaluation. This is unsurprising since, after the brief career of PAR, formal systems of policy evaluation have been out of favor. This is not to say, however, that there has been no interest in evaluation or that it is not conducted. Indeed, as was noted previously, the designers of the FMI were well aware of what they saw as a need for program evaluation (Gray & Jenkins et al. 1991). This led to a small but sustained effort in the Treasury to encourage and facilitate regular evaluations in departments. This involved departments in developing and testing an evaluative methodology, which in turn led to the publication by the Treasury of a guide to policy evaluation (Treasury 1988). These efforts were coupled with authoritative ministerial statements on the necessity of institutionalizing evaluation into expenditure bids and decisions. However, to date there is little evidence of these evaluations becoming an institutionalized part of the public *expenditure* process.

Where the United Kingdom differs from countries such as Canada and the United States is that there is no clearly identifiable community of policy evaluators either within or outside government nor, other than in an indirect sense, is there an established requirement for the regular evaluation of policies and the linking of the results of these into the budgetary process. However, some departments do make a rigorous attempt to conduct evaluations and, in the wake of the FMI, evaluation in certain particular guises *is* important in structuring relationships between departments and the Treasury. For example, there is now a considerable performance indicator industry to inform public accountability (published as part of the annual Public Expenditure White Papers) and resource bids. The utility of such indicators as a reflection of regular evaluative activity or as a means of measuring program effectiveness may be questioned (Flynn et al. 1988). However, there can be no doubt that these indicators are seen as important and that the Treasury uses them in assessing departmental budgetary bids (Carter 1991; Thain & Wright 1990).

Over and above performance indicators, however, there is also evidence that the climate of the 1980s and the culture fostered by the FMI has led some departments to strengthen their evaluative activities either by developing internal evaluative capabilities or by engaging external management consultants to evaluate their programs. Hence, in a recent examination of the conduct and management of government programs aimed at facilitating local economic development, Bovaird et al (1991) note that departments such as Trade and Industry (DTI) and Environment (DOE) had made significant efforts to conduct ex-post program evaluations. However, these activities are not as comprehensive as the monitoring and appraisal techniques that usually characterize evaluation in these areas and they are not so much contributions to budgeting as simply tools to be employed in the traditional bargaining process described above. Hence, as Bovaird et al note, evaluations have been commissioned to ward off aggressive Treasury scrutiny during the PES round; those programs considered most vulnerable have been "evaluated most frequently" (1991, p. 109).

It is possible that Whitehall behavior may change in the new world of executive agencies. However, since these agencies will be governed by Treasury disciplines and departmental allocations, the prospect of a new world where organizational budgeting and evaluation will be linked seems remote. Agencies will operate under the existing managerial paradigm and the routines that dominate the public expenditure process.

Budgets and Evaluation Assessed

In their study of budgeting in British central government Heclo and Wildavsky (1981) argued that PES was a bastion of incrementalism, i.e., a device through which the center and the departments conducted ritual-

istic bargaining games. This may still be true, although much has
changed: the political and economic environments, the relationships
between the major players in the budgetary game and the language and
routines by which this game is played.

The last point is important. To force departments to discuss issues in
cash terms *is* to amend their behavior. To talk of *managers, efficiency,
delegated responsibility* and *accountability for resources* at least changes
the terms on which the old game is now played and may alter the game
itself in a permanent fashion, leading to the cultural change often spoken
of at the center of Whitehall. Hence, in recent years, the lingua franca of
budgeting has been the language of cost and management accounting
rather than that of planning and rational decision making. Such a new
language has its purpose in serving both the political and managerial
functions of the budgetary process. In political terms commitment to such
objectives such as lower inflation, a smaller state and less intervention
requires paradoxically a strong center and a tight control of budgets and
financial management. Recent budgetary and financial management
initiatives have been designed to achieve these objectives. In such a
world, evaluation and performance measurement are useful only as far
as they facilitate these aims, i.e., legitimate evaluations are ones that serve
rather than question the system.

In Schick's terms (see above, Ch. 1) it therefore appears that the United
Kingdom has never really achieved the status of a mature budgetary
system. At best it has flirted with planning and then for numerous reasons
abandoned it or consigned it to the back burner. Subsequently it has
firmly embraced the control function and sought to refine this through
increasingly sophisticated systems of financial management. This appears to be management within an immature budgetary system or one
which Schick describes as insular or "back to basics" (1988, p. 532). This
has limited the actual and potential role that evaluation is able to play.
The effect on the development of auditing will now be explored.

Public Sector Auditing in the U.K.

The Development and Role of Public Sector Audit

Audit is one of the oldest and most firmly entrenched financial
activities in government, not least because of its link with *accountability,*

i.e., the holding of the government to account for the way it uses and disposes of public funds. The audit function is therefore generally linked to the power of legislatures to scrutinize the actions of the executive. How far such scrutiny should probe the substance as well as the process of policy is arguable. However, there is little doubt that the audit function (and the organizations and processes associated with it) provide legislatures with one of their strongest weapons to explore the conduct and content of public policy.

In the United Kingdom, budgetary process audit represents what Likierman sees as "the essential final stage in the public expenditure cycle" (1988, p. 163). However, to what extent auditing links systemically with budgeting is more difficult to assess. Undoubtedly constitutional and parliamentary procedures set out guidelines for checking that funds are authorized and expended in the proper manner. This involves the examination and approval of accounts and the passing of judgments on the propriety of actions. Yet this seems not to link up with or influence the budgetary cycle (PES).

Government organizations are subject to both *internal* and *external* audit. For the purpose of this discussion it is the latter that is of the most interest since it is here that audit achieves its greatest powers and, through value-for-money study, comes close to conducting evaluations. However, the role of internal audit should not be overlooked, especially since recently there have been attempts to strengthen and widen its scope and function.

Traditionally internal audit exists as an adjunct to financial control. Its objectives vary according to context but in central departments, governed by Treasury guidelines, include the examination of the appropriateness and adequacy of accounting, financial and other controls, reviewing the compliance of the organization with established policies and procedures, ensuring the safeguard of assets and monitoring the reliability of financial data (Likierman 1988, pp. 164-5). The underlying purpose is therefore to promote good housekeeping. Historically there is little evidence of any link with evaluation and its contribution to budgeting has been one of ensuring the presence of internal controls. However, in the changing world of delegated budgets and financial management, the traditional function of internal audit is being widened. It has frequently been argued that in the United Kingdom public sector the quality of internal audit is low and that its functions should be expanded to assist new financial regimes. Consequently there have been moves by the Treasury to strengthen the role of internal audit to assist the development of new management techniques and undertake value-for-money studies. To date, however, it seems that such a revamped role is likely to be limited (Wilson 1987).

But what *is* the task of audit? Traditionally, it encompasses what Fielden terms *financial* and *regularity* audits (1984, p.218). Financial audit involves an assessment of the adequacy of financial systems to ensure that rules are followed and controls properly applied. Regularity audit is designed to ensure that departments and public sector bodies incur only such expenditures as have legislative approval and that they also serve Parliament's intentions. However, as Fielden also observes, recent critics have argued that as the political and financial environments have changed such functions may require extension. Such critics draw attention to the growth of government, to frequent failures by the executive to give attention to policy implementation, to an increasingly complex body of legislation hastily pushed through Parliament and to a general weakening of parliamentary powers of scrutiny and accountability. Such developments are reinforced by concerns with waste and inefficiency in the public sector and the effectiveness of programs. On such a basis there have been calls to extend audit functions to deal more forcefully with *value-for-money*, and especially *efficiency* and *effectiveness* of programs.

If auditing is to assume this new role it may need to be organized, staffed and operated in a way significantly different from before. It is also likely to be drawn further into the political arena. Not surprisingly this alarms those with a traditional view of audit and has led to debate in the audit profession over the scope and nature of VFM auditing. Some argue that if VFM work is defined as covering economy, efficiency and effectiveness it must inevitably lead to a questioning of program objectives (i.e., policy). Those who see themslves as objective technicians rather than policy analysts resist this interpretation (Fielden 1984). Until recently this view has held sway; but there is some evidence now of a move within audit agencies in the United Kingdom to adopt the more penetrative approach associated with Canada, Sweden and the United States. Some of the evidence for this view is discussed below.

External Audit in U.K. Central Government: Historical Background

In terms of financial scrutiny the U.K. Parliament's most important arm is the Committee of Public Accounts (PAC) and it is to the PAC (and through the PAC to Parliament) that the National Audit Office (NAO) and its head, the Comptroller and Auditor General (C&AG), report. The PAC is one of the longest established committees of the House of Commons (over one hundred years). The origins of the office of C&AG go back even further (to the fourteenth century) and since the late ninteenth century, in theory at least, the C&AG has been independent of government and responsible only to Parliament (Likierman 1988, p. 166).

Audit has therefore evolved in the United Kingdom as part of the parliamentary scrutiny process. Since 1866 when the Exchequer and Audit Act formally established the Exchequer and Audit Department and empowered its head, the C&AG, to examine accounts on behalf of Parliament, the audit system has been based on financial and regularity audits of government departments. However, by the mid-1960s serious questions were raised about the efficiency and effectiveness of the system of external audit. A study by Normanton (1966), for example, compared state audit in a number of countries and found U.K. arrangements seriously wanting, especially in contrast to those in the United States. This fueled increasing doubts about the independence of the C&AG from the executive, the scope and scale of his operations, the Treasury's influence on the staffing of the Exchequer and Audit Department and on the way accounts were presented, and the limitations of regularity audit, which said little about the efficiency and effectiveness of expenditures.

Although these criticisms persisted, reform proposals were firmly resisted by the center of government and, initially, drew little support from Parliament. Garrett (1986) attributes this to low interest coupled with a lack of support facilities to allow members to keep abreast of financial matters. However, the criticisms gathered strength and centered on the independence of the C&AG and his staff from the executive, the widening of his jurisdiction to agencies outside the central departments, and the need to formalize the audit link with Parliament.

These efforts came to a head in 1981 when the Public Accounts Committee published a special report calling for new audit legislation to ensure parliamentary accountability. This legislation would establish a

National Audit Office and institutionalize arrangements to ensure the C&AG's independence and links to Parliament. The initial reaction of the government was to resist these proposals. For once, however, the House of Commons united to put pressure on the executive to increase parliamentary power. In 1983 a private member's bill passed through the House of Commons to be enacted as the National Audit Act. Under it the National Audit Office was established (to replace the old Exchequer and Audit Department) with both it and the C&AG being formally established as officers of the Commons. The act also empowered the C&AG to widen his brief to economy, efficiency and effectiveness of departmental operations. However, it was also stated that he was not entitled to question the merits of departmental policy objectives (Garrett 1986, p. 424).

The struggle to create the NAO is significant since it indicates how the scope and nature of public sector audit in the United Kingdom has been dominated by political battles between Parliament and the executive. In this context the argument of the reformers is that accountability can only be served by strengthening the audit function and through this the power of Parliament. Against this the executive would claim that increasing the powers of audit (and evaluation) puts unnecessary checks on the executive, possibly limiting its capacity to govern. As we shall see below, this issue becomes crucial as audit moves into the areas of effectiveness and value-for-money studies.

External Audit in the 1980s: The Operations of the NAO

With its renewed regularity audit function and its new remit to embrace value-for-money studies, the NAO set out to change its structure and operating processes. Since its inception it has aimed to recruit graduates and to ensure these obtain accounting qualifications. It has also sought to break away from formal civil service pay scales and has been active in using and developing new technologies. The NAO has therefore attempted to create a new image and to develop an effective style of working that differs from the old Exchequer and Audit Department.

However, with regard to the links between audit, budgets and evaluation the greatest interest must be the NAO's move into statutory value-for-money audits. In the NAO there is a growing emphasis on this work whether relating to individual departmental programs or interdepartmental activities. In organizational terms the NAO has been structured so that its staff covers (and has access to) the activities of specific departments. From information emerging from these sections a strategy for VFM audit is drawn up and priorities for investigation established.

If this portrays the NAO primarily in an inquisitorial role this would not be wholly accurate. While the NAO does indeed see part of its task as exposing and highlighting inefficiencies, it also seeks to facilitate and improve departmental systems and operating practices. Thus, while frequently critical, the NAO also discusses its work with the departments involved and indeed clears reports with them before publication. Thus, although the NAO has right of access to departmental staff and papers, it also depends on departmental cooperation to continue its work successfully on a long-term basis. This shapes the NAO's investigations. Hence reports may be edited to avoid departmental embarrassment, especially in areas where the NAO is seeking to facilitate improvement in systems and procedures.

The NAO's VFM work therefore covers a variety of departments and differing activities (e.g., in agriculture, environmental matters, health and transport). In all these areas detailed studies have been conducted, often involving a great deal of fieldwork and frequently the use of external consultants. Yet how deeply do such studies go in examining the effectiveness of activities? As Garrett points out, this area is fraught with technical and related difficulties. This not only involves establishing the relationship of outcome to objective but also examining and, if possible, measuring a program's impact (1986, p. 426).

Such factors undoubtedly cause problems for the NAO in extending its remit, not least because VFM work differs from traditional audit in having a more flexible methodology. In its early days the NAO attempted to deal with this issue by concentrating efforts on areas of control weaknesses or of waste and extravagance (i.e., to use it to pursue traditional audit functions). The NAO would now claim that it has extended VFM audits to larger-scale studies in major areas of government activity. Here the intention is to go beyond investigations of economy, i.e., resource consumption, to deal with wider questions of efficiency and effectiveness. However, to all this the NAO sets out a coda:

> All NAO value for money examinations avoid questioning the merits of policy objectives which are for Ministers and Parliament to decide. This does not preclude, however, an examination of the completeness and accuracy of the information on

which these decisions were based nor does it prevent an investigation of the implementation of the agreed policy and its impact (National Audit Office 1988).

The NAO therefore faces a dilemma as it seeks to broaden the functions of state audit work. As a body external to government accountable directly to Parliament, it has considerable power and legitimacy. However, if it seeks to expand its functions to encompass genuine effectiveness measurement work, the basis for this legitimacy weakens not only in terms of its relationships with departments but also within Parliament since party pressures are likely to be brought to bear if it moves into sensitive areas. There is also the problem that the NAO's findings lie in the public domain, i.e., its reports are published. Thus the NAO's activities have been restricted primarily to areas of management and financial control that do not put great strain on government-Parliament relationships. In the view of the PAC its function is to deal with matters of *financial accountability*. Any wider interpretation of this function would compromise this position, leading to frictions between the PAC and the executive.

Other State Audit Bodies: The Audit Commission

The National Audit Office is not the only public sector auditor in the United Kingdom. As was noted above, the Audit Commission also exists as an independent body with responsibilities for the audit of local authorities and for conducting value-for-money studies in the areas for which local government has responsibility. Its terms of reference are now to be extended to the National Health Service (NHS).

The Audit Commission emerged via the Local Government Finance Act of 1982. In its early days under its first Director of Audit, John Banham, it demonstrated a firm commitment to move beyond the traditional role of audit to promote the gospel of the 3Es (economy, efficiency and effectiveness) and to develop VFM studies. During this period the Audit Commission's relationships with the government were often strained, especially when it adopted a critical stance on subjects such as local government finance (Gray & Jenkins 1990). More recently the Commission has taken an active role in attempting to improve the managerial capacity of local authorities and to assist them in adapting to a rapidly changing political climate where many responsibilities for delivering services (e.g., education, housing) are being removed from their direct control.

Like the NAO, the Audit Commission is an external audit body and has run into difficulties when attempting to advance the development of management systems in the public sector. This has been particularly so in its attempts to develop VFM or effectiveness work. As McSweeney (1988) has observed, there has often been a scarcity of output data and a lack of standards against which performance can be judged. This has led to problems of comparability (e.g., what is a good or efficient local authority?) arising from studies the Commission has conducted and political arguments concerning the "objectivity" of its findings.

Nevertheless, the Commission has been active in promoting a consistent methodology of effectiveness and efficiency measurement. This makes it possible to see the Audit Commission as an evaluative agency. Henkel (1991), for example, has argued that it has adopted such a role not least in studying the impact of local government services on the public and demonstrating an increased concern with effectiveness issues. Yet, as she also notes, as in the NAO, policy is not officially the Commission's concern and its preferred mode of action in the current climate is to act as a change agent, facilitating local authority accommodation to a rapidly altering political environment. Thus, the Commission faces particular difficulties not found with the NAO as most of the bodies it deals with are elected and party political. To move outside the traditional audit role is therefore to place itself in a vulnerable position where the legitimacy of its findings (and its intentions) may be called to question. In Henkel's view (1991), one of the strengths of the Audit Commission is not only its recognition of this fact but also its efforts to impose a managerial perspective on a political world. Its successes, however, reflect also on the relative political weakness of U.K. local government during this period.

Audit and Accountability in a Political Climate

The above discussion illustrates the difficulties faced by audit bodies as they attempt to extend their role and functions. Traditional audit claims a consistent and generic methodology. In the world of VFM audit this is no longer the case and studies are conducted in an arena of greater uncertainty and political sensitivity. Such dilemmas are well charted in the policy evaluation literature. How far they can be accommodated by audit without threatening its traditional claim to independence is an important question. Consequently, to broaden their functional base in any effective way audit agencies may have to restructure their values and approaches.

This leads to the issue of accountability, as the case for extending audit's role is often made on the basis of increasing accountability. This rhetoric has accompanied the development of programs such as the Financial Management Initiative (accountable managers) as well as other recent developments in the public sector such as local management for schools, universities and hospitals (accountable teachers, professors and doctors). Similarly, the rationales for the Audit Commission and the revamped NAO rested on the need to make local government and the executive, respectively, more accountable.

Although the term accountability appears throughout this debate, it is often used in different ways by different participants and is underpinned by different assumptions and meanings (Gray & Jenkins 1985, Ch. 6). For example, while traditional forms of audit reflect well-defined forms of accountability (financial, regulatory), efforts to develop effectiveness audits and VFM work widen the concept into the areas of policy and political accountability. In many ways this might be desirable. However, it also indicates why such developments cause problems and why, when faced by critical reports from bodies such as the NAO and the Audit Commission, the executive in the United Kingdom has attempted to narrow the parameters of what it is and should be accountable for. Hence, at the center accountability is often defined narrowly (i.e., in a managerial or technical fashion) with the function of audit restricted to serve this. In contrast, advocates of greater public scrutiny define accountability more broadly and politically. This perspective extends the language of audit, rejects the traditional limits placed on it and seeks to extend its functions. As a result it increases the potential for conflicts within organizational and political systems.

Budgeting, Auditing, and Evaluation in the U.K.: Systemically United or Loosely Coupled?

In his account of budgeting, auditing and evaluation in the Federal Republic of Germany, Derlien (Ch. 4) highlights the fact that the Bonn policy making process is essentially a two track system that does not integrate policy making and budgeting. He does find, however, that there is a greater congruency between budgeting and auditing systems. Segsworth's discussion of Canadian experience also indicates a certain lack of unity and disjointedness in the historical pattern of developments. His account indicates that in Canada there may have been two distinct and incompatible bases of budgetary reform. On the one hand central agencies and the executive have dominated the main budgetary system, while on the other, internal audit and evaluation policies have been directed exclusively at departments. He concludes that "in the past, it is clear that there was no successful integration of these processes" (Ch. 5).

This paper comes to a similar if more extreme conclusion: British experience is not so much twin-track as multitrack, not so much out of sequence as almost disconnected. Brought together, these three accounts suggest that there is rarely one integrated system in which budgeting, evaluation and auditing are drawn together. Rather there are different subsystems in operation (dominated by different actors and different histories) that are, at best, what organization theorists refer to as "loosely-coupled". Further, the dominating influences that have shaped such systems are political and historical centering on the control of the budgetary process. Auditing and evaluation can be understood only in terms of how they relate (or fail to relate) to the budgetary system.

Crucial to all this is the concept of *ownership*. In the United Kingdom (and in many other systems) the executive "owns" the budget. There may be fighting within departments over how the cake is divided, but the center is jealous of its property rights. In political terms budgetary control appears essential to maintain a power base and to achieve goals in the ways the center defines them. In contrast, audit in Britain is owned primarily by Parliament and is employed as a device in the power game between Parliament and the executive. In constitutional terms this is perfectly acceptable. Parliament has the duty of scrutiny and a strong audit facility may be necessary to check a powerful executive. However, what this means is that, other than in a token and symbolic way, audit does not become part of the budgetary process. As presently constructed it is a subsystem that serves Parliament. Moves to increase its effectiveness (i.e., to move it toward evaluation) will be resisted since this will challenge executive power.

In such a world both major parties (i.e., legislature and executive) would claim to conduct audit and evaluations but these are separate activities, conducted by different organizations on different terms. Audit in the budgetary process is usually internal, focusing on regularity and propriety; overall goals are not questioned and the process is directed down the governmental organization rather than upward to the top. In contrast external audit, while also taking on basic auditing tasks, has recently sought to widen its compass and ask deeper questions. It is this that has brought it close to conducting evaluations, an activity that not all auditors are happy with.

Evaluation in the budgetary process is designed to serve the executive, is usually carried out internally and is structured to serve political goals. In certain circumstances it may not be carried out at all. Evaluation in audit is conducted by independent organizations (independent, that is, of the executive) and is designed to further the cause of scrutiny. Such activities have the potential to be destabilizing in political terms, especially since they may question the assumptions on which decisions and policies are based.

This picture is not new or peculiar to the current U.K. administration. It represents the outcomes of historical developments in the executive itself and in executive-legislative relationships. However, in the current era there may be particular consequences of the operation of such a loosely coupled system driven by an executive-dominated budgetary process. Indeed *politics may shape budgeting*, i.e., budgetary systems and budgetary development may be products of particular types of politics.

The idea of politics having shaped budgeting during the Thatcher era is worth exploration. While it is too simple to describe Thatcherism as the search for a "free economy" through a "strong state" (Gamble 1988), there is little doubt that recent U.K. governments, driven by strong ideological commitments, have sought to strengthen central controls in order to achieve major political objectives. Such a stance has placed high value on commitment, action and simplicity. It has been underpinned both by a distrust of intermediate institutions (e.g., local government, health agencies and professional groups) and the state itself as agents of change and also by a touching faith in market mechanisms. This type of politics has led to a particular rhetoric - freedom, choice, efficiency, markets, customers - and a particular style of action - committed, rigorous, certain.

Such a form of politics can be seen in operation in the U.K. budgetary world. Goals are taken as clear and the only issue is how these are to be implemented within a cash-controlled system. Public organizations are assumed to be inherently inefficient and hence have a seemingly infinite capacity to make savings. Performance is judged against targets, usually budgets. Objectives are rarely questioned or alternatives sought, nor is evaluation, other than in cost terms, thought necessary.

In such a world budgeting has become less simple as simplistic and, in a paradoxical fashion, the search for control has, in many ways, resulted in its loss. Historical accounts of budgeting indicate that budgets must be designed to cope with uncertainties and, indeed, that the process itself may involve the management of uncertainties. As such there is a limit to control. Indeed an obsession with control may prove counterproductive.

With these thoughts in mind we can return briefly and finally to the example with which this paper began, i.e., the British National Health Service (NHS). For the NHS the problem may well be a budgetary one, especially since there has been little analysis or evaluation of its performance. In political terms, however, the faults are self-evidently managerial; for these, conviction politics provide a certain solution. Here evaluation is unnecessary; indeed it would be a sign of political weaknesses. Audit may improve matters but even here this may be on the government's terms (i.e., the scope of the Audit Commission to examine value for money issues is limited). So the loosely coupled systems of budgeting, auditing and evaluation coexist perhaps in an even more fragmented form than before. Disjointed, they wait (probably in vain) for a new type of politics to draw them together in a different fashion.

References

Barnett, J. (1982). *Inside the Treasury*. London: Andre Deutsch

Bovaird, T., D. Gregory, & S. Martin. (1991). "Improved Performance in Local Economic Development." *Public Administration*, 69/1, 103-19.

Carter, N. (1991). "Learning to Measure Performance: The Use of Indicators in Organisations." *Public Administration*, 69/1, 89-101.

Clarke, Sir Richard. (1978). *Public Expenditure, Management and Control* (edited by Sir Alec Caincross). London: Macmillan.

CM 555 (1989). *Working for Patients*. London: HMSO.

Fielden, J. (1984). "Presures for Change in Public Sector Audit." Ch. 11 in A. Hopwood & C. Tompkins, eds., *Issues in Public Sector Accounting*. Oxford: Philip Allan.

Flynn, A.C., A.G. Gray, W.I. Jenkins, & B.A. Rutherford. (1988). "Making Indicators Perform." *Public Money and Management*, 8/4, 35-41.

Flynn, A.C., A.G. Gray, & W.I. Jenkins. (1990). "Taking the Next Steps: The Changing Management of Government." *Parliamentary Affairs*, 43/2, 159-78.

Gamble, A. (1989). *The Free Economy and the Strong State*. London: Macmillan.

Garrett, J. (1986). "Developing State Audit in Britain". *Public Administration*, 64/4, 421-3.

Gray, A.G. & W.I. Jenkins. (1982). "Policy Analysis in British Central Government: The Experience of PAR". *Public Administration*, 60/4, 429-50.

Gray, A.G. & W.I. Jenkins. (1985). *Administrative Politics in British Government*. Brighton: Harvester Wheatsheaf.

Gray, A.G. & W.I. Jenkins. (1989). "Policy Evaluation in a Time of Fiscal Stress: Some Reflections on British Experience". *Knowledge in Society*, 2/4, 20-30.

Gray, A.G. & W.I. Jenkins. (1990). "Policy Evaluation in British Government: From Idealism to Realism". Ch. 3 in R. Rist, ed, *Program Evaluation and the Management of Government*. New Brunswick, N J : Transaction Publishers.

Gray A.G., W.I. Jenkins with A.C. Flynn and B.A. Rutherford. (1991). "The Management of Change in Whitehall: The Experience of the Financial Management Initiative". *Public Administration*, 69/1, 41-60.

Heald, D. (1983). *Public Expenditure*. Oxford: Martin Roberston.

Heclo, H. & A. Wildavsky. (1981 edn). *The Private Government of Public Money*. London: Macmillan.

Henkel, M. (1991). "The New 'evaluative' state." *Public Administration*, 69/1, 121-36.

Hennessy, P. (1989). *Whitehall*. London: Secker & Warburg.

Likierman, A. (1988). *Public Expenditure: The Public Spending Process*. Harmondsworth: Penguin Books.

McSweeney, B. (1988). "Accounting for the Audit Commission." *Political Quarterly*, 59/1, 28-43.

National Audit Office (1988). *The Role of the NAO*.

Normanton, E.L. (1966). *The Accountability and Audit of Governments*. Manchester: Manchester University Press.

Pliatzky, L. (1982). *Getting and Spending*. Oxford: Blackwell.

Port, J. (1990). "Devolved Budgeting." *Public Finance & Accountancy*. 9 February, 11-13.

Schick, A. (1986). "Macro Budgetary Adaptations to Fiscal Stress in Industrialised Democracies." *Public Administration Review*, 46/2, 124-34.

Schick, A. (1988). "Micro Budgetary Adaptations to Fiscal Stress in Industrialised Democracies." *Public Administration Review*, 48/5, 523-33.

Thain, C. & M. Wright. (1988). "Public Expenditure in the UK since 1976." *Public Policy and Administration*, 3/1, 1-18.

Thain, C. & M. Wright. (1990). "Running costs in Central Government." *Financial Accountability and Management*, 6/2, 115-31.

Treasury (1986). *Multi-Departmental Review of Budgeting: Executive Summary and Final Report*. HM Treasury.

Treasury (1988). *Policy Evaluation: a Guide for Managers*. London: HMSO.

Wilson, T. (1987). "Management Evolution in the Civil Service." *Public Finance &*
    Accountancy, 15 May, 6-9.
Wright, M., ed. (1980). *Public Spending Decisions*. London: George Allen and Unwin

4

Two-Track Processes:
Budgeting, Auditing, and Evaluation in the
Federal Republic of Germany

Hans-Ulrich Derlien

Previous research has revealed that evaluation has been closely linked to innovations in the budgetary process at least in some countries (Rist 1990). A broader scope is adopted here by looking at evaluation as only one albeit important element in the system of budgeting and auditing. To what extent, for example, do evaluations of programs, which are frequently quite costly, affect the state budget and how does evaluation fit in with more traditional monitoring mechanisms like auditing and accounting? Although it has already been indicated (Derlien 1990a) that budget law has been a complementary factor in institutionalizing evaluation in Germany and that the link between budgeting and evaluation is a feasible one, this paper takes up the subject again, this time from a systems perspective.

The paper has four sections. First, the relevant terminology used in Germany is explicated and basic organizational traits of the budgeting and auditing system at the level of federal government are described. Since the broader policy making system in Bonn does not systematically integrate programmatic policy making and budgeting (i.e., it is "two-track"), it is no surprise that evaluation is linked primarily to program development, while financial auditing is predominantly a phase in the budgetary cycle. Second, the paper investigates the historical development of the bugetary system and the role of financial auditing. Budgeting and accounting practices have developed over a period of 250 years to serve a number of functions. Among these the program function of the budget was institutionalized only in 1969, whereas most of the norms determining the system were devised to serve parliamentary control functions that were gradually imposed on the management function budgeting and auditing served in the monarchic state. This might explain the peculiar role the German Federal Court of Audit plays in auditing budget operations. Third, the paper analyzes the selective criteria according to which this institution, which has its roots in the absolutist state, operates today. The final section summarizes the findings by asking, from a systemic perspective, why evaluation is not more firmly linked to budgeting in the Federal Republic of Germany (FRG).

Elements of the System

Conceptualizing budgeting, auditing and evaluation as systematically interrelated is facilitated by adopting a cybernetic model. In this model budgeting corresponds to the planning phase and, after the implementation of the (annual) budget has been completed, accounts are drawn up and information fed back to the planning/budgeting phase through mechanisms that are customarily termed "auditing" or "monitoring". Accounting and evaluation, but also audits focussing on conformity with budgetary law, are among the most customary of these feedback mechanisms. However, the practical terminology in the various countries might differ from these general terms and translating the terminology from German into English loses some of the meaning. It seems appropriate, therefore, to clarify the national terminology, and thereby some of the implicit philosophy, before turning to the central actors and their role in the budget cycle.

Terminology

There are various words used in German for the English "budget". As well as "Budget", "Etat" and "Haushalt" (literally household) are customary. The *budget* is usually defined as a periodic, detailed and systematic compilation of estimated revenues and planned expenditures of a public corporation, which to a certain extent is binding for the operations of the state organs. The words "detailed" and "systematic" refer to the requirement that budget items be quantitatively and qualitatively (by denominating their purpose) specified and put together in the budget according to certain principles, for instance according to institutional responsibilities or programmatic coherence. The definition, furthermore, implies that the budget is formally legislated, and therefore binding, and that this has to happen in certain intervals, usually annually (but as in the case of Bavaria this may be biannually). Apart from the annual budget, the government has, since 1967, also prepared annually a five-year financial plan. This is basically a projection of the current budget with little determining power for next year's budget (Nachtkamp 1976, Wille 1977); it is also less detailed than the annual budget and submitted to Parliament only for informational purposes.

The mechanism corresponding to *auditing* is in German "Rechnungsprüfung" (literally: checking accounts). Like the English word "auditing", the German expression refers to financial matters, but is confined to formal aspects. Substantive financial checkups are termed "Finanzkontrolle" (Zavelberg 1990). As a theoretical term, auditing applies also to checking and communicating results of public activities that would not necessarily imply financial operations. Another way of stating this peculiar selectivity of auditing when limited to financial operations would be to outline the objects and criteria of auditing (see below). Financial auditing presupposes *accounting* (Rechnungslegung). Again, it is significant whether the accounting categories are restricted to financial operations or include outputs or even impacts.

The German word for *evaluation* is "Erfolgskontrolle", although the term "program evaluation" is gaining ground in German. Recently the relationship between auditing and evaluation has been discussed (Rürup & Färber 1985; Blasius 1989), indicating that evaluation has developed in a context different from budgeting and auditing. While evaluation is primarily related to program development and its institutionalization was brought about in the process of expanding state intervention programs in the late 1960s, auditing is tied to budgeting. Also, the federal government never really attempted to apply a system of integrated budgeting, connecting program development and financial planning in a systematic way. Thus, decision making in Bonn follows a *two-track* system.

This does not mean that there is no political relationship between a government's program and its budget. Political considerations enter the financial middle-range plan and the annual budget through politics on all levels of decision making. For instance, empirical evidence (Treiber

1984) proves that incoming governments will affect the budgetary base, i.e., those allocations that are continued from one budget year into the next without critical questioning; also, political exigencies may drive a government to draft an extraordinary budget (Nachtragshaushalt) during the fiscal year or exceed established budget limits in urgent and unforeseen situations. In response to the reunification of Germany, five supplementary budgets were legislated in 1990. The political rationale of this procedure is that items which years ago have entered the budget through politics may continue to claim political legitimacy unless questioned. Thus, traditional budgeting is politico-logical and therefore subjected to rationalist criticisms and confronted with reform models that ultimately aim at an integrated system of policy planning and budgeting, in which all budget items are deduced from national goals or explicit policy priorities.

In principle, evaluation could be related to budgeting, if the finance ministry in preparing the annual budget requested evaluation studies from the departments. This, however, is almost never done. The incongruency between auditing and evaluation observable in Bonn does not originate from the two-track system as such, but has theoretical reasons, too, because the concept of evaluation is not limited to financial programs; in fact, evaluation is often concerned with regulatory policy without financial implications.

Central Actors in the Budget Cycle

Drafting the budget is an executive matter. It is the *Ministry of Finance* and its budget division that is in control of all informational sources and operations involved in preparing the annual budget. On the request of the finance ministry, the individual departments submit budget proposals. In asking for budget proposals (Haushaltsvoranschläge) in December of each budget year, the Ministry of Finance issues guidelines, which are based on previous discussions within various commissions preparing revenue estimates, economic forecasts and coordinating federal and state fiscal policies. In spite of the guidelines, the sum of the departmental budget proposals, as in most other countries, regularly exceeds the estimated revenues. Consequently, the Ministry of Finance negotiates with the ministries, occasionally ending in the Cabinet. Here the finance minister is in a strong position rooted in paragraph 26 of the Procedural

Code (Geschäftsordnung), which states that he can only be overruled by the Cabinet if the chancellor does not back him.

What is submitted to Parliament for legislation is a draft in which 8000 budget items are classified in a threefold way. The coding, on which electronic data processing relies when systematic aggregates are produced and attached to the budget, is functional, macroeconomic and institutional. The functional classification, introduced in 1957, involves nine traditional and nonprogram delineations of the policy area. The macro-economic classification, developed in 1969, follows the logic of national accounting and, apart from distinguishing three types of revenues, differentiates six categories of expenditures with special emphasis on different types of investments. However, the most important, and historically oldest, classification is the institutional system, which follows departmental jurisdictions. A departmental budget (Einzelplan) is composed of chapters (Kapitel), of which the first contains all expenditures (for instance salaries) consumed or invested (buildings) in the department itself.

The institutional classification is powerful because it reflects the communication patterns between the budget division of the finance ministry, which is internally differentiated according to ministerial budgets, and the departments. The same pattern is repeated in the *parliamentary budget committee* (Haushaltsausschu), which is the main actor during the appropriation process. While the policy committees of Parliament are almost completely excluded from the working of the budget committee, thus deflecting political and programmatic considerations, the individual reporters (Berichterstatter) of the latter are specialized in departmental budgets (Sturm 1988). Whereas the plenary discussions of the Bundestag, which basically serve party political publicity functions, do not substantially affect the shape of the budget, the budget committee is the central actor in the parliamentary phase. However, it rarely changes the government's budget proposal by any significant amount. Even here it is impossible to disentangle genuine parliamentary influence from government suggestions to improve the budget draft since, when it has reached Parliament in September before the financial year, premises are likely to be outdated for exogenous reasons.

During the implementation phase the focus of activity shifts toward the spending departments, although the Ministry of Finance is in a position to control the spending process through regulations and withholding consent to certain spending items. This requirement of consent (Haushaltssperre) is legislated for, in part, for specific spending categories, or can be imposed at the discretion of the Ministry. At the end of the fiscal year the executive, through the Ministry, prepares a complicated system of accounts (Rechnungslegung) submitted to the *accounts committee* of the Bundestag, which is a subcommittee of the budget committee, and to the Federal Court of Audit. This is the primary basis of auditing (Prüfung) by the *Federal Court of Audit* (Bundesrechnungshof; BRH). As every postwar federal government was discharged by Parliament, it is the BRH that dominates this final phase of the budgetary cycle. Until 1969 the BRH reported exclusively to the government, which reflected the executive bias derived from its absolutist origins; since the 1969 budgetary reform the BRH reports simultaneously to Parliament and the government, and in 1985 the balance was redrawn again by having the president of the BRH elected by parliament instead of having him appointed by government. The auditing report prepared by the BRH is published in parliamentary proceedings and a shortened version handed out to the press which publishes it widely. It is only through this publicity that the Federal Court of Audit has some effect on future government planning and budgeting, because it has no formal sanctioning power of its own. However, the influence of the auditors is not limited to ex-post auditing, but extends to concomitant auditing, which takes the form of advice during budget preparation. Furthermore, in each ministry there is an extension of the Federal Court of Audit (Vorprüfstelle), which on a sampling basis carries out some financial auditing during the fiscal year. What the Federal Court of Audit does not engage in, however, is evaluation beyond traditional conformity and financial auditing. The auditing criteria will be analyzed in more detail below.

According to German public law, the budgetary system (including auditing) is highly formalized. The constitution itself contains important rules (Art. 109 ff.) for determining budget principles and budgetary legislation since 1967. Article 109, for example, has required the federal government to promote economic equilibrium, and entitles the Bundestag to legislate common budgetary principles for the federation and states. The position of the Federal Court of Audit is laid down in Art. 114 and will be dealt with below.

The procedures of budgeting and auditing are laid down in the Federal Budgetary Code (Bundeshaushaltsordnung of 1969). Evaluation became only indirectly institutionalized, when the Ministry of Finance issued an administrative regulation in 1973, which interpreted Section 7 Federal Budgetary Code, concerning cost-benefit analysis, in such a way as to include also ex-post analysis. As the departments have to submit cost-benefit analyses for "important measures" if requested by the Ministry, the administrative regulation of 1973 also puts the Ministry in a position to request evaluation studies. However, the ministry seldom does this for political reasons, and the BRH recently criticized this deviation (Bundesrechnungshof 1991, 43 f.).

Historical Developments of the Present Budgeting and Auditing System

Today's textbooks ascribe five normative functions to public budgeting, which may serve us here as a heuristic tool to understand the historical evolution of the present budgetary system (Rürup & Körner 1981, 40).

The *program function* emphasizes that the budget should refer to public tasks and should reflect the political program of government. This function was emphasized in the 1960s when it became apparent, that the state operates far beyond merely securing law and order, but intervenes in socio-economic structures and processes. The program function is underlined in the parliamentary budget debate, which as a rule turns out to be a general debate about government policy.

Second, a *macroeconomic policy function* can be attributed to the budget. Since the concept of Keynesian economic policy was adopted in Germany in the 1967 Law on Stability and Growth of Economy, the state has been obliged to keep macroeconomic processes under control and to tailor its budget according to the economic requirements.

Third, the *financial management function* stresses the input side of the budget and postulates that the budget should be concerned with the long-term financial consequences of government operations and with balancing revenues and expenditures.

Fourth, the budget serves a *parliamentary political control function*. It should enable parliament to judge government operations against the aims postulated in the budget and to make the government politically accountable for its macroeconomic policy and fiscal management, the political program behind the budget and its administrative guidance.

Finally, the budget fulfils an *administrative control function* for the government by programming the executive's operations during the budget year and by setting financial constraints for administrative activities.

Historically, these functions developed in reverse order, since the (absolutist) state with its administrative control needs developed prior to parliamentary democracy (Derlien 1987). Consequently, parliamentary budget rights had to be pushed through, *after* core executive institutions like the finance ministries and audit courts had been established.

The Absolutist State and the Administrative Control Function

In creating the absolutist state after the Thirty Years' War and the political neutralization of the estates, a standing army was established as one pillar of the modern state and a financial administration, the sitting army, as a second to secure its financing by levying taxes and carrying through mercantilist economic policy (Rosenberg 1958). In Prussia, permanent taxation became the rule at the beginning of the eighteenth century, when the Prussian state consisted of two administrative branches: the War Commission and the Domesne Chamber (fused in 1723). In 1689 the first budget was prepared to enable the ruler to control the (military) administration. Since 1713 Prussia practiced precise and periodic budgeting, and in 1714 the Prussian accounting chamber (Oberrechnungskammer), the forerunner of the present courts of audit in the federation and the states, was established.

Constitutional Monarchy and Political Control Function

During pre-constitutionalism (1815–1848) the estates achieved participatory rights in the various German territories, partly by influencing tax legislation, partly by co-determining the tasks for which specific taxes were levied, and, in other territories, by influencing the whole spectrum of state expenditures. In the course of the 1848 revolutions parliamentary budgetary rights were extended and codified. Since then, German tax legislation has been separated from annual budget legislation. Although parliamentary budgetary rights did not mean much in practice (the Prussian Prime Minister von Bismarck, after rejection of the military budget in the diet, ruled between 1862 and 1866 without legislated budgets), the budget gradually acquired a parliamentary control function.

In 1872, after the creation of the second German Reich, budgetary rights were also granted to the Reichstag, but because the Reich's budget was rather small and consisted overwhelmingly of military expenses, political influence was peripheral. Nevertheless, Prussian administrative budgetary techniques were adopted by the Reich administration owing to the close links between the prime minister and Reich chancellor.

Weimar Republic and Financial Management Function

After 1918, during the first German Republic, the existing administrative budgetary and auditing techniques were codified in the Reichshaushaltsordnung in 1922, which persisted until 1969. During the Weimar Republic, reparation payments, inflation and economic depression made financial management more important, and in 1927 the president of the then Reichs-Rechnungshof was installed Reichssparkommissar (commissioner for saving). The court of audit itself maintained its affiliation to the executive branch.

The budgetary principles developed by 1922 were strongly shaped by parliamentary control needs as reflected in the principles of annuality (instead of five year military budgets), publicity (no secret parts), and particularly the principles of comprehensiveness (no separate funds), and the temporal and material (aim) specification of items. Financial management needs, on the other hand, were dominant in the principles of balancing the budget, of gross accounting (displaying all cash flows) and of economy and efficiency.

Federal Republic and Economic Policy Function

During the Second Republic after 1949, the basic principles and structures of the state apparatus of the Weimar Republic were restored and the budgetary code of 1922, along with the constitutional norms referred to above, continued. Due to budget expansion and the undeniable impact of the state budget on economic performance, there was a pressing need to improve budgeting in order to make fiscal policy an instrument of macroeconomic policy. Thus, constitutional amendments of 1967 and 1969 created a unitary information base for the then 20,000 local government budgets, the eleven state budgets and the federal budget. This helped to coordinate the fiscal policies of the three layers and to tailor the budget to the economic needs. The macroeconomic policy function was achieved technically by introducing the economic system of item classification for all public budgets. Furthermore, under the influence of integrated budgeting systems abroad (e.g., United States and France), theorists in Germany began to emphasize the program function of the budget. However, the functional classification never reached the level of sophistication required for a true program budget.

Assessment of Functionality

Although empirical research on the relative importance of the individual functions attributed to the budget is lacking, it can be argued that the economic management function is the most important for drafting the budget, followed by the financial management function. For the program function to become stronger, the technical prerequisites of an appropriate central policy planning system and a more sophisticated functional item classification are lacking. The administrative control function probably contributes to the persistence of the institutional budget classification. Since the parliamentary control function rests outside the executive, it hardly clashes with the other functions mentioned, more so because since 1969 the executive orientation of the Federal Court of Audit has become more favorable toward parliament. This has not meant, however, that the BRH has engaged in evaluation.

There has been no significant attempt to reform the budgetary system since 1969. It is indicative that neither Schick (1988) nor Caiden (1988) nor De Visscher (1989) mention any German budget innovation in their surveys. Consistent with the character of a two-track system, budgetary processes were hardly affected by government policies in the 1980s to de-bureaucratize and privatize public activities. In view of the massive public debt burden for restoring East Germany, fiscal management might even gain dominance in the future. So far, moreover, there is no overriding budget philosophy in Parliament (Sturm 1985). Established routines and pragmatism still prevail in budgetary Bonn. As we shall see, the same applies to auditing.

Court of Audit and Auditing Practice

The position of audit offices vis à vis the Cabinet and Parliament has been of utmost importance in the development of evaluation systems in

Europe and the United States (Derlien 1990b). This section deals with the constitutional position of the German Federal Court of Audit (BRH), its functions and its auditing practice. From this discussion, and the ruling doctrine of auditing, we may obtain an additional explanation of the separation of auditing and evaluation in Germany.

Position of the Auditing Office

The earlier historical account indicated a gradual reorientation of the central auditing institution from the executive in favor of parliamentary affiliation (Wittrock 1986). This process links up with the functional differentiation of auditing in a more restricted backward-oriented sense and of giving advice for future decisions of budget makers.

Historical reorientation. As the BRH is historically rooted in the absolutist bureaucracy, it is evident that it first served an administrative control function for the ruler. Since its inception in 1713, in Prussia it functioned independently of the bureaucratic structure and was used by the king to fight corruption and to improve the budget by learning from previous budget implementation. From its inception the institution obviously contributed to a rudimentary separation of powers, at least in the executive branch. Unlike the Prussian constitution of 1850, the 1871 and 1919 Reich constitutions did not guarantee the existence of an audit office, but merely stated the obligation of the finance minister to lay the accounts. The exact position of the audit office, appointment power and communication lines, thus, had to be defined in special legislation. Parliaments after 1848 pressed toward parliamentary affiliation in order to execute fully their newly gained budget rights, while the monarch and, later on, the executive branch adhered to its executive orientation.

In 1872 the Prussian diet passed a law, which secured only independence and the principle of collegial decision making, but sacrificed the obligation to report to the diet. The same pattern was repeated at the Reich level, although Prussian members of Parliament claimed more parliamentary access to the information stored in the audit office. The reorientation of the supreme audit institution did not take place until the Weimar Republic; in 1922 the Court of Audit was allowed to produce reports on request of the Reichstag and was given the authority to ask the government to pass on its regular reports to the Reichstag. In general, though, the political distance between the Court of Audit and the Reichstag was great.

After 1949, it was again a parliamentary initiative that induced the reorientation of the audit office toward Parliament in the budgetary reforms of 1969. The constitution now rules that the BRH has the obligation to report simultaneously to the federal government and Bundestag (as well as to the Bundesrat, the federal chamber). When in 1985 the Federal-Court-of-Audit-Law was amended, Parliament underlined the reporting function and in addition took the right to appoint the president of the Federal Court of Audit and its vice president. Previously, the presidents were appointed by the federal president on request of the federal government; the BRH presidents were regularly former state secretaries.

Differentiation of functions. Although in practice any auditing report serves as a basis to improve future decisions, it makes a difference to the influence of the audit office whether this advisory function is implicit or explicit. The 1969 budget code entitled the BRH to add to its auditing report suggestions for future budgetary improvements. Besides this, it was empowered to give special advice on request of the Bundestag, Bundesrat and the federal government. In response, in 1970 the Cabinet decided to appoint the president of the Bundesrechnungshof ad personam Commissioner for Economy in Public Administration, thereby taking up the 1927 concept of Reich's Savings Commissioner. This decision was to establish a more personal, trusting relationship between the president and the government beside the advisory function of the court as such (Wittrock 1989). Thus, presently the BRH enjoys relative independence from the various branches of government and is regarded by some people as a fourth constitutional power. It has acquired a multifunctionality reaching from traditional legal and financial auditing to routine and personnel advisory functions.

Auditing Practice

Article 114, Section 2 of the constitution states that the BRH has the task to check the annual accounts prepared by the Ministry of Finance and to examine compliance with the standards of economy and regularity (Wirtschaftlichkeit und Ordnungsmäigkeit). Auditing subjects are not only federal ministries, but also QUANGOS and QUAGOS and even

Länder administrations, if these implement federally financed legislation. It is also important to note that auditing does not take place only
after the implementation of the annual budget, but accompanies budget
implementation through preaudits. Furthermore, the BRH may interfere
in current operations if it believes that new regulations affecting the
budget are objectionable.

One way of classifying auditing practice in Germany is to distinguish
between accounts auditing, administrative auditing and constitutional
auditing. *Accounts auditing* (Rechnungskontrolle) concentrates on the
annual partial and summary accounts prepared by the finance minister.
Figures are checked as to their mathematical correctness, their consistency with receipts and their compliance with regulations for compiling
accounts. The target of accounts auditing is the administrative office that
produced the individual account.

Administrative auditing checks compliance with laws and regulations.
Here, the main yardsticks are legality and the principle of economy
(Wirtschaftlichkeit). This type of auditing is addressed to administrative
decision makers with some degree of discretion and responsibility.

Constitutional auditing asks whether the political will of the legislature was fulfilled. Although the ensuing audit report is addressed to
parliament (as well as the federal government and the federal chamber),
this type of auditing is not regarded as a political matter. Even calling a
budgetary behavior unconstitutional has no political consequences unless Parliament declines to discharge the government or even appeals to
the Constitutional Court. The political assessment of the report is left to
the parliamentary accounts committee, a subcommittee of the budgetary
committee, and to Parliament as a whole.

Another way of specifying types of auditing and auditing criteria is to
distinguish auditing of formal aspects, the accuracy of accounts, expenditure conformity with the budgetary law, and material auditing.

The first three criteria all concentrate on compliance with some sort
of norms, be they norms of budgetary behavior (legality) or norms of
mathematical operations (accuracy). However, material auditing
("sachliche Prüfung", literally auditing of the substance matter) is the
most crucial, because this assesses the standard of economy and efficiency (further, see below).

What these criteria mean in practice can best be read from some
examples drawn from the annual report of the BRH as submitted to

Parliament. This report divides into two chapters: general remarks and specific remarks. General remarks typically deal with, e.g.:

- budget excess, in particular spending without qualifying entitlement;
- weaknesses of budget-related practice and procedures like accounting for federal property (1976 report) or applying cost-benefit analysis (1991);
- criticism of increasing fiscal burdens due to interest payments for public loans (1985, 1991), that would narrow the margins of fiscal policy in future budget years.

Specific remarks refer to individual ministries and reveal what, besides accuracy and legality checks, is meant in practice by *economy auditing*. For instance, the Foreign Office was criticized in the 1978 report:

- that "partly serious violations of the principles of orderly budget execution" had been detected. Numerous technical equipment, in particular entertainment electronics had been purchased under misleading declarations and were privately used. But, the audit office complains, the minister did not undertake anything to have the damage restored by those responsible and has not initiated disciplinary or legal measures under the penal code.
- The ministry had built up a staff reserve for the embassies containing, among others, thirty one posts of higher civil servants. Some of these positions, however, were not used for the declared purpose, but the incumbents were partly occupied in the ministry itself, partly delegated to parliamentary party factions (!).
- Embassies kept too much cash and, due to shifts in the exchange rates, lost considerable amounts of money.
- German car drivers were sent abroad to embassies, although one could have used native car drivers. On the other hand, native car drivers had been used, where for security reasons Germans should have been employed (report 1985).

As to the Defense Ministry, which regularly is extensively covered, the 1985 report castigated it, including as follows:

- The ministry had not succeeded to build up a sufficiently large supply of bread in case of defense as deficient wrapping necessitated that part of the supply had to be abandoned. Furthermore, the production of bread in bakeries of the Bundeswehr is regarded uneconomical and should be privatized, which would save 100 million DM per annum.
- The ministry had purchased in 1979 twelve Navy helicopters for six frigates employed in 1982. Until 1987 the ministry had not managed to install the helicopters, which made the complete weapon system ineffective.

Ambivalence of economic rationality. Economic rationality is a particular problem in the auditing field. For example, a fictitious audit by the BRH of the Bamberg Symphony Orchestra might read as follows:

1. Thirty per cent of the orchestra are inactive during large parts of the concert. A more even activity of all musicians, in particular of the drums, would increase efficiency.

2. Eight violins are used in a violin section, when three would have be sufficient.

3. A more balanced way of playing instead of changing between full power (tutti) and low parts (pianissimo) would increase efficiency.

4. Inspection of the individual instruments shows that the triangle is by far the cheapest solution. An increased application of this instrument is recommended.

This case is clearly imaginary and exaggerated. However, it should demonstrate that in order to assess the validity of such an audit, we need a conception of economic rationality, and some notion of the objectives of a measure. This is equally necessary for applying the maximum-principle (effectiveness, resources being constant) as well as the minimum principle (economy, output constant). Very often, though, the objectives of public activities are less than precise. This applies to the goal specification in the budget as well as to other sorts of entitlements, because the description of policy objectives is often the product of political compromise and therefore necessarily blurred. In these cases auditors can do nothing but apply the minimum principle without regard to the implicit goal expectations or potential negative side effects. This ambivalence between maximizing and minimizing principles may also be induced by treating economy and efficiency on the same logical level within the budgetary code (Wirtschaftlichkeit und Sparsamkeit), although, as every economist knows, saving is just one way of interpreting the principle of economic rationality. While this restricted interpretation of the standard of economy allows an assessment of individual decisions and projects, it is obviously no basis for evaluating programs in terms of their impacts.

Auditing beyond the budget? Auditing is part of the parliamentary discharge procedure and serves parliamentary control functions by keeping individuals in the executive branch accountable for their budgetary behaviour. But German auditing philosophy does not extend to program evaluation. There are several reasons for this. First, the German admin-istrative culture does not think in terms of programs. Practitioners have not yet learned that a law can also be conceived of as a program. This might have contributed to the tradition of perceiving laws as eternal, although in reality they are quite frequently amended. Second, from the point of view of financial auditing, there is a gap between legislated programs and the budget. As auditing is undoubtedly related to budgeting and as accountability has to do with accounts, only the budgetary consequences of legislation are reviewed, while the laws themselves are not part of the budget. Third, the political will expressed in legislation is customarily regarded as sacrosanct by the audit office. Thus, it is fre-quently argued that assessing the achievement of politically decided goals implies political judgments and oversteps the boundary into politics (Kisker 1989). However, there are some signs that auditors regard it as legitimate for them to refer to politically set goals (Geist 1984; Selmer 1990). Given the notorious imprecision of goal declarations, however, the BRH might be justified in warning of the danger in substituting the auditors' operationalizations for the politicians' will.

More recently it is increasingly acknowledged, that the Federal Court of Audit could take the results of budgetary audits as the occasion to request program evaluation of legislation without necessarily carrying through these evaluations (Zavelberg 1990). In line with this reasoning, the president of the federal audit office in his capacity as commissioner for economy in administration recently published a study (BWV 1990), in which the state of program evaluation in the executive branch was analyzed. This recommended that the minister of finance should request evaluation studies more frequently when preparing the budget, and measures were suggested to strengthen the institutionalization of the evaluation function in the federal ministries. Thus it might be argued that the BRH is in the process of opening up and strengthening evaluation capacities in the executive branch (Rürup & Färber 1985; Diederich et al. 1990). It is, however, doubtful whether the BRH is willing or capable of carrying through major evaluations with sufficient regularity.

Why Evaluation Is Not Linked to Budgeting and Auditing

There seems to be a tendency toward congruency between budgeting and auditing systems. Since program budgeting has never developed in

Germany, one cannot expect program evaluation to be part of the auditing process. Furthermore, despite the economic policy and program functions recently attributed to the budget, the budgetary system is, for historical reasons, devised primarily for the function of administrative and parliamentary control and emphasizes administrative and political accountability. The surpreme audit office has been shaped by this administrative control function and has only recently become a "subsidiary organ" of the legislative branch. No wonder, therefore, that the auditing process serves first the needs of these subsystems. Nevertheless, evaluation has developed in the German federal government, even if this has had almost nothing to do with budgeting, and takes place outside the auditing process (Derlien 1990a).

The Interest of Program Administrators in Evaluation

Previous research has revealed that in many countries a second shift to institutionalize evaluation in the policy making process came into existence at the end of the 1970s (Rist 1990). One characteristic of this second evaluation movement was that functiionally, evaluation became more closely related to budgeting. Institutionally this change was facilitated and made more visible by the important role central institutions such as finance ministries and auditors have been presently playing (Derlien 1990b).

Initiatives to evaluate intervention projects and programs in Bonn originated with program administrators. However, specialized parliamentary politicians outside the budget committee have felt the need to be regularly informed about the performance of their legislation. Thus, several hundred reports have been requested by Parliament in order to learn about the implementation of legislation (Derlien 1975a; Schindler 1986). Both groups of program specialists, those in the departments and those in Parliament, were attracted to evaluation because they were concerned about the operation of substantive policies. Thus, the information function of evaluation has been dominant.

Of course, evaluation studies could have been used by the officials of the finance ministry to find out which programs were inefficient and where spending could be curbed. However, not only is there no procedure to utilize evaluation studies initiated by program specialists, but also financial specialists lack the capacity to analyze the numerous reports.

In addition, it is difficult to draw conclusions from individual reports and prioritize programs. Logically this would presuppose cost-benefit analyses across various evaluation studies of programs designed to achieve different goals. Only in the extreme case of clearly deficient programs could one have considered stopping the program and spending the funds for different purposes. It is very rare for an evaluation to declare a program altogether inefficient precisely because evaluations are tailored to the needs of the program managers. The inquiries of the Federal Court of Audit, on the other hand, display a strong tendency to neglect programmatic aspects of the programs and rather concentrate on monetary inputs, minimization of costs, and abiding to budgetary law.

Two-Track Budgeting

The missing link between evaluation and budgeting has institutional causes. Not only is there no procedural connection between evaluation and budgeting, the budget structure itself and the organizational separation of budgeting and program development account for the lack of utilization. As budgeting in Germany is not comprehensive in the sense of the planning-programming-budgeting model, the budget process is not formally connected with policy making. There is hardly any systematic relationship between annual incremental budgeting projecting last year's figures into the next period and setting policy priorities. Thus, what has been observed in other countries - the most important factor shaping next year's budget is last year's budget - also holds for the FRG. Evaluation cannot enter the budgetary process as long as program development and budgeting are not linked in a systematic way.

Program administrators and members of Parliament are related to the budget process predominantly through intra-departmental budgeting. The program administrators request their budgets with programmatic concerns in mind and defend their previous budget by emphasizing the political priority of their projects. Parliamentary standing policy committees, which are specialized according to departmentalization of the executive, link up to support the budgetary position of their government departments. Whereas in the United States there is a variety of appropriations committees for a number of departments, the German parliamentary committees do not link to the one appropriations committee. Here the relationship between members of Parliament belonging to policy committees and those specializing in budget matters is even looser than the interaction between policy departments and finance ministry. Thus, the evaluation reports requested by Parliament are addressed to the policy committees and dealt with there. Members of the small budget committee rely on the testimony of government officials and the advice of representatives of the Federal Court of Audit, who participate in the committee meetings, but do not focus on program issues. This division of labor is repeated within the parliamentary factions, where budget specialists lead a life of their own. Even pressure groups have little chance to influence decision making in the parliamentary budget committee, so they address themselves to relevant departments instead.

Dominance of Institutional Budgeting

Closely related to the two-track system is another technical element of the budgetary process: the institutional system that dominates the budget process both organizationally and systematically. The national budget is based on the departmental institutional budgets. These in turn comprise individual budget items that have some declared aims, but are not combined into programs. In principle, it would be possible to organize budget items contained in a ministerial budget in a programmatic way. This, however, has so far been attempted only in the Ministry of Agriculture (Derlien 1975b). Further, programming budget items within an individual ministerial budget does not allow any tailoring of programs crossing departmental jurisdictions. There are organizational reasons why the younger functional systematization, designed to strengthen the programmatic function of the budget, has limited practical use and has remained underdeveloped. All central actors involved in the budget process (the Ministry of Finance, the Cabinet, the parliamentary budget committee, the Federal Court of Audit, and the parliamentary review committee) are internally specialized according to the institutional system of the budget. There is no programmatic specialization either in the finance ministry or in the parliamentary budget committee. These central experts normally stay in their positions for a number of years and are extremely familiar with the ministerial sub-budgets (Zunker 1972).

Administrative reformers tend to abandon structures and replace them with new ones, that have never been put into practice before. This is not merely a risky strategy for change, it is also bound to engender resistance on the part of those who are operating the system. One has to understand that the structures of the budgetary system in the FRG fulfill certain purposes that few want to give up. Focusing on institutions instead of programs clearly has organizational merits, not least extremely stable communication patterns (departmental boundaries change very seldom). Rearranging the system according to programs would mean that the network of contacts used for establishing the annual budget would change with policy changes and would need rearranging after every change in government. Furthermore, with programs that crosscut departmental boundaries, representatives of the finance ministry would have to deal with various departments and their representatives. This means not only that the communication network would become more complicated but also that, in the case of allocation conflicts, the finance minister would ultimately have to deal with two or more Cabinet ministers. This would complicate conflict resolution and, for instance, aggravate package deals.

In sum, budgeting, auditing and evaluation, which ideally are integrated in a system, are more fragmented in Bonn than may be the case in other Western capitals. This is so because first of all budget and program are neither organizationally nor logically integrated; at best, they are politico-logically linked by implicit considerations. The resulting two-track system, according to the principle of congruency between decision making and feedback processes, was bound to keep auditing and evaluation separate, too. The former has historically developed concomitant to budgeting and the functions it served in the various constitutional systems. Evaluation, which is related to the program (and insufficiently developed) function of the budget, is not yet related to auditing. Auditing practice is still fundamentally shaped by the requirements of administrative and parliamentary control functions with their emphasis on legal compliance and responsibility and accountability for organizations and not for programs. Also, economic rationality tends to be interpreted according to the minimum principle. Evaluation, on the other hand, had its origins in program development of the late 1960s and is functionally related to the information needs of those actors in the departments and in Parliament responsible for substantive policy, not for the budget.

Even in terms of recruitment, professional socialization and role understanding the worlds of auditors and evaluators differ. While the auditor, like his colleague in the Ministry of Finance, tends to be a jurist, his role understanding is shaped by the budgetary code and he moves primarily inside the institutional setting of the budget cycle. Evaluators are, however, involved in a policy network of economists and social scientists in the departments, in Parliament and in the research community.

With this absence of organizational integration of evaluation and auditing within the BRH and consequently a lack of social integration of both communities, the only realistic hope to bring both functions, practices and groups of specialists closer together is some form of informational integration. Evaluation results could at least routinely be communicated to and analyzed by those administrative and political actors running on the budget track.

References

Blasius, H. (1989). "Finanzkontrolle und Gesetzgebung," *Die öffentliche Verwaltung*, 42, 298-306.

Bundesrechnungshof (1991). "Bemerkungen zur Haushalts-und Wirtschaftsführung," *Bundestags-Drucksache* 12/1150.

BWV (Bundesbeauftragter für Wirtschaftlichkeit in der Verwaltung) (1990). *Erfolgskontrolle finanzwirksamer Manahmen in der öffentlichen Verwaltung*. Stuttgart/Berlin/Koln: Kohlhammer.

Caiden, G.E. (1988). "The Vitality of Administrative Reform," *International Review of Administrative Sciences*, 54, 331-57.

De Visscher, C. (1989). "The Modernization of Budgetary Techniques and Financial Control," *International Review of Administrative Sciences*, 55, 323-64.

Derlien, H-U. (1975a). "Das Berichtswesen der Bundesregierung - ein Mittel der Kontrolle und Planung," *Zeitschrift für Parlamentsfragen*, 6, 42-7.

Derlien, H-U. (1975b). "Probleme des neuen Planungssystems im Bundesministerium für Ernährung, Landwirtschaft und Forsten", *Die Verwaltung*, 8, 363-71.

Derlien, H-U. (1990a). "Program Evaluation in the Federal Republic of Germany," in R.C. Rist, ed, see below, 37-52.

Derlien, H-U. (1990b). "Genesis and Structure of Evaluation Efforts in Comparative Perspective", in R.C. Rist, ed, see below, 147-76.

Diederich, N. et al. (1990). *Die diskreten Kontrolleure. Eine Wirkungsanalyse des Bundesrechnungshofs*. Berlin: Westdeutscher Verlag.

Geist, B. (1984). "Auditing Government Policies", *International Journal of Government Accounting*, 9-11.

Kisker, G. (1989). "Rechnungshof und Politik," in H.H. von Arnim, ed, *Finanzkontrolle im Wandel*. Berlin: Duncker und Humblot, 195-220.

Nachtkamp, H-H. (1976). *Mehrjährige Finanzplanungen und mittelfristige Zielprojektionen der Bundesregierungen*. Baden Baden: Nomos.

Rist, R.C. (ed) (1990). *Program Evaluation and the Management of Government. Patterns and Prospects Across Eight Nations*. New Brunswick, N.J.: Transaction Publishers.

Rosenberg, H. (1958), *Bureaucracy, Aristocracy and Autocracy. The Prussian Experience 1660-1815*. Cambridge Mass.: M.I.T. Press

Rürup, B. and G. Färber (1985). "Kontrollorientierte Ansätze einer Budgetreform," *Die Verwaltung*, 18, 173-200.

Rürup, B. and H. Körner (1981). *Finanzwissenschaft. Grundlagen der öffentlichen Finanzwirtschaft*. Dusseldorf: Werner-Verlag.

Schick, A. (1988). "Micro-Budgetary Adaptations to Fiscal Stress in Industrialized Democracies," *Public Administration Review*, 48, 523-33.

Schindler, P. (1986). *Datenhandbuch zur Geschichte des Deutschen Bundestages 1980 bis 1984*. Baden Baden: Nomos.

Selmer, P. (1990). "Zur Intensivierung der Wirtschaftlichkeitskontrolle durch die Rechnungshöfe," *Die Verwaltung*, 23, 1-24.

Sturm, R. (1985). "Entscheidungsstrukturen und Entscheidungsprozesse in der Haushaltspolitik - zum Selbstverständnis des Haushaltsausschusses des Deutschen Bundestages," *Politische Vierteljahresschrift*, 26, 247-69.

Treiber, H. (1984). *Politik unter der Oberfläche. Politikwissenschaftliche Analysen von Bundesausgaben 1952-1980*. Frankfurt.

Wille, E. (1977). "Mittel- und langfristige Finanzplanung," in Fritz Neumark et al. (eds), *Handbuch der Finanzwissenschaft*, Vol. I (3rd ed.), 427-74. Tübingen.

Wittrock, K. (1986). "Parlament, Regierung und Rechnungshof. Zur Geschichte einer schwierigen Dreiecksbeziehung," *Zeitschrift für Parlamentsfragen*, 17, 414-22.

Wittrock, K. (1989). "Der Rechnungshof als Berater - Aktuelles und Historisches zu einem interessanten Thema," *Die öffentliche Verwaltung*, 42, 346-9.

Zavelberg, H.G. (1990). "Performance Auditing in the Federal Republic of Germany," *International Journal of Government Auditing*, 5-7, 16.

Zunker, A. (1972). *Finanzplanung und Bundeshaushalt. Zur Koordinierung und Kontrolle durch den Bundesfinanzminister*. Frankfurt.

5

Out of Sequence and Out of Sync: Budgeting, Auditing, and Evaluation in Canada

Bob Segsworth

The evolution of budgeting in Canada demonstrates an interesting pattern. For a century after independence from Britain in 1867, we see a gradual development of colonial principles as budgeting evolves in the new sovereign state. Beginning in the late 1960s, however, the pace of reform of the budget process quickens dramatically with at least three major overhauls and the introduction of a large number of related initiatives. During this latter period, the Parliament of Canada adopted a significantly different definition of auditing that expanded its nature and role. By the 1980s, the Office of the Comptroller General had succeeded in developing a clear policy on program evaluation and took responsibility for the development of evaluation capability throughout the government of Canada. The auditing and evaluation reforms took place at different times and did not coincide with the major revisions to the budget system.

Another important element of difference is the institutional responsibility for the three functions. Treasury Board Secretariat takes a lead role in the preparation of the expenditure budget. The Office of the Comptroller General is responsible for ensuring the implementation of government policy on evaluation. The Office of the Auditor General is regarded as the most important source of pressure to reform both external and internal auditing.

This chapter provides an overview of the evolution of the expenditure budget process, the development of the audit function and the establishment of evaluation capability in the government of Canada. It also examines some recent initiatives of the federal government in terms of their impact on budgeting, auditing and evaluation.

Three specific objectives emerge from the framework presented in the introduction of this book. The first is to determine whether the sequence of budget system changes in Canada follows Schick's model of budget reform in the twentieth century. The second is to indicate whether the changes to the auditing function and the development of an evaluation capability synchronize with the major budget reforms. Finally, the chapter assesses whether Canada has a "mature" budget system into which the auditing and evaluation functions are integrated effectively.

Historical Background

At Confederation, the Canadian budgeting processes reflected British practice with some adaptation. Four elements of the British tradition were, and remain key features. They are:

1. The creation of a single consolidated fund, the Consolidated Revenue Fund into which all public revenues were deposited;

2. A cash basis for accounting;

3. An annual limit imposed by Parliament on the financial authority of the government;

4. A requirement that the government specify the purposes of its requests to Parliament for appropriations.

The system's informality was evidenced by the fact that John Langton served as deputy minister of finance, secretary of the Board of Treasury and auditor general of Canada simultaneously. However, the 1878 Consolidated Revenue and Audit Act was the beginning of a lengthy process of formalizing expenditure management in Canada. It established the auditor general as an independent officer of Parliament with both pre- and postaudit responsibilities. The act did little to formalize the annual expenditure budget process.

In response to Sir George Murray's 1913 Report, which was highly critical of financial management within the Government of Canada, an order-in-council (PC 2402) was issued to establish formal procedures for the estimates review process. This change was not sufficient to ensure effective control of the public purse and the Royal Commission on Government Organization (1962, p.128) described the situation as one in which

> votes were over-expended; expenditures were charged to the wrong vote; liabilities were incurred which committed in advance almost the entire amount of the votes appropriated by Parliament in the succeeding year; expenditures were made out of revenues; and other questionable practices were often in evidence.

As a result of previous pressures for reform and the effects of the Great Depression Parliament responded in 1931 with major amendments to the Consolidated Revenue and Audit Act. These revisions reaffirmed the primacy of Treasury Board in financial management, broadened the postaudit responsibilities of the Office of the Auditor General, created the new position of comptroller of the Treasury and required a new standardized vote structure for the estimates.

By the 1930s the Treasury Board had assumed control over departmental spending. It provided a central cheque issuance system and required that uniform accounting practices be used in all departments. In addition, the Treasury Board received responsibility for "establishment control". This meant that the Treasury Board could unilaterally decide the size of the Public Service and the number of persons employed by each department or agency annually.

The amendments to the act removed any remaining preaudit controls from the jurisdiction of the auditor general. At the same time, the auditor general's postaudit mandate was expanded considerably (Clark 1938). His reports, submitted to Parliament annually, were normally referred to the Public Accounts Committee of the House of Commons for detailed review. In comparison with the United Kingdom, the Canadian Public Accounts Committee was relatively weak. This was hardly surprising given that the Chairman of the Committee was a member of the governing party and the majority of members, including some Cabinet ministers, were government representatives.

The Comptroller of the Treasury assumed responsibility for the preaudit function. The mandate of this new position reflected two basic concerns: to ensure that all public expenditures were legal and that sufficient uncommitted funds remained in the appropriate accounts to cover committed expenditures. The comptroller of the Treasury took over the former preaudit staff of the auditor general and these worked in the various departments and agencies of the federal public service. The comptroller of the Treasury reported to the minister of finance. The Treasury Board was empowered to deal with appeals from departments of Comptroller of the Treasury decisions.

The revised vote structure was based on the notion that "the more detailed the estimates are, the greater the control will be" (Clark 1938, p. 397). Additional reforms in 1937 reflected the control orientation and a desire to improve the quality of information provided to Parliament as part of the estimates process. By the 1930s then, the first major budgeting reform of the twentieth century (i.e., the control function described in Chapter 1) had become well entrenched in Canada.

A straightforward expenditure budgeting process remained largely intact for more than thirty years following the 1931 amendments to the Consolidated Revenue and Audit Act. Each fall, the minister of finance requested departments to prepare their estimates for the following fiscal year and to submit them by a specific date. Within departments, estimates were developed by branch heads based upon current expenditures and activities and were reviewed ultimately by the responsible minister. Departmental requests, with appropriate documentation and support, were forwarded to the Department of Finance for review and comparison with previous expenditures. After the Department of Finance had completed its work, the material was submitted to the Treasury Board, which was expected to examine these submissions in the context of probable revenues and government policy initiatives. As part of its examination, the Treasury Board frequently called upon other ministers and permanent officials to appear and to explain or justify requests. Once the Treasury Board completed its work, it submitted the estimates to the Cabinet for review. After approval was received from the Cabinet, the estimates were presented to the House of Commons early in the session for debate and ultimately, for approval. Once the necessary Appropriations Acts were passed, the government had the legal authority to spend. At the end of the fiscal year, the auditor eneral would conduct his audit and report his findings to the House of Commons in his *Annual Report*.

The only major alteration to the budgeting system between 1931 and 1961 was made by the Financial Administration Act in 1951. This statute defined which structures of the public service (crown corporations, departments, boards and commissions) were subject to particular sets of financial controls and delegated a great deal of Cabinet authority to the Treasury Board. Thereafter, a larger number of Treasury Board decisions no longer required the approval of the Cabinet before they could be implemented. By 1961, therefore, the expenditure budgeting system was clearly defined. It included:

1. A single consolidated revenue fund;

2. A standardized appropriations structure with detail provided by standard object of expenditure;

3. Secondary control based upon Treasury Board allotments in terms of objects of expenditure;

4. A centralized system of recording commitments in relation to appropriations and allotments;

5. An independent preaudit;

6. Standardized accounting and reporting systems;

7. Limited delegation of authority to departments and agencies;

8. Accounting on a cash basis;

9. An independent postaudit by the auditor general.

The criticism of the entire procees, of which there was a great deal, crystallized in the report on *Financial Management* of the Royal Commission on Government Organization in 1960. In general terms, the Royal Commission argued that the control orientation had become too dominant. Central agencies, especially the Treasury Board and the Comptroller of the Treasury, were overly involved in minutiae with the result that departments and agencies were unable to manage their own affairs and the system paid too little attention to efficiency and managerial effectiveness. The Commission also noted that the Estimates presented to the House of Commons were inadequate and inappropriate for the purposes of informed debate.

In addition, financial management in Canada appeared to lag behind developments in the United States. The commission found little evidence of a performance budgeting emphasis on managerial efficiency, work measurement and cost analysis within the Canadian Public Service and very few departments had developed a meaningful internal audit infrastructure.

The commission outlined a series of recommendations to reform the budget system. The emphasis was on the creation of a process in which managers would have the freedom to manage while central agencies and senior bureaucrats would be able to hold them accountable. The new emphases were upon efficiency and effectiveness within the context of longer-term planning. This was the direction the budget system would take by the end of the decade.

The Planning-Programming-Budgeting Era

The 1966 Treasury Board publication, *Financial Management*, provided an indication of the response of the government of Canada. It indicated a desire to adopt a Planning-Programming-Budgeting System in Canada. Several factors encouraged such a change, including the apparent success of PPBS in the United States, the Treasury Board's desire to resist the decentralization trends recommended by the Royal Commission, and the election of a rationalist prime minister, Mr. Trudeau. In addition, the 1967 amendments to the Financial Administration Act and the passage of the Public Service Employment Act and the Public Service Staff Relations Act established the Treasury Board Secretariat as a distinct department with its own minister, the president of the Treasury Board, and gave it overall responsibility for financial management and personnel policy.

The *Planning-Programming-Budgeting Guide* (Treasury Board 1969) confirmed the government's decision to introduce PPB in a comprehensive manner. The guide (p.8) outlined the six basic concepts to be introduced:

1. The setting of specific objectives;

2. Systematic analysis to clarify objectives and to assess alternative ways of meeting them;

3. The framing of budgetary proposals in terms of programs directed toward the achievement of the objectives;

4. The projection of the costs of these programs a number of years in the future;

5. The formulation of plans of achievement year by year for each program; and

6. An information system for each program to supply data for the monitoring of achievement of program goals and to supply data for the reassessment of the program objectives and the appropriateness of the program itself.

With a series of reforms to the Cabinet and its committee structure, the expenditure budget process was revised (Robertson 1971). Initially, the Cabinet, and in particular the Priorities and Planning Committee, developed an outline of key government priorities and set relatively crude expenditure guidelines. This material was used by the Treasury Board to produce more refined and precise guidelines, which were forwarded to departments. Departments were expected to prepare and submit to the Treasury Board their expenditure requests by vote, standard object-of-expenditure, and by program, with the appropriate supporting documentation. It was expected that departments would not normally exceed the guidelines, although, in practice, they did so frequently. At this point, negotiations took place between the policy analysts of the Treasury Board Secretariat and departmental officials.

These negotiations reflected an innovation in the budgeting process. In effect, departments submitted two expenditure budget submissions. The A budget contained departmental estimates of the costs involved in continuing existing activities with adjustments for inflation and, where appropriate, volume increases. The B budget submission contained departmental requests for funding of new programs or enriched funding of existing programs. Virtually all attention in discussions with Treasury Board analysts at this stage concentrated on the B budget submissions of departments. Departments were required to provide multiyear (usually five) forecasts of planned expenditures and to support such projections with relevant documentation. This was to be a control against the "thin edge of the wedge" tactics employed by wily departmental officials attempting to push new policy proposals through the expenditure budget process. Once the Treasury Board review was completed, formal recommendations were submitted to the Cabinet, after which the estimates were introduced in the House of Commons and the necessary Appropriations Acts were passed.

Policy planning, including formative evaluation, was a key element of PPB. Consequently, departments increased their policy staffs significantly. The Planning Branch of the Treasury Board Secretariat added staff and conducted a number of interesting long-term planning studies.

In addition, a number of other changes were experimented with in order to supplement PPB efforts.

Several departments attempted to introduce Management by Objectives (MBO). This seems to have been a logical step because MBO's emphasis on setting and attaining objectives appeared to be compatible with PPB. The Treasury Board also launched an ambitious initiative - the Operational Performance Measurement System (OPMS). OPMS was a performance measurement system that applied a "hierarchy of proxy measures" (Kernaghan and Siegel 1987, p. 529) to enable departments and ministers to obtain systematically useful data on program and operational efficiency as well as some indicators of program effectiveness.

By the mid-1970s, all was not well with PPB, MBO, and OPMS in the Canadian Public Service. The reasons were varied (Segsworth 1972). PPB required a large number of highly skilled economists who were not available when PPB was introduced, there was considerable resistance to the changes from line departments who saw the new system as part of an attempt by the Treasury Board Secretariat to enhance its position as a control agency, and the complexities of PPB and OPMS were beyond the capacities of the public service at that time.

The most serious difficulty, however, lay with the rapid growth of federal expenditures. Between 1965 and 1978 real government spending on goods and services had increased from $15.2 billion to $26.4 billion (Auld and Miller 1982). Total gross public debt had increased from $27.5 billion in 1966 to $80.0 billion in 1978 (McCready 1984) and showed no signs of slowing down. There was a perception that the introduction of PPB had contributed to such expenditure increases. If the A budget was assured, then the only real question was how big an annual increase in expenditures would result from the reviews of the B budget submissions.

A number of individuals and groups expressed the growing concern about this trend. Among them was the auditor general. He used the media and his annual reports to pressure the government for reform. In his 1976 *Annual Report* (p. 9), for example, he stated that "I am deeply concerned that Parliament - and indeed the Government - has lost, or is close to losing, effective control of the public purse".

The mounting criticism pushed an uncertain government into a number of initiatives. Not surprisingly, one of them was the formation of yet another Royal Commission - The Royal Commission on Financial Management and Accountability. Its mandate included the examination of financial management in the government of Canada and the formulation of recommendations for reform.

The government also responded to the long-standing requests of the auditor general to expand the mandate of the Office of Auditor General. In 1977 the Auditor General Act was passed by Parliament. It established the Office as a separate employer largely free of central agency controls. It defined the nonrenewable term of office as ten years and, most important of all, altered the traditional responsibilities. The financial statement and compliance audit elements remained, but the "3 Es" - economy, efficiency, and effectiveness - were added. The act gave the auditor general the responsibility to "report instances where money was spent without due regard to economy and efficiency or where satisfactory procedures have not been established to measure and report the effectiveness of programs, where such procedures could appropriately and reasonably be implemented". This provided the legal authority for the Auditor General's practice of developing and conducting comprehensive audits.

A third response was the creation in 1978 of the Office of the Comptroller General (OCG). This initiative was an acceptance of both Auditor General and Royal Commission recommendations that a chief financial officer for Canada be appointed. According to Kernaghan and Siegel (1987), the OCG has two major responsibilities: to develop and oversee financial management policies within the federal public service and to give substance to the Treasury Board policy on program evaluation and to engage in meta-evaluation.

Even more significant than these government initiatives was a series of changes made by the Treasury Board in the 1970s to deal with performance measurement, internal audit and program evaluation. In 1973, the Treasury Board reviewed the performance management systems and practices of the departments and agencies of the federal public service and in 1976, Treasury Board Circular 1976-25, (*Measurement of the Performance of Government Operations*) required all departments and agencies to develop adequate and reliable performance measurement systems and to have them in place by 1980. The focus of performance measurement was to be primarily one of efficiency. Indicators such as productivity, cost-efficiency ratios, error rates, and waiting periods for benefits/decisions were characteristic examples included in reports to the

House of Commons by the president of the Treasury Board in 1977 and 1979.

Although some improvements to the internal audit function had resulted from the Royal Commission on Government Organization during the 1960s, serious deficiencies still existed. The *Financial Management and Control* study of the Office of the Auditor General in 1975 found that several problems remained. A Treasury Board review largely confirmed these findings and in 1978 the Office of the Comptroller General issued *Standards for Internal Financial Audit in the Government of Canada*. This document increased the direction given to internal audit groups and departments and elevated the status of the function considerably.

PPB was an attempt to implement a planning-oriented budgeting system in Canada. It was never fully implemented, and it was by most standards a failure, yet it left a significant legacy. The recognition of failure was most important because it provided an impetus for a large number of internal reforms such as the policy on performance measurement, revised internal audit standards, a policy on evaluation, an expanded role for the Office of the Auditor General and the postaudit function, and the creation of the Office of the Comptroller General. It also was important because the failure of PPB helped to create the perception that something had to be done to control expenditures. These changes led the way to what Schick (1988, p. 532) described as the "only major innovation to have taken root in industrialized countries" after the third wave of budgetary reform.

The Policy and Expenditure Management System (PEMS)

The Progressive Conservative government of Mr. Clark responded to the deficit problem, in part, by creating PEMS, a new budget system that was adopted with some modifications by other governments in the 1980s. The objectives of the new system were to integrate policy making and expenditure decision-making processes, to decentralize decision making authority while increasing the Cabinet's control over policy and expenditure decisions and to provide more time for the planning process.

This new system featured four key elements - a fiscal plan, expenditure limits (or envelopes), a re-organized Cabinet committee system and an altered set of departmental submissions including strategic overviews (later called strategic memoranda), multiyear operational plans (MYOPS) and budget-year operational plans (BYOPS).

The Fiscal Plan described the government's fiscal policy over a five-year cycle. In order to prepare this document for approval by the Cabinet Committee on Priorities and Planning, the minister of finance sought a great deal of information such as revenue projections, assessments of the economy, the effects of different policy options on monetary policies, borrowing requirements and tax policy and estimates of expenditure requirements before making his final recommendations. The policy committees of the Cabinet outlined sectoral priorities and the Cabinet Committee on Priorities and Planning provided an indication of overall government priorities. The approved document established government-wide expenditure targets, allocated specific targets to the various envelopes and outlined the strategy of the government to deal with the revenues-expenditures relationship. The expenditure sections of the Fiscal Plan were published as *Part I, The Expenditure Plan* when the *Main Estimates* were tabled in the House of Commons. The entire *Fiscal Plan* was made public when the minister of finance presented the annual budget speech.

The future-oriented features of the Fiscal Plan were altered gradually by the Mulroney government after 1984 so that by the end of the 1980s only the next fiscal year was reported, with few exceptions. The planning aspect of the process appeared to have been discontinued. Furthermore, by 1988, only five of the eleven Cabinet committees were directly involved in PEMS. The three policy committees - Economic and Regional Development, Social Development, and Foreign Policy - were responsble for the Economic and Regional Development Envelope, the Social Development Envelope and the External Affairs and Aid and Defense Envelopes respectively. The Treasury Board, a coordinating committee, was responsible for the Parliament Envelope and the Services to Government Envelope. Priorities and Planning, a key coordinating committee, was responsible for the Fiscal Arrangements Envelope and the Public Debt Envelope.

Priorities and Planning played a particularly important role. Chaired by the prime minister, this committee established the overall direction of government policy, approved the Fiscal Plan and established the expenditure levels for each of the eight envelopes. In addition, this committee ratified decisions taken by the policy committees of the Cabinet.

The policy committees, as well as the two coordinating committees involved in PEMS, were responsible for allocating the expenditures to the various departments, agencies and programs funded by the envelopes within their jurisdiction. Basically, all existing programs expected to receive funding at reference levels and unless there was some significant change in government policy, the A base was maintained. In some cases, these committees were provided with policy reserves, that were to be used to fund new programs or to enrich the funding of some existing programs. Policy committees could create additional policy reserves by reducing their expenditures on existing programs. As Kernaghan and Siegel (1987, p. 538) put it, "one of the most significant innovations of this system was the power it gave the policy sector Cabinet committees to make budgetary and policy decisions in their sectors as long as they stayed within their set expenditure limit".

Another important change from past practice was the treatment of tax expenditures, which had become a very popular policy device in the 1970s. Under PEMS, the envelopes reflected tax expenditures as well as cash expenditures. Although departments could continue to use tax expenditures in lieu of grants or other incentives, they were no longer "free" and showed up in their envelope as an expense. Put simply, the basic notion was that the amount of money available to departments was fixed. If departments and ministers wished to increase expenditures on some activity, they had to find it within their envelope.

In addition to the policy reserves, two additional reserves were created. The operating reserve was designed to finance cost overruns of existing approved programs, which resulted from unforeseen circumstances and involved large sums of money. The Treasury Board expected departments to absorb relatively minor overruns. The reserve for statutory overruns was established to deal with unpredicted cost increases of statutory programs for which, in many cases, costs were linked to inflation, federal-provincial agreements and/or unemployment rates.

The Treasury Board was given the job of maintaining the envelope accounts. In addition, it prepared regular reports on the status of the various reserves and provided assessments of the accuracy of the projected costs of proposals submitted to Cabinet committees for consideration.

Departmental activities involved in the preparation of the annual expenditure budget produced three interrelated submissions - the strategic overview, the multiyear operational plan, and the budget-year operational plan. The strategic overview, a major departmental planning document, was submitted annually to the appropriate policy committee in March (Brown-John et al., 1988). Since 1984, they have been replaced by less formal ministerial strategic memoranda in which the minister describes priorities and desired policy changes. The Cabinet committee reports became part of the annual priority-setting exercise of the government.

The MYOPS were submitted to the Treasury Board each year at the end of March. The time frame involved plans over the next three fiscal years. Typically, MYOPS contained information on at least four elements. The first involved a discussion and statement of the department's long-range objectives and strategies in the context of existing approved policies and programs. The second element was primarily descriptive. It outlined the various programs and activities of the department and demonstrated how they were related to the attainment of departmental objectives. The third section provided an assessment of the anticipated results and benefits of the existing programs of the departments. Finally, the MYOPS contained a review of past and projected trends of demand for these programs and their associated costs. Overall, these MYOPS were important sources of information for Treasury Board staff in the calculation of the reference level expenditure projections for each department used in the development of the Fiscal Plan.

The BYOPS were submitted to the Treasury Board each October in preparation for the upcoming fiscal year. Brown-John et al. (1988) describe them as documents from each department that contain an outline of updated financial resources, a description of key operation goals, an explanation of the relationship between the estimates and the department's management structure and a detailed evaluation plan.

After 1985 the spring and fall exercise was replaced by an annual review of both the MYOPS and BYOPS. Changes to the BYOPS submitted by departments in October result in adjustments to their MYOPS, which are forwarded to the Treasury Board Secretariat at the same time. The effect of government restraint was that departments and the Treasury Board saw no reason to continue the earlier process since there was so little "new" money available for departments to build into their fall BYOPS once spring MYOPS approvals had been received.

The result of this new budgeting system was a cycle of some four and one-half years involved in the creation of each fiscal year's expenditure budget. Although PEMS was described (Kernaghan and Siegel 1987, p. 536) as "a marriage of the policy-making and expenditure management systems" that attempted "to force politicians to consider the budgetary implications of their actions", this was a marriage that did not succeed. Despite the alterations introduced by Prime Minister Mulroney since 1984, PEMS did not meet the government's commitment to introduce restraint and assist in reducing the annual deficit significantly.

One reason for this was that the system had not encouraged departments to practice restraint. If a department initiated policy changes that produced savings, the savings went into the policy reserve, which was controlled by the appropriate policy committee. If efficiency improvements were introduced and resulted in cost savings, these savings were returned to the Treasury Board for reallocation. As Schick (1988, p. 527) put it, "the incentive (to save) is diminished somewhat by giving the savings to the policy envelope - which typically consists of a number of government ministries - not to the ministry from which the funds were taken".

As we shall see later, the federal public service had created, during the same period as PEMS, a capability for performance measurement, program evaluation, internal audit and an expanded external audit. Despite this apparent capacity to uncover more economical, efficient and effective ways of attaining objectives and ensuring better financial and managerial control, the budgeting system did not appear to be able to utilize fully these functions to meet the restraint objectives set for it by the Progressive Conservative government. In January 1989, the prime minister announced, yet again, a new (or perhaps revised) budget system for the government of Canada.

The Current System

In the spring of 1988, the prime minister suspended the operation of PEMS. He felt that the system had not been successful in helping his government to meet its expenditure restraint objectives. Subsequently, we were informed that Mr. Mulroney and his advisers had been impressed by the British and Australian experiences in coping with their deficits. The prime minister had become convinced that he would have to take a more active role directly if his government were to succeed in dramatically reducing the annual deficit.

To date, no formal replacement for PEMS has been announced. What has occurred is a restructuring of the Cabinet committee system that reflects the increased concentration of financial decision-making power in the hands of the prime minister and his closest Cabinet colleagues. The number of policy committees has been increased by four. The membership of Cabinet committees has been reduced to the eight to twelve-member range. Policy committees no longer have any decision-making authority regarding expenditures. Their function is purely advisory. When that advice takes the form of a recommendation to initiate new programs and policies, it is vetted by the new Expenditure Review Committee.

The Expenditure Review Committee is chaired by the prime minister. The minister of finance and the president of the Treasury Board are members. According to the *Background Paper* (Privy Council Office 1989, p. 1), "it is mandated to ensure that the Government's expenditures continue to be directed to its highest priorities, and that expenditure control continues to contribute to deficit reduction". This committee has jurisdiction over the reserves and its decisions are forwarded to the Committee on Priorities and Planning for ratification.

The Operations Committee sets the agenda for the policy committees and Priorities and Planning. It provides the first Cabinet-level review of new initiatives proposed by ministers and refers such initiatives to the policy committees for discussion, the departments for more development or to Priorities and Planning for discussion and decision.

Treasury Board responsibilities continue to be much the same as they were under PEMS. It maintains responsibility for the annual process of preparing the estimates for submission to the House of Commons. In addition, it retains responsibility for operating reserves as well as a small program reserve.

Senior officials in the Treasury Board Secretariat have indicated privately that it is not yet clear how this new system will unfold. Some ministers are unhappy to have lost control over policy reserves and to have only an advisory function in this revamped structure. Certainly, the view of central agency officials involved in the budgeting system is that no firm decision has been made regarding what will replace PEMS. Although the Expenditure Review Committee review of expenditure submissions involves a line-by-line, program-by-program examination, the current practice does not allow analysts to develop the competing views on expenditure decisions to assist this Cabinet committee in carrying out its responsibilities. Ideology, as opposed to analysis of alternatives, may be a more important factor in expenditure decision making than was the case under PEMS. It may well be that the current system reflects the type of relatively minor adjustments that Schick (1988) has noted. On the other hand, it is also possible that the government of Canada may see another major overhaul of its budgeting system in the future.

Although the expenditure budget process is a lengthy and rather complex one that is currently, once again, being reformed, it has been influenced by a variety of other developments. Certainly, auditing and evaluation may impact on the budgeting system. In addition, the Treasury Board launched an interesting initiative, Increased Ministerial Authority and Accountability (IMAA), which impacts directly on departmental and central agency budgeting processes. The sections that follow outline briefly the development and role of internal and external auditing, program evaluation and IMAA in the current Canadian budget system.

Internal Auditing

The absence of a serious internal audit capacity within the government of Canada was noted with concern by the Royal Commission on Government Organization as early as 1960. Despite some efforts to improve the situation, the auditor general reported in 1975 that serious deficiences still remained. These conclusions led to a review of departments by the Treasury Board and the publication in 1978 by the Office of the Comptroller General of *Standards for Internal Financial Audit in the Government of Canada*.

The 1979 the *Final Report* of the Royal Commission on Financial Management and Accountability had a great deal to say about the internal audit function in most federal departments. It noted that the scope of audits was narrow, standards were unsatisfactory and follow-up was fragmented or inconclusive because of reporting weaknesses.

Despite the work done by the Treasury Board and the Office of the Comptroller General, it became apparent that two basic changes in internal auditing were viewed as essential. The first was to expand the scope of the audit. The second was to elevate the status of the internal audit function to ensure that audit planning and audit reports reached senior managers within departments.

These changes were reflected in 1982 in the revised *Standards for Internal Audit in the Government of Canada* issued by the Office of the Comptroller General. This document described Treasury Board policy on the subject as follows (p. 4):

> Departments shall have an independent internal audit function that carries out a systematic review and appraisal of all departmental operations for purposes of advising management as to the efficiency, economy and effectiveness of internal management policies, practices and controls.

The revisions required all departments to conduct internal audits on all aspects of their operations. They required auditors, in particular, to express opinions on systems, procedures and controls, reliability and adequacy of decision-making information, the utilization of available information in decision-making and compliance with statutes and regulations. This revised policy also required departments to audit each operation at least once every three to five years.

The *Standards* also had some impact on the status of the function. They suggested that the head of the internal audit group should report directly to the deputy minister. They required that an annual report summarizing the results of the year's audit activity be submitted to the deputy. In addition, they obliged the internal audit groups within departments to follow up on recommendations and to report their findings to their deputy ministers.

This expanded internal audit function may have produced a system more capable of revealing problematic areas, and a lack of efficiency and economy in departmental operations. It remains the responsibility of senior managers to respond to the findings of internal audit reports. In terms of the budgeting process, the role and/or impact of this augmented capacity is not clear.

Budget officials in the Treasury Board Secretariat are not normally interested in the contents of departmental internal audit reports. The policy committees of the Cabinet do not normally receive even summaries of internal audit reports. To date, the new Expenditure Review Committee has expressed little interest in the specific results of the work of internal auditors. Although the Treasury Board Secretariat during the past two years has assisted in the development of audit criteria regarding such matters as user fees and capital planning, it appears that the internal audit function has little impact on the central agencies and cabinet committees involved in the budgeting process.

If the internal audit does have an impact, it must occur within departments, i.e., it must affect the annual budget submissions of the departments to the Treasury Board. Officials have told me that this happens, but they have been unable to provide much in the way of documented evidence to support their claim.

External Auditing

In Canada, the external auditor for government departments and most crown agencies is the auditor general. He is perceived as an influential actor in the development of financial management policies, including budgeting systems. This perception has continued, and may have increased, since the passage of the Auditor General Act in 1977.

The 1977 statute continued the requirement that the Office of the Auditor General maintain its traditional function of auditing the financial statements of the Government of Canada and departments and of assessing the extent to which departmental practices complied with legislative, central agency and other applicable directives. In addition, the act introduced the notions of economy, efficiency and effectiveness - the 3 Es - to his mandate. According to Kernaghan and Siegel (1987, p. 579):

> Economy is defined as obtaining the appropriate goods and service needs at the best possible price. Efficiency is defined as arranging resources in such a manner as to obtain the maximum output from the resources employed. Effectiveness is defined as maximizing the attainment of a desired output.

These 3 Es constitute the conceptual bases of value-for-money auditing in Canada, which has become a major tool in the auditor general's annual examination of the financial practices of government departments and agencies.

One consequence of the application of this new mandate by the auditor general has been a change in the format of the annual reports. To a considerable extent, the horror stories of earlier times have been replaced by two types of chapters. The first contains the reports of comprehensive audits conducted on selected programs or departments. The second contains commentary resulting from government-wide reviews conducted by the Office of the Auditor General on such matters as the purchase and use of computer equipment. The Annual Report is no longer restricted to financial activities. It may include the auditor general's views on such subjects as the personnel appraisal systems of departments and the strategic planning capability, or lack thereof, found in government agencies.

In general, there is little disagreement regarding the right of the auditor general to examine and comment upon matters related to the concerns of efficiency and economy. There has been considerable controversy regarding the role of the auditor general in dealing with effectiveness issues. Although the 1977 Act is restrictive, Kernaghan and Siegel (p. 580) note that the previous Auditor General J.J. Macdonnell "took the position that all programs should have indicators to measure their effectiveness and that his office ought to have responsibility to comment on the existence (or non-existence) and adequacy of those indicators". His successor, Kenneth Dye, appears to share his predecessor's belief and has developed more fully another area of interest - access to policy advice received by ministers (Segsworth 1990).

Over the past two decades, the auditor general has been a proponent of change and many of his suggested reforms have been adopted. The format of the Estimates has altered dramatically. The government has created a chief financial officer in the position of comptroller general. The mandate of the Office of the Auditor General has been extended considerably. His concerns about financial management and expenditure levels have struck sympathetic responses in many parts of Canadian society.

Certainly, departments appear to accept his recommendations. The report of a comprehensive audit on the Department of Fisheries and Oceans Atlantic Operations, Inspections and Corporate Functions included in the 1988 *Annual Report* provides a useful example. In it, the auditor general makes ten specific recommendations and the department formally concurs with all of them. The same document also indicates that such acceptance by departments is more than lip service. In following up the recommendations of his 1986 audit of the Pacific Region, the Auditor General (13.167) concludes:

> Overall, the management of the Pacific Region has made progress, resolving or addressing the observations from our 1986 Report with noticeable improvements to information and management systems. A number of areas, by their very nature, will require continued attention by management and will be reviewed by us during the normal cycle of our audits.

In terms of the budgeting system, apart from the form of the Estimates, it is much more difficult to determine the effects of the activity of the Office of the Auditor General. Officials in his office argue that the reports and studies have generated savings due to increased efficiency, better management and improved accountability within departments. At the same time, they acknowledge that they cannot quantify the effect of their work on federal expenditures. Within the Treasury Board Secretariat the prevailing view appears to be that the work of the Auditor General has not had a major effect upon the budgeting system. Treasury Board officials state, however, that the work of the Auditor General is essential to ensure financial control over departments and to enhance political accountability.

Program Evaluation

The 1977 policy on program evaluation issued by the Treasury Board reflected the previous failure of the government to create a successful evaluation capability and system within the public service despite numerous initiatives in the 1960s and 1970s. This policy did not take on substance until the Office of the Comptroller General published the *Guide on the Program Evaluation Function* and *Principles for the Evaluation of Programs by Federal Departments and Agencies* in 1981.

The policy establishes four basic evaluation issues - program rationale, impact and effects, objectives achievement, and alternatives. It requires all departments to establish an evaluation capability and to develop and submit for approval evaluation plans. It establishes clearly that the client for evaluations is the deputy minister.

Once the policy went into effect, evaluation activity developed rapidly. By the mid 1980s, departments were conducting well over 150 evaluation studies per year (Office of Comptroller General 1989a). The vast majority of such studies concentrated on issues of improved efficiency and program documentation. There was a small minority that focused more closely on issues of progam rationale and resulted in termination or major revision of programs (Rayner 1986).

Based upon a decade of experience under the 1977 policy, the Office of the Comptroller General (OCG) issued a *Government Program Evaluation Plan* in 1988. One key finding in this annual plan was that there was a need to rationalize the demand for evaluation. The *Plan* (p. 2) noted that "departments as a whole must improve their coverage and selection of issues to meet government-wide evaluation requirements as well as their own." In addition, the *Plan* reported that in some departments, the shortfall between planned and completed evaluations was as high as fifty percent.

In order to respond to these issues and others, the OCG identified specific action requirements under nine different headings including Expenditure Programs, and Treasury Board and other Cabinet-Requested Evaluations. In these cases, OCG takes on a stronger coordinating and follow up role than has been the case in the past.

A recent development in terms of program evaluation policy occurred in July 1989 when OCG issued *Working Standards for the Evaluation of Programs in Federal Departments and Agencies.* This document refines and clarifies many of the issues presented in the 1981 *Guide* and *Principles* publications. The *Working Standards* is designed to achieve two objectives (p. ii):

> By using a common language and agreed upon criteria, these standards will provide departments with a workable basis for internal self-assessment and quality improvement of evaluation practice. At the same time, they provide the OCG with a basis for making disciplined professional judgements of evaluation practice in individual departments.

The *Evaluation Plan* and the *Working Standards* seem to reflect some slight change in evaluation policy in Canada. One the one hand, they appear to promote more frequent rationale and/or impact-based evaluations at the expense of the managerial efficiency studies, which have been so common. Perhaps even more important is the suggestion that the deputy heads of departments, the formal clients of evaluation in the federal public service, may have lost some of their control over the implementation of evaluation policy in their own departments. Certainly the interests of external agencies such as the Treasury Board are referred to more frequently than was the case in the past.

In the context of the budgeting system, evaluation appears to have played a minor role at the center of the process. The Treasury Board is not overly interested in the vast majority of evaluation studies. Although summaries of evaluation reports were submitted to the policy committees of the Cabinet under PEMS, the evidence appears to be that they had little impact on committee decisions regarding the budget. More recently, Treasury Board officials have expressed the opinion that the Expenditure

Review Committee may call for evaluations of programs of interest and that the evaluation reports may play a more important role in its decisions on expenditures. Although summaries of evaluations are supposed to be included in the Part IIIs of the Estimates, it appears that members of Parliament have not yet seized upon this information to any great extent to assist them in fulfilling their parliamentary responsibilities.

Because evaluation policy makes the deputy minister the client, evaluations have reflected departmental priorities and concerns. It is not clear that the impact of the hundreds of evaluation studies completed to date upon departmental budget submissions has been significant. Officials in the Treasury Board Secretariat have expressed the view that evaluation within departments has not had much impact on the budgeting system. They note, however, that recent consultations with the OCG may lead to evaluations that are more directly useful to budget officers within the Secretariat.

Increased Ministerial Authority and Accountability (IMAA)

One of the more interesting recent initiatives in the federal public service is Increased Ministerial Authority and Accountability (IMAA). It is a Treasury Board effort to respond to the primary concerns raised by Royal Commissions, which have examined the operations of government in the recent past in the context of current resource constraints.

In its January 1988 *Report* on IMAA, the Treasury Board highlights two fundamental objectives. The first reflects the basic philosophy of the Royal Commission on Government Organization. IMAA is designed (p. 1) "to give ministers and senior managers the increased authority and flexibility they need to deal with changing circumstances and manage effectively with limited resources". Like the Royal Commission on Financial Management and Accountability, IMAA attempts (p. 1) "to enhance the accountability of Ministers and senior managers for the achievement of results, both in program delivery and in the implementation of Treasury Board policies". One interesting characteristic of the approach is that it is more results-oriented than has been the case in the past. Less concern is expressed with departments following procedural rules that exist in the various administrative manuals.

The initiative involves two simultaneous efforts. The first is a review of Treasury Board policies that might impede effective departmental management. The second is the negotiation and signing of Memoranda of Understanding between the Treasury Board and ministers and deputy ministers. The policy review responds to constraints that have been identified by the auditor general and senior managers such as too many central agency rules, overly extensive reporting requirements, an overly complex classification process and a lack of clarity in accountability policies (Treasury Board 1988). To date, the relaxed or revised policies have dealt with a number of these concerns. By giving departments greater freedom in expenditure management decisions, the Treasury Board received only 3,500 submissions from departments in 1986-87, a decline of 1,600 from the 1983-84 fiscal year. The multiyear human resource planning requirements have been streamlined. A capital carryover provision has been built into the budgeting process. Common services policy is in the process of major revision. In return for such greater freedom, the Treasury Board is requiring departments to sign Memoranda of Understanding (MOUs).

These MOUs are three-year agreements between the Treasury Board and the departments. In return for delegated authority in such areas as financial and personnel management, departments take on specific obligations.

One of these obligations is the preparation and submission to the Treasury Board of an Annual Management Report. This report typically includes a review of the departmental environment, a statement of actual performance as compared to targets in the MOU and Treasury Board policy, an explanation of the variances from the targets and an outline of changes proposed to meet expected performance levels. In addition, the report includes summaries of audit and evaluation plans, a description of follow-up action taken and updates to audit and evaluation plans. Once the report is received, a meeting is arranged involving the deputy minister of the department concerned, the secretary to the Treasury Board and the comptroller general to review the report and discuss any areas of concern.

A second obligation involves a commitment by the department to conduct internal audits and/or evaluations of departmental programs and activities of interest to the Treasury Board. The reports of these evaluations and audits are submitted to the Treasury Board for review.

Finally, departments agree to undergo a major accountability review near the end of the third year of the agreement. The focus of this review is the extent to which the department has met the targets set for it in the

MOU. The expectation is that after high-level meetings have taken place, the MOU will be revised and extended for another three-year term.

By July 1989, eight departments had signed MOUs with the Treasury Board. Twelve major departments and eighteen smaller agencies were considering their options.

In terms of the budgeting system, IMAA offers a number of interesting features. It appears that evaluations will be more rationale and/or impacts oriented and that they may play a more important role in resource allocation decisions. Internal audits may also play a more prominent role than has been the case in the past. The most interesting initiative, however, is the three-year funding guarantee. In essence, an MOU provides a department with a guarantee that its A base (reference level) budget will be maintained for the three years of the agreement. If a department can economize, become more efficient or revise or terminate programs and save money by doing so, it can keep the savings and use them to respond to departmental priorities and needs. IMAA clearly provides an incentive for departments to manage their operations more efficiently, economically and effectively. It is, however, too soon to come to any conclusions regarding the success of this Treasury Board initiative. IMAA is still in its infancy, but it appears to provide advantages to departments that want greater autonomy and to central agencies that are preoccupied with accountability and expenditure restraint concerns.

In the summer of 1990 a response to concerns regarding the overly bureaucratic character of IMAA emerged - the Shared Management Agenda. In essence, the Shared Management Agenda reduces the IMAA time frame from three years to one. It involves far less extensive agreements between the Treasury Board and departments than is the case with IMAA. One senior Treasury Board official expects that IMAA will continue with a revised focus on more strategic concerns. Other officials, however, see the Shared Management Agenda as an initiative that will kill the IMAA experiment.

Conclusion

The Canadian experience with budgeting systems in the twentieth century does not conform to the model developed by Schick. Schick suggests three phases of reform in which first control, then management, and finally planning are emphasized by the budgeting process. By the third phase, states have established budgeting systems capable of performing all three functions successfully. As a result, when the fiscal environment changes, as it has in the 1980s, there is no need for major reforms to the existing budgeting system. All that is required are minor adjustments to the system to accommodate new environmental pressures and revised government priorities.

In the Canadian case, this did not happen. The budgeting system in place until the 1960s was one that reflected a strong control orientation. The system that replaced it emphasized planning. In other words, budgetary reform in Canada did not move through the performance budgeting phase on its way to the mature, planning-focused systems such as PPB.

From this perspective, it is relatively easy to explain the rapid failure of PPB. Because there was no performance budgeting phase in the Canadian experience, the federal government did not acquire the infrastructure and capability that was reflected elsewhere in performance measurement systems and internal auditing. When PPB was formally adopted, the system had to attempt to develop both the planning capability required by the third reform phase and the managerial efficiency infrastructure and processes required by the second management phase, which had been skipped.

PPB was not a mature budgeting system. Rather than developing planning capabilities in the 1970s, the Canadian Public Service was forced to develop performance measurement systems, and internal auditing policy and capability. Thus, much of the internal effort in Canada during the years of PPB went into creating the capacity necessary for the second rather than the third phase of budgetary reform.

In this context, it is PEMS that might well be seen as the third phase of budgeting reform in Canada. By the early 1980s the focus of the budgeting process in terms of functions was clearly on planning. The Fiscal and Expenditure Plans, the annual priority-setting exercise and the development of a serious policy on, and capacity for, evaluation provide examples of this.

If PEMS rather than PPB constitutes the third reform phase in Canada, then one would expect that the changes introduced by Prime Minister Mulroney since 1984 and especially in January 1989 are the types of adjustments suggested by Schick in his 1986 and 1988 articles. In addition, Canada's experience in transforming its budgeting system may demonstrate the need to evolve progressively through the three phases.

In other words, it appears that a country cannot successfully reform its budgeting system by skipping a phase.

As the Canadian budgeting system and related processes have evolved, one sees evidence of two distinct and incompatible bases of reform. In terms of the budgeting process, central agencies such as the Treasury Board and the Cabinet and its committees have taken on major roles in the development of priorities and in the setting of expenditure levels. At the same time, the internal audit and evaluation policies are directed almost exclusively at departments. In the past, it is clear that there was no successful integration of these two processes.

Indeed, one might argue that the budgeting systems did not provide any incentive to departmental management to cooperate fully with the central direction especially in a time of resource constraint. It makes little sense for managers to commit a great deal of time and effort to become more economical, efficient and effective, if the resulting savings are returned to other areas of government. PEMS did exactly that. Economy and efficiency savings were returned to the Treasury Board. Effectiveness savings were returned to the appropriate policy committees for redistribution. From a department manager's perspective, there appeared to be no positive return on his investment. In this context, it is perhaps not too surprising that the government's expenditure control efforts were frustrated even under PEMS and that the Prime Minister decided to make changes to the budgeting system.

Certain features of IMAA appear to resolve some of these contradictory goals. The three-year funding guarantee provides department managers with some sense of financial stability, which should assist them in planning more realistically. The return of economy, efficiency and effectiveness savings to the department offers an incentive to senior managers to develop and utilize their performance measurement, internal audit and program evaluation capabilities more fully. The requirement that some audits and evaluations be undertaken which reflect the interests of the Treasury Board ensures that a broader perspective to policy development and financial management is applied within departments.

The evidence regarding utilization of evaluation and internal audit in the Canadian budgetary system is not as clear as one might like. It appears that, if they have been utilized, such utilization has occurred at the departmental, rather than the systemic, level. Recent steps to adjust the budgeting system suggest positive moves that will result in a closer and more meaningful relationship between the auditing and evaluation functions and the budgetary system in the future. These adjustments may also reduce the extensive variability between departments in terms of the extent to which the audit and evaluation functions have more important roles to play in the management process.

References

Auditor General of Canada (1976). *Report of the Auditor General of Canada to the House of Commons Year Ended 31 March 1976*. Ottawa: Supply and Services.
Auditor General of Canada (1988). *Report of the Auditor General of Canada to the House of Commons Year Ended 31 March 1988*. Ottawa: Supply and Services.
Auld, D. and F. Miller (1982). *Principles of Public Finance: A Canadian Text*. Toronto: Methuen.
Brown-John, C., A. Leblond and D. Marson (1988). *Public Financial Management: A Canadian Text*. Scarborough: Nelson.
Clark, W. (1938). "Financial Administration of the Government of Canada," *Canadian Journal of Economics and Political Science*, 4/3.
Kernaghan, K. and D. Siegel (1987). *Public Administration in Canada: A Text*. Toronto: Methuen.
McCready, D. (1984). *The Canadian Public Sector*. Toronto: Butterworths.
Office of the Auditor General (1975). *The Financial Management and Control Study*. Ottawa: Supply and Services.
Office of the Comptroller General (1978). *Standards for Internal Financial Audit in the Government of Canada*. Ottawa: Supply and Services.
Office of the Comptroller General (1981a). *Guide on the Program Evaluation Function*. Ottawa: Supply and Services.
Office of the Comptroller General (1981b). *Principles for the Evaluation of Programs by Federal Departments and Agencies*. Ottawa: Supply and Services.
Office of the Comptroller General (1982). *Standards for Internal Audit in the Government of Canada*. Ottawa: Supply and Services.
Office of the Comptroller General (1988). *Government Program Evaluation Plan*. Ottawa: Supply and Services.
Office of the Comptroller General (1989a). *Federal Government Evaluation Studies Completed as of May 15, 1989*. Ottawa: Program Evaluation Branch.
Office of the Comptroller General (1989b). *Working Standards for the Evaluation of Programs in Federal Departments and Agencies*. Ottawa: Supply and Services.
Privy Council Office (1989). *Background Paper on the New Cabinet Decision-Making System*. Ottawa: Privy Council Office.
Rayner, M. (1986). "Using Evaluation in the Federal Government," *Canadian Journal of Program Evaluation*, 1/1.
Robertson, G. (1971). "The Changing Role of the Privy Council Office," *Canadian Public Administration*, 14/1.
Royal Commission on Financial Management and Accountability (1979). *Final Report*. Ottawa: Supply and Services.
Royal Commission on Government Organization (1960). *Management of the Public Service, Report 2: Financial Management*. Ottawa: Queen's Printer.

Schick, A. (1988). "Micro-Budgetary Adaptations to Fiscal Stress in Industrialized Democracies," *Public Administration Review*, 48/1.

Segsworth, R. V. (1972). "PPB and Policy Analysis: The Canadian Experience," *International Review of Administrative Sciences*, 38.

Segsworth, R. V. (1990). "Auditing and Evaluation in the Government of Canada: Some Reflections," *Canadian Journal of Program Evaluation*, 5/1.

Treasury Board (1969). *Planning, Programming, Budgeting Guide*. Ottawa: Queen's Printer.

Treasury Board (1988). *Increased Ministerial Authority and Accountability: Introduction and Progress Report*. Ottawa: Supply and Services.

6

Many Reforms, Little Learning:
Budgeting, Auditing, and Evaluation in Spain

Eduardo Zapico Goñi

Public spending in Spain has increased sharply during the first twelve years of post-Franco democracy. From 1975 to 1987 spending escalated from 25 to 42 percent of GDP. This is a similar increase to that of other EEC countries since the 1960s (Alcaide 1988, p. 2). Although by the end of the 1980s and beginning of the 1990s spending increases have moderated, the effect of the tax reform of 1979 and succeeding tax measures, including the introduction of Value Added Tax (VAT), has not been enough to cover spending. Therefore the public deficit has grown and debt interests have become a greater share of the deficit. Furthermore, demographic growth and the poor quality of public services (especially health and education), have placed further pressures on public spending. Much criticism has been made of the Ministry for the Economy and Finance for not curbing public spending. This ministry is not only responsible for the budgetary policy, but also maintains a rigid formal control on the whole budgetary procedure by means of two of its units: the Directorate General of the Budget, responsible for budget formulation, and the General Audit Office, responsible for budget follow-up and audit.

When the first Socialist government since the civil war came to power after the 1982 elections, the Ministry for Economy and Finance attempted to improve efficiency in the public sector rather than privatize or deregulate it. As part of this strategy, the ministry made several important efforts to integrate budgeting, financial information systems and auditing in such a way that the allocation and use of resources might be improved. Further, the Ministry of Public Administration also initiated studies and experiments to modernize public services. In the following pages these efforts and initiatives will be examined.

The aim of this chapter is to describe and analyze first the budgetary procedure, and second the audit and evaluation system in Spanish government. Both sections focus on reforms introduced by the Socialists during the 1980s. For clarity of presentation each section has been divided according to the functions and roles played by the responsible units and other main participants in these aspects of financial management. The main questions are: how does financial management function today, and how well are auditing, program evaluation and budgeting integrated? However, first it is necessary to examine how these processes operated before the arrival of democracy.

Revenue Budgeting and Tight Control under Franco's Regime

In Spain, as in other countries of continental Europe, the legal perspective is the main concern of civil servants: "the traditional legalistic orientation of the Spanish Administration is prone to view and interpret social reality through legally-biased lenses, reminiscent of similar developments and cultures in the German and Italian (and French) public bureaucracies" (Wollman 1984, p. 709). The Ministry for Finance and spending officials in Spain are therefore mainly concerned with the legality of spending procedures while compliance control has monopolized the attention of authorities responsible for budgeting. This traditionally legalistic culture was reinforced during Franco's regime when budgeting in Spain was revenue driven. Until the approval of the democratic Constitution in 1978, budgeting and financial management corresponded to the so-called revenue budgeting practices typical of poor governments. "Despite Spain's status in the early and mid-1970s as a relatively wealthy country, its central government budgeters engaged in the same 'revenue budgeting' practices that are characteristic of budgeting in 'poor' American cities" (Gunther 1980, p. 51).

Gunther argues further that this paradox is explained by the unwillingness or inability of the Spanish Government to increase taxation and hence public investment. However, what is important here are the consequences of these budgetary practices for the budgetary process itself, including auditing and evaluation. Revenue budgeting means that the volume of revenues received determines the volume of expenditure estimated. This promotes rigidity and emphasizes an almost exclusive concern in budgeting and financial management with tight controls on spending (Wildavsky 1975, p. 11).

During the late 1970s, public spending in Spain increased very quickly and almost equaled the average (as a percentage of GNP) of industrialized countries (Comín 1988, p. 87). However, budgetary and financial management capacity did not adapt accordingly. Hence, the functioning of budgeting at the end of the 1970s could be described as incremental; the main concern of agencies was in executing or consuming the whole budget authorization, which was essential for obtaining further funds. Here financial control was mainly a rigid ex-ante inspection on every expenditure to verify compliance with financial regulations and the avoidance of overspending (Argüello 1979, p. 280).

However, by the early 1970s some form of program evaluation had been introduced into the Spanish government. An interministerial commission was created to develop evaluation methodology and coordinate other units responsible for the evaluation of investment projects. This constituted a first step toward the introduction of cost-benefit analysis. Yet there were several serious limitations to this initiative. The analysis was only applied to capital investments. Evaluations focused on individual investment projects considered in an isolated way and global program effects were not considered. Further, due to measurement difficulties, it was not feasible to evaluate social projects (Lozano 1982, p. 111 et seq.) while there was a lack of coherence between the project costs estimated for the purposes of evaluation and the budgetary costs (a line-item budget was applied). Personnel costs were not allocated within the budget according to the center in which civil servants worked, but the center paying the salaries (Carreño & González Finat 1979, p. 139). Finally there was a lack of motivation and capacity for performing across-the-board evaluations within the Spanish administration (Barea & Carreño 1971, p. 325 & 138).

It is clear, therefore, that during the 1970s, the Ministry for Finance (today called Ministry for the Economy and Finance) emphasized spending control rather than auditing or evaluation. Budget formulation was largely an exercise in administrative calculations (i.e., projections of the amount of spending implied by administrative decisions, new laws, and inflation). The focus was almost exclusively on the legality of procedures. During the first half of the 1980s, however, directly after the Socialists came to power in 1982, the Ministry for the Economy and Finance tried to introduce program budgeting. This was the result of a new Budget Act, Ley General Presupuestaria 1977, which set out the main guidelines for future budgetary reform. The law thus obliged government to formulate and apply its budget by program, "taking into account . . . the goals and objectives (to be) achieved" (Ley General Presupuestaria 1977). By the end of the 1980s, the emphasis of budgetary reform had shifted from budgetary format to budgetary process. The current intention of the Ministry for the Economy and Finance is to modify the rules of the budgetary game (to encourage multilateral negotiations) and to integrate the roles played by budgeters, auditors and other actors within this game. These latest reforms will be discussed below in more detail.

The Budgetary Reforms of the Socialist Government

General Overview: Law and the Reality of Budgeting

From a legal viewpoint, the Spanish budgetary process is clear and well structured. It has well-defined phases, beginning with the estimation and allocation of revenue and expenditure according to government policy, followed by the monitoring of budget execution according to well-established regulations. The primary regulation commands: "the main official centres of the nation and the spending ministries will transfer to the Ministry for (the Economy and) Finance . . . the corresponding drafts regarding expenditure, properly justified and adjusted to the laws which must be applied and to the directives approved by the Government" (Ley General Presupuestaria, Art. 54). The spending ministries present their requests for the following year through their budgetary offices. Subsequently, the Ministry for the Economy and Finance (MEF), through the Directorate-General for the Budget (DGB), revises these requests and balances them against revenue estimates and economic projections. The MEF then integrates all these with the programs and projects for public investment. At this point, the draft budget is submitted to the Council of Ministers, and once approved by the Council of Ministers, is sent to the Parliament as a draft law for approval, amendment or rejection. After it has been approved by the Parliament, it becomes law on 1 January.

The General Audit Office (Intervención General de la Administración del Estado - IGAE) is the unit of the MEF responsible for monitoring budget execution and undertaking the audit of budgetary management. Here "the aim is to assess both the degree of usefulness of resources . . . available to the goals assigned to each expenditure, and the achievement of these objectives" (Official Journal of the State 1986). At the end of the process, the Court of Auditors, which is responsible for external control, examines the budget accounts and the quality of budgetary management on behalf of the Parliament. However, as is the case in many other countries, the actual process of formulating the budget is more complex and interactive than the formal methods prescribed by law or suggested in official studies or textbooks.

In reality the budgetary process in Spain has developed at two different overlapping levels. At the political level, the main budgetary headings (spending aggregates) and the most relevant or controversial figures are discussed. This level is characterized by the high status of the participants within the political hierarchy (ministers, state secretaries, etc.), by the political criteria used in negotiations and by the major influence exerted by the government's macroeconomic program. The more technical procedures involved in the budgetary process are obviously carried out at lower levels. Here the decision-making criteria are, theoretically, purely technical, and negotiations are based on budgetary resources for services. The processes at these two different levels have developed simultaneously and interact continually, generally through the state secretary for Finance and the undersecretaries within the spending ministries. See Figure 6.1.

Budgeting within Spending Centers: Fulfilling Formalities for the Ministry for the Economy and Finance

As Table 6.1 shows, the first step toward formulating the draft budget within spending ministries is taken after the state secretary for finance has held a meeting with undersecretaries representing all spending ministries, in which he informs them of the general guidelines for the formulation of the budget. This meeting allows the undersecretaries to estimate their financial needs within a specific macroeconomic framework. Then each ministry's budgetary office, in collaboration with spending centers, starts to estimate budgetary needs. During the months of May and June, the budgetary offices formulate a preliminary budget in collaboration with the spending centers. As will be shown below, spending programs should, legally, be evaluated at due time. However, in reality this is overlooked. Rather, most of the work involves fulfilling the formalities requested by the Ministry for Economy and Finance. Budgeting within spending centres is perceived as a constraint rather than a policy instrument or a management tool. Interest in the budget, as a document or as a process, is merely formalistic and reactive. Budgetary offices possess only sufficient resources to carry out operational budgetary routines and to ensure that budget formulation within spending ministries follows the bureaucratic instructions from the MEF (see below). Nevertheless, one important function of budgetary offices is the representation of their ministries during the process of negotiations with the Ministry for the Economy and Finance. As will be shown, these negotiations are shifting from bilateral to multilateral to encourage interministerial coordination.

Budgeting within the Ministry for the Economy and Finance:
Toward Program Budgeting and Budgetary Integration

Since the end of the 1970s, and more specifically since 1982, the Ministry for the Economy and Finance has attempted to rationalize the budgetary system. These reforms have focused on the introduction of program budgeting, the computerization of budgetary procedure and the introduction of new methods for financial control and auditing. The main advances involved computerization and spending control. There have also been some changes in the budget format and several elements of program budgeting have been introduced, such as the definition of objectives and performance measurement. However, there is widespread recognition that the new budget format is not very useful, either for monitoring or for decision-making within spending ministries.

Table 6.1: Overview of Budget Formulation

(1)	Definition of macroeconomic scenario Priority setting by Functional Commissions for Public Expenditures Formulating instructions for budget preparation	March/May

(2)	Estimation of budgetary needs
	Presentation of proposals to the
	    Directorate-General for the Budget (DGB)
	    and of investment project proposals to the
	    Committee for Public Investment
		May/June

(3)	Evaluation and approval of investment
	    projects and proposal to the DGB to
	    include them in the Budget
		April/May

(4)	Negotiation and proposals for distribution of
	    budgetary funds according to priorities
	    set by the Commissions for Programme
	    Analysis
		April/May

(5)	Adjustment of estimates and presentation of the Draft Budget to the Council of Ministers	June/July
(6)	Adaptation to additional expenditure and political demands	September
(7)	Presentation of the Bill to the Parliament	September 30
(8)	Parliamentary debate and approval of the Budget Law	Oct/Dec

The changes introduced in the late 1980s and early 1990s have not aimed simply to develop and apply a new budget format. Since 1988–89, several innovations have restructured the budgetary process itself, while a new system for monitoring program execution is currently being implemented. A sample of budgetary programs has been selected for a systematic examination of the extent to which program objectives have been achieved. In addition, the Ministry for Economy and Finance has formulated general guidelines to be observed by spending units on adopting this new follow-up system (Ministerial Order, 11 April 1989). Recent pilot schemes involving investment programs (e.g. roads, airports, railways, etc.) are leading the way for other programs. Furthermore, the Auditor General (IGAE) has carried out audits of budgetary programs to evaluate whether the execution of the budget is consistent with the new format. The intention of the IGAE is to identify any difficulties arising from ambiguous objectives, irrelevant performance measures and weak information systems. This has meant that since the end of the 1980s the IGAE has participated in the formulation of the draft budget. So far, however, its presence is rarely taken into account and at no time are auditing reports considered during budgetary negotiations. Officials of the DGB have explained that this is due to the "lack of relevance of the auditing report for budgetary management" (Zapico 1989, p. 173). Thus, there has been little integration of auditing with budgeting.

The main effect of the reforms, however, is more original since it aims for a shift from bilateral to multilateral budgetary negotiations. In 1989, the Functional Commissions for Public Expenditure (Comisiones Funcionales del Gasto Público) were formally institutionalized. These six commissions are responsible for establishing priorities among multiple objectives and for proposing initial resource allocations. Their members are top-level officials dealing with (1) effectiveness and control of public spending and management; (2) taxes, public spending and employment; (3) budgeting and human resources; (4) policies for social protection; (5) the budget and the single European market perspective; and (6) regional policy and infrastructure (Sánchez Revenga 1989). The intention of the MEF in creating these commissions is to avoid bilateral confrontation with each spending ministry, i.e., by transferring the responsibility to reduce expenditure to these commissions. Once the position of the MEF has been presented, the heads of spending centers should negotiate among themselves and distribute funds among different services with regard to budgetary programs in a context of "zero-sum negotiations", i.e., an increase in any program is balanced by a decrease in another. The change aims at encouraging goal-oriented, generic and interdepartmental discussions.

Sectoral issues are resolved by other commissions referred to as the Commissions for Programme Analysis (Comisiones de Análisis de Programas). These commissions, which are of a more technical nature, are chaired by the secretary-general for planning and budgeting. Their task is to distribute budgetary funds among the different spending programs by reviewing the objectives and resources defined for each of these programs.

This process can involve requests for program reports and relevant analytical studies. These reports and studies may also have been produced by other participants within the budgetary procedure. One of these participants is the Committee for Public Investment (CIP), which is also an interministerial body falling under the Ministry for the Economy and Finance. Currently, the CIP receives instructions regarding its activities from the Functional Commissions. According to the results of its studies and evaluations, the CIP reports to the Directorate-General for the Budget (DGB) on the projects that comply with the conditions and priorities set by the commissions, without establishing quantitative limits. At a later stage, the DGB decides on the inclusion of these projects in the budget according to the availability of funds. The approval of the Committee for Public Investment is a necessary condition, but this alone is not sufficient. Using the above measures, the Ministry for Economy and Finance aims to verify whether the coordination between investment plans and the budget is operative. Therefore, these new multilateral negotiations do not mean that the Ministry for the Economy and Finance no longer maintains firm control of the formulation of the budget.

The introduction of the six functional commissions has had a clear if limited effect. The formulation of the budget is still essentially based on bilateral contacts very similar to those described in the case of other countries (Wildavsky 1966, Lord 1973). In June and July, the budgetary offices in spending ministries and the DGB remain in constant contact with the aim of reaching agreement as to the final amount to be allocated to each program and budgetary head. The budget figures are in fact estimated according to the base of the previous budget. Not all the requests made by the spending ministries are within the limits imposed by the MEF. In order to limit requests by spending ministries, the officials of the DGB initially review the requests very broadly and then contact spending ministries. The ensuing negotiations are coordinated by one of three different Deputy Directorates within the DGB according to the nature of the activities to be financed: General Affairs, Social Affairs, and Economic Affairs. In July and August, the budgetary figures and the negotiating positions are usually close to their definitive form (see Table 6.1).

The Process of Appeals: Hierarchical Arbitration

Should no agreement be reached between spending centers and the DGB, responsibility for the settlement of conflicts is passed on to the next hierarchically superior level. The appeal process varies according to each case and year. As has been illustrated, at the first level, the officials of the budgetary office of spending ministries negotiate directly with the deputy directors-general for the budget. The latter study the proposals according to reports from their officials. These reports provide an initial review of the documentation. Subsequently, joint negotiations ensue between budgetary offices and spending centers on the one hand, and the deputy director-general for the budget and these spending centers on the other.

In the case of failure to resolve conflicts at this level, the DGB is included in the negotiations. In general, he focuses on the most likely decisions within the next hierarchical stage. Positions are normally taken and defended strongly. The emphasis of the debate is on requested increments that are beyond the limits anticipated by the DGB. The nature and outcome of these discussions is reported to the undersecretary of the spending ministry.

In practice, the DGB plays only a technical although fairly important role. The personal character of the director-general and his capacity to persuade may serve to reduce the number of appeals for the arbitration of his hierarchical superior (the state secretary for finance). Nevertheless, negotiations are not definitively concluded until the state secretary or the minister for finance has approved the outcome. However, important decisions may also be taken at other levels. Once it has been established that there is no further possibility of agreement through negotiations between spending ministries and the MEF at the technical level, negotiations are raised to the political level. Ultimately it is the minister of economy and finance, in close cooperation with the state secretary for finance, who has the main responsibility for the formulation of the budget, and he is directly involved throughout the entire process.

Before the summer holidays, usually at the beginning of August, the Council of Ministers debates the first global version of the budget. It discusses the main elements of the budget and the macroeconomic framework. After the holidays, the Council of Ministers decides on the aggregated distribution of budget resources. Finally, it agrees on the directives for new adjustments to the investment plan and to the percentage increase in civil servants' salaries and fixes the budgetary limits for each major sector or function. During the 1980s, this was always carried out within a framework of reducing the public deficit. Throughout September, meetings are held within the Council of Ministers to take account of new circumstances. At this stage and the following parliamentary debate the social partners (trade unions and employers' associations) focus their efforts.

The institution possessing the authority to approve the draft budget is the Council of Ministers. Yet, by the time proposals are lodged with the council, most solutions have already been anticipated. The minister of economy and finance sends the draft budget to the various departments and holds bilateral meetings with each minister in order to solve existing conflicts before consulting the council. If responsibility for the resolution of a disagreement concerning the allocation of funds is passed on to the Council of Ministers, the ministers involved present their positions and debate the issue multilaterally. However, in general, agreement is achieved during informal meetings prior to the session of the Council of Ministers. Ultimately, however, it is the prime minister who has the final say.

The Budgetary Process and Parliament: A Ritual

Once the Council of Ministers has approved the draft budget, it is sent to the Parliament (Las Cortes). The Budgetary Commission of the Congress is responsible for examining the budgetary documentation and for preparing discussions and decisions for the plenary session of the Congress. This process takes place between the first of October and the end of December. The debates focus on large areas of expenditure and spending centers. The presentations made by ministers during the plenary sessions are based on programs. Nevertheless, the regulations of the Congress (10 February 1982) demand discussion or debate by sections (or line items). All amendments implying an increase in expenditure on one budgetary item must be presented in combination with a parallel decrease in another form of expenditure in the same section. The formal rigidity and slowness of this process (the aim of which is to guarantee that parliamentary groups are able to maintain control over their members), the centralization of power within the Group of Speakers (Junta de Portavoces) and the concentration of competences within the Board of the Congress (Mesa), all serve to assist the majority in gaining its way (Arias Salgado 1987).

At the end of November, the draft budget is sent to the Senate, where it is debated by a special procedure for twenty days, including Sundays and holidays. The Senate has in fact been referred to as an "Echo Chamber" because its amendments are usually very similar to those presented in the Congress. Members tend to discuss geographical implications of public spending. If the Senate modifies the proposal made by the Congress, the Congress still has final decision power. Once approved by Parliament the draft budget is sent to the government. The Ministry for Relations with the Parliament is responsible for sending it to the BOE (Official Journal of the State) for publication after being signed by the king.

Auditing and Evaluation: Developing Processes

Since 1982, simultaneously with budget reforms introduced by the Directorate General of the Budget, the Socialist government has also undertaken a series of reforms on auditing and evaluation. We will now examine the effect of these reforms in the framework of the roles played, or to be played, by other important budgetary participants.

Auditing and Evaluation in Spending Centers: The Missing Links

Before 1991, there were no internal auditing services subordinate or reporting to spending center managers. Generally, spending centers have not had the financial information systems nor the statistics necessary for evaluating performance. However, there are some exceptions. The Ministry for Public Works and Transport, for example, has been a pioneer creating the first Directorate-General for Auditing within a ministry and developing one of the most advanced information systems. Further, internal evaluation units may also play an important role in policy making. Some spending centers with economic or investment portfolios (such as the Directorate-General for Railway Infrastructure) have carried out cost-benefit analyses that draw on evaluation methodology. However, the influence of such studies on the formulation of the budget has usually been indirect (Zapico 1988) and even when new programs have been set up (e.g. in the context of rural development and agriculture or social policy), the studies necessary for designing these programs have often not been systematic evaluations.

The quality of analysis depends on several factors including the size of the ministry, the nature of the activity (technical or economic), the professional group that has the most influence within the department concerned, and the size of the departmental budget. There are usually qualified personnel within the administration, especially within the economic departments, but they tend to have a narrow professional or sectoral orientation rather than a programmatic one, and are not usually integrated into the budgetary process. This is illustrated by the functioning of the interministerial Public Investment Committee (CIP). The CIP neither elaborates nor takes into account systematic programme evaluations or cost-benefit analyses, but rather distributes resources for public capital investments on the basis of complex mathematical formulae.

The potential role of the budgetary office within program evaluation. By law, the budgetary offices must carry out a considerable number of different functions within their ministries. These include:

1. The development of the instructions for the formulation of the budget received from the Ministry for the Economy and Finance (MEF);

2. The formulation of the draft budget for its department;

3. The formulation of objectives and program expenditure, including projections over several years;

4. The monitoring and evaluation of programs;

5. The management of budgetary modifications during the financial year; and

6. Reporting on ministerial projects and resolutions that influence public spending (Real Decree 1979).

In theory, therefore, budgetary offices are well placed to play an important evaluative function. However, according to recent research, programs are not evaluated. At best there are only financial and accounting analyses of the degree of efficiency achieved in the execution of the budget. In any case, public managers are not interested in the outcome of this type of analysis and do not use it in budgetary decision making. As the head of a budgetary office put it: "instead of analyzing the distribution of personnel and other resources, the Budgetary Office is dedicated to filling out accounting tables and checking total aggregates" (Zapico 1989, p. 145).

In general, investing ministries, such as those for Transport, Health and Social Security or Public Works, have more powerful budgetary

offices than other ministries. These are capable of gathering and analyzing program information independently of the spending centers. They
can therefore perform their own estimates with regard to expenditure and
even program outcomes. As a result, these ministries are able to bring
more technical rather than intuitive arguments to the negotiations with
the Ministry of Finance.

One of the main problems of the budgetary offices is the lack of a
technical capacity to budget. The insufficiencies in human and technical
resources and the low number of qualified and motivated officials mean
that work is directed toward routine tasks to the detriment of real
long-term concerns. Moreover, senior personnel within the budgetary
offices often lack sufficient training to undertake program evaluation.
For example, officials of the Service for Evaluation and Follow-up of the
Budget are not civil servants from the top professional groups (Cuerpos)
and, generally, do not have university backgrounds! Furthermore, civil
service selection examinations and the university curricula of candidates
are not related to evaluation and policy analysis. Only one out of the
thirteen officials working in the budgetary office of the Ministry for
Foreign Affairs had a university background. At the Ministry for Science
and Education, only four out of the thirty eight officials had such a
background. At all the other ministries, there was usually a ratio of one
official with a university background to two without. Budgetary offices
therefore consider that they do not have enough resources to do the work
required of them in this field, and usually complain of this in one form
or another: "there is a lack of human resources and data processing
equipment, and there is a need for more training in informatics" (Ministry
for the Interior); "the human and material resources available are not
enough to develop cost accounting, there is a need for more personnel
with backgrounds in public accounting and private accounting" (Ministry for Public Administration) (Zapico 1989, p. 149 et seq.).

It is quite apparent that whatever the potential for budgetary offices in
evaluation, they do not have the skills, information, procedures, and cost
accounting systems to realize it. Moreover, it seems that the need for new
methods to be developed for evaluating public programs is not generally
felt.

External program evaluation. At this stage, it is still possible to argue
the case for spending centers to contract out program evaluation to
universities. Traditionally, however, Spanish universities have been in-

stitutions for teaching rather than for research (Alba Tercedor quoted in Wollman 1984, p. 713). Even scientific achievement has been perceived in a philosophical and theoretical fashion, allowing empirical research (fieldwork) to appear second rate and ancillary with little scientific reward. In these circumstances, it is easy to understand the late introduction of program evaluation (especially public policy-oriented program evaluation) in the curricula and research programs of Spanish universities. Nevertheless, at the end of the 1980s, several masters' programs in public administration (especially in the new universidades autónomas such as that in Barcelona (UAB)) had introduced courses on program evaluation and were carrying out research in this field. However, any increase in the use of program evaluation research in the administration will still take many years.

Even if some kind of evaluation is carried out within budgetary offices, other spending center services or in external research centers or universities, the allocation of resources is so much shaped by negotiations about the additional funds demanded by spending ministries beyond the base of the previous budget, that it is hard to see how evaluation is to make an impact. As we shall see below, it is not as though traditional auditing has had a direct influence on budgetary decisions.

The General Audit Office: Moving toward Auditing for Budgeting

Falling under the Ministry for the Economy and Finance (MEF), the General Audit Office (IGAE) has traditionally been responsible for ex-ante control of expenditure. The work of the IGAE is based on an extensive network of delegated auditors (Interventores Delegados: ID). These are officials of the MEF located within the spending ministries. Their task is to analyze and control all administrative decisions with financial consequences; they guarantee that expenditure is carried out according to financial regulations, and their signatures are necessary to validate committed expenditure and payment. Simultaneously, the ID monitors budget execution to ensure that it does not exceed the limit authorized and examines the requests for supplementary budget resources, as well as preparing the final account after budget execution. This is then incorporated by the MEF in the General Ledger of the State and subsequently revised by the Court of Auditors and Parliament. Until the mid-1980s, the forms of control exercised by the ID emphasized the concern for the financial regularity of the execution of the budget. During the 1980s, new tools and methods (statistical random-sample methods, audits, etc.) were introduced to reduce the heavy workload and to complement traditional controls.

In theory, the IGAE can provide valuable information for the use of the officials of the DGB, based either on the experience and knowledge of the IDs or on the program audits. Since it is the ID who monitors budget execution, his knowledge of the financial problems of his spending ministry could therefore be very relevant for officials of the DGB when examining the requests for funds from the spending ministry within which the ID in question works. However, it was not until the end of the 1980s that this interaction between the DGB and the IGAE began to be encouraged.

Since 1987 the General Audit Office (IGAE) has been requested to carry out audits of budgetary programs so that the appropriateness of the resources in relation to the objectives of each center could be estimated. According to the IGAE's guidelines, the objectives pursued within program auditing are:

1. To determine whether the financial information is presented according to accounting principles (Financial Auditing);

2. To determine whether the management of public funds respects current law (Regularity Auditing);

3. To evaluate whether management has been economical and efficient (Efficiency and Economy Auditing); and

4. To evaluate the degree of effectiveness and achievement of objectives (Auditing of Results) (IGAE 1987, p. 11).

The manual for program operative control (i.e., program auditing) sets out procedures to allow the assessment of whether "the objectives, policies and procedures of the centre under analysis are rational and appropriate, the determination of the reasons for non-continuous follow-up of programmes and objectives, and the identification of the information required for improving the budgetary system" (IGAE 1985, p. 3). The IGAE also set out the requirements for effectiveness and efficiency auditing. Among other things, the auditor general declared it was necessary that "objectives are clearly defined . . . that internal control is adequate for the follow-up of objectives . . . and that the objectives may be related to resources" (IGAE 1985, p. 9–10). However, since these conditions are rarely fulfilled, many of the officials of the IGAE have found it impossible to complete the reports according to the norms prescribed by this Operative Control Manual.

A new manual followed the Budget Law of 1989 (Ley General de Presupuestos Generales del Estado para 1989), which authorized the Ministry for the Economy and Finance to establish a system for evaluating and auditing the efficiency of budgetary programs. Although more comprehensive than its predecessor and identifying clearly the delegated auditors as responsible for program auditing, the procedures proposed by this guide are much as before. The conclusions and recommendations of program auditing reports are sent to the IGAE, which then sends them to the DGB. During budget formulation, officials from the IGAE, DGB and the spending centers meet as working groups for program follow-up (Comisiones de Analisis de Programas). So far, several programs possessing objectives that are easier to measure have been selected as pilot cases for budgetary program audits (public construction work on roads, airports, dams, railways, etc.), but until 1991, the outcome was not particularly successful. Several weaknesses in integrating the spending managers with the IGAE (auditing) and the DGB (budget) make rapid progress unlikely. There are also very simplistic notions of what is required to make the system work. In this respect, the IGAE has not changed its approach to the problem of auditing within the public sector; it sees it as essentially a procedural matter based on rather normative and mechanistic assumptions.

It can also be argued that the work to be carried out is far too extensive to be left in the hands of the delegated auditors (ID). Even if it is assumed that objectives and measurements and information systems are well designed and functioning, it is very difficult for this work to be carried out properly by the ID. They usually run small offices (usually two or at the most three senior civil servants). Questioning, redesigning and implementing internal information systems for goal achievement, as well as other components of integrated budgeting, require great effort, a large amount of resources, and also demand new know-how and skills. This is particularly so if one considers that, traditionally, inspection procedures in Spain have focused on guaranteeing control rather than learning.

In short, this second guide *Guía de Control Financiero de Programas* (IGAE 1989) proposes a similar solution to that proposed by the manual issued in 1985 and will no doubt confront the same problems. Little learning has been achieved and the capacity for integrating the main budgetary actors (budgetary officials, auditors, public managers) has not been improved.

The General Inspectorate of Services: The Push for Auditing of Administrative Procedures

The General Inspectorate of Services (GIS) falls under the Ministry for Public Administration and has traditionally been a unit for inspecting the legal compliance of personnel and administrative procedures. However, since 1987, it has developed into an important unit for internal control and the auditing of administrative procedures.

In the mid-1980s, a study led by the GIS on the organization of Spanish administration detected several weaknesses, including a lack of organizational analysis and evaluation (Valero 1991, p. 106). In response it indicated the need for "Inspecciones Operativas de Servicios" (IOS): the scrutinizing and/or auditing of standard administrative procedures. These IOS inspections include making recommendations for improvements within the units analyzed. The methodology applied is based on that used by multinational auditing and consulting firms. The work is carried out by teams drawn from the Inspection Service and the unit under inspection. The implementation of recommendations is also the responsibility of these teams.

This Inspectorate (GIS) does not carry out program evaluation as such, but reviews and scrutinizes personnel, formal structures, the rationality of procedures and the administrative matters (Valero 1991, p. 107). However, its conclusions are not integrated into or used in budget formulation, the main reason being the lack of coordination between the Ministry for the Economy and Finance and the Ministry for Public Administration.

The Court of Auditors: A Judicial Control

This court carries out traditional external financial control on behalf of Parliament by examining and analyzing the General Ledger of the

State by way of delegation from the Parliament. At the end of each fiscal year, the administration sends its accounts to the Court of Auditors in order to make it possible for this court to formulate the annual report on the General Ledger of the State. After this report has been presented to the Joint Commission (the Parliament and the Senate), debate is entered into within this commission. Should the Parliament finally not approve the report, the Court of Auditors is required to present a new report on the General Ledger of the State.

However, the utility of this audit of the General Ledger is limited. The court has traditionally carried out such examinations from a judicial and formal perspective, without paying attention to the soundness of the management of public sector spending. The members of the Parliament have neither the time nor the technical expertise necessary for a real debate, and the time lag between the end of the fiscal year to which the ledger refers and the debate robs the exercise of any interest. As a result, Parliament acts to legitimate rather than control spending (Fernández 1985, p. 252).

For these reasons, the Court of Auditors is not particularly useful to the Parliament in evaluating government performance and debating the formulation of the following year's budget. Parliament does not in fact approve the spending management of the government, but approves the General Ledger as a formal document, i.e., the financial regularity of the ledger. The information presented in the General Ledger is not particularly relevant to the search for efficiency and effectiveness. However, during the 1980s, important legal changes were introduced. New laws of 1982 and 1988 relating to the Court of Auditors established efficiency and effectiveness as part of its audit scope. Nevertheless, this court is already overloaded due to its exclusive role in the examination of the General Ledger, reporting on the finances of political parties and the Fondo de Compensación Interterritorial (Fund for Balancing Regional Governments). Even if it was able to carry out efficiency and effectiveness audits, the time taken for its reports to be considered in Parliament would render its work of historical value only.

Conclusions: Many Reforms but Still a Long Way to Go

After years of revenue budgeting, the new Spanish democratic regime has introduced tax reforms and adapted spending to demands for public services and infrastructure. It has also adapted budgeting and public spending controls. Up until the beginning of the 1980s, the main concern of the Ministry for Finance was the financial regularity of spending. After 1982, budgetary reforms focused on changing the budget format (program classification) and then the process of resource allocation in an attempt to move from bilateral to multilateral negotiations and the integration of auditing into budget formulation procedures.

It was not until the end of the 1980s and the beginning of the 1990s that these reforms began to yield any results (Zapico 1989, Sánchez Revenga 1989). It is widely accepted that the new budget format is simply a reclassification of the previous one, the budgetary process still suffers from the lack of integration of its main actors (budgeters, auditors and line managers), and auditing and evaluation are still in a very early phase of development. Nevertheless, there has been at least more discussion on priority setting in spending. Furthermore, auditing by the IGAE has introduced efficiency and effectiveness criteria, mainly into the auditing of public enterprises and autonomous agencies with activities of a commercial nature. However, even in those cases where some form of evaluation does exist (economic or investment centres), results are not sufficiently linked or used in budgeting. Little has been done by the MEF to develop methodologies and learning capacities for program evaluation within spending centers. Medium-term advances in this respect may come from the universities, some of which have been quite active recently.

Most organizational conditions for effective coordination of budgeting and auditing are already satisfied. Main financial management units DGB (Budget) and IGAE (Audit) belong to the Ministry for the Economy and Finance. They are both responsible to the secretary for finance. The sources and type of information they use are similar, and the financial data base is the same. Annual Budget Laws demand the integration of budget formulation and auditing. Furthermore, the technical skills of the personnel working in these two units are very similar. Officials holding higher positions belong to the same professional group of civil servants and have very similar backgrounds.

In fact the traditional functions of the two units were once integrated. Line-item budgets were consistent with the type of spending control that traditionally had been done by the IGAE (compliance with financial regularity). It was at the moment of reforming budgeting and auditing that lack of integration arose. Each unit tried to introduce reforms individually. It seems that they perceived these reforms as their sole responsibility and reserved full credit for the result. In other words, interdependence for the effective management of change has not been recognized in practice. The effective integration of new auditing and budgeting procedures has been seriously constrained by lack of incentives to cooperate between these two units during the introduction of changes. One clear condition for succesful integration of auditing and budgeting is the encouragement of voluntary consultation and cooperation to complement hierarchical arrangement.

On the other hand the integration of program evaluation, done by spending centers, into budgeting is very weak. Conditions for integrating existing program evaluation into the budget cycle are not satisfied from most points of view (technical, organizational, legal, etc.).

There are several factors that explain the limited success of these reforms. First, the initial general lack of awareness of the need to integrate budgeting, auditing and evaluation has given the reforms a *symbolic and mimetic nature*. Until the end of the 1980s, the real intention seems to have been the pretense of rationality. Program budgeting or the integrated budgetary system represents an ideal budgetary model that legitimates, simply by the use of its name, the improvement of budgetary performance. This could explain the across-the-board uniform choice of this budgetary model. However, the validity of the application of this model to various different public organizations has never been questioned.

Second, *no attention has been paid to behavior and cultural values*. Officials responsible for budgetary and audit reforms have never been sufficiently aware of the reward/punishment system actually at work in the Spanish Administration. Reformers and the Ministry for Economy and Finance have assumed the existence of hierarchical relationships with and within spending ministries, and have therefore centralized and imposed their technical ideal solution on everyone.

Third, *legal rationality predominates*. Everyone accepts the need to shift from a concern with legality to a concern with results, but reform efforts by the Ministry for Economy and Finance have been based primarily on new laws, regulations and manuals on procedures. This continues, despite the fact that there is an awareness that the legalistic approach has important weaknesses. The legalistic and hierarchical traditions are so deeply rooted in the awareness of officials of the

Ministry for Economy and Finance that they continue to propose new norms in the belief that the success of the reform is guaranteed once the correct norms are formally established. The next version of this approach is in a draft of a new Reglamento de Control Financiero (Regulations for Financial Control), which enforces a responsibility to comply with the law, and even to achieve goals, on spending managers. Although the importance of formal responsibility systems should not be underestimated, such systems are not sufficient in themselves to ensure the successful implementation of reforms. It seems that the Spanish Ministry for Economy and Finance has not learned from previous experience.

Fourth, there is a *lack of organizational capacity for learning*. It is very clear to authorities within the Ministry for Economy and Finance what is desirable within budgeting and financial management. However, such authorities do not know how to implement what is desirable; the IGAE, for instance, prescribes for efficiency and effectiveness audits without making appropriate changes to organizational design (capacity for financial management, financial information system, etc.) to enable these audits to take place. Traditional formal links do not encourage learning. The failure to integrate line spending managers into the budgetary process further limits learning, and self-evaluation has not even been considered as a way toward improvement.

Fifth, there is *weak political support*. During the 1980s, there was a certain impulse and willingness within the Ministry for Economy and Finance to support the use of efficiency and effectiveness criteria in budgeting. However, this interest is not shared by the spending ministries or Parliament. The success of future budgetary reforms, including the integration of auditing and evaluation, will require high-level political support to guarantee effective implementation.

Finally, there have been *too many differentiated reforms*. Since the 1980s, a great many executive centers (IGAE, DGB, GIS) have been trying to modify their traditional functions and working methods. Yet, many changes have not had relevant integrative effects. The reforms represent differentiated initiatives produced in separate centers. Virtually none of these centers has learned from the reform experiences of the others.

These weaknesses are not exhaustive (although dealing with them could go a long way to remedying the shortfall of Spanish practice compared to other countries). At the heart of the problem however, lies the lack of learning in comparison to the efforts and the number of proposals made. For almost a decade, we have seen many reforms and innovations within budgeting and auditing without there having been one single attempt to assess the real effects of such reforms. Perhaps their lack of impact is a widely accepted fact. If this is the case, the fear of exposing the failure of such reforms might block the way toward a learning process whereby the Ministry for Economy and Finance becomes capable of integrating budgeting, auditing and evaluation in Spain.

References

Alcaide, J. (1988). "El Gasto Público en la Democracia Española," *Papeles de Economía Española*, 37.

Argüello, C. & Palacios, J. (1979). "El Presupuesto por Programas en España," *Hacienda Pública Española*, 50.

Arias Salgado, R. (1987). *El País*, 10 February.

Barea, J. & Carreño, A. (1971). "Pasos para la Implantación en España de un Presupuesto por Programas," *Hacienda Pública Española*, 11.

Carreño, A.M. & González Finat, A. (1979). "El Primer Presupuesto por Programas del Ministerio de Obras Públicas y Urbanismo," *Hacienda Pública Española*, 58.

Comín, F. (1988). "Evolución histórica del Gasto Público," *Papeles de Economía Española*, 37.

Fernández Carnicero, C.J. (1985). "La Cuenta General del Estado ante el Tribunal de Cuentas y ante el Parlamento." Congreso de los Diputados, *Funciones Financieras de las Cortes Generales*. Madrid: Publicaciones del Congreso de los Diputados.

Gunther, R. (1980). *Public Policy in a No-Party State. Spanish Planning and Budgeting in the Twilight of the Francist Era*. Berkeley: University of California Press.

IGAE (1985). *Guía para el Control Operativo de Programas*. Madrid: Ministerio de Economía y Hacienda.

IGAE (1989). *Guia de Control Operativo de Programas*. Madrid: Ministerio de Economia y Hacienda.

Lord, G. (1973). *The French Budgetary Process*. Berkeley: University of California Press

Lozano, J.M. (1982). "Apuntes de Catedra de Hacienda Pública," Universidad Complutense de Madrid, Lectura tema 6.

Official Journal of the State (BOE) (1986). N. 96. Madrid.

Sánchez Revenga, J. (1989). *Presupuestos Generales del Estado y aspectos básicos del Presupuesto General de las CEE*. Barcelona: Editorial Ariel S.A.

Valero, J.J. (1991). "La Eficacia en la Administración: Estrategia y Factores de Resistencia." Paper presented in the conference: *Jornadas para la Modernización de las Administraciones Públicas*, Cuenca.

Wildavsky, A. (1966). *The Politics of the Budgetary Process*. Boston: Little Brown.

Wildavsky, A. (1975). *Budgeting: A Comparative Theory of Budgeting*. Boston: Little Brown.

Wollman, H. (1984). "Policy Research in Spain," in Thurn, G. et al., *Development and Present State of Public Policy Research: Country Studies in Comparative Perspective*, working document discussed at a workshop at the Wissenschaftszentrum Berlin on December 9, 1984.

Zapico, E. (1988). *Financial Management Reform in Spanish Central Government.* Madrid: EIASM.
Zapico, E. (1989). *La Modernización Simbólica del Presupuesto Público.* Madrid: HAEE/IVAP.

7

Connected or Separated?
Budgeting, Auditing, and Evaluation in Sweden

Rolf Sandahl

Whether the practice of evaluative analysis is to be regarded as a long-standing or a new phenomenon in Sweden depends on the meaning attached to the term "evaluation". If the concept is understood as one that embraces both an ex-ante and an ex-post activity it would be safe to say that evaluative analysis has been around for a fairly long time. The fact that the ex-ante form of evaluative analysis - but to some extent also the ex-post form - has a long track record may be explained with reference to the "Swedish model" in which a consensus between all interested parties is normally sought before decisions affecting major reforms are finally approved. In concrete terms, Sweden possesses a well-developed parliamentary committee apparatus which refers legislative proposals to virtually all affected parties for review.

But even if the concept of evaluation is reserved for ex-post activities, Sweden was still one of those countries which, along with the United States and Canada, comprised the "first wave" of countries, that developed policy evaluation (Derlien 1990). Expert groups, institutes, councils and similar bodies were drawn into various areas of policy in order to institutionalize these ideas. Attempts were also made to integrate evaluation activities into the budget process. For example, Sweden was one of a number of countries that attempted to introduce program budgeting in the late 1960s. At the same time, a new type of auditing - performance auditing - arose, which was concerned not with financial transactions but with the achievements of activities.

The purpose of this paper is to describe the processes of budgeting and performance auditing in Sweden. It will also consider the ways in which policy evaluation is rooted in the budget process and performance auditing, and the possible correlations between performance auditing and the budget process. Further, the paper will discuss whether the intention to integrate evaluation with decision making is founded on a realistic view of the decision-making process. At present, considerable energy is being devoted to changing the Swedish budget process so that policy evaluation is integrated into it. This in turn puts certain demands on ministries, agencies and politicians.

The concluding discussion will deal with the question of whether or not the prerequisites for the fulfillment of these demands are present. However, the paper begins by describing the formal Swedish budget process, and then proceeds to deal with the attempts, both past and present, to integrate concepts of evaluation into this system.

The Swedish Budgetary Process

The Formal Process

In September each year, government agencies submit requests for appropriations to their respective ministry. It is important to note here that Swedish central government administration differs from that usually found in other countries. There is a clear division between ministries and state agencies. The greater part of the work carried out by ministries in other countries is done by agencies in Sweden. These agencies have a considerable degree of autonomy.

When the appropriations requests have all been submitted, work on the budget at ministerial level begins. This takes the form of negotiations between the various ministries concerned and the Ministry of Finance. The former may be thought of as acting in their agencies' interests as specified in their appropriations requests, while the Finance Ministry attempts, as far as possible, to hold ministerial demands within the limits of the resources available and the government's overall fiscal and economic strategy. At this stage routine matters are dealt with at executive level, i.e. between ministerial specialists in the field and their opposite numbers at the Ministry of Finance. Only matters of exceptional importance are dealt with higher up the hierarchical structure.

The interministerial negotiations come to an end in late autumn. By the beginning of the following January, the government is ready to lay its Budget Bill before Parliament. The main body of the bill is essentially a statement of aggregate incomes and proposed expenditures; activities are set out in a series of appendices. The first appendix, titled Financial Forecast and the National Budget, contains both a statement of the government's proposed intentions - along with supporting arguments - regarding the various spheres of government activity, and an assessment of the projected course of development of the Swedish economy at home and abroad. Broadly speaking, the remaining appendices include more detailed accounts of the activities corresponding to the various departmental spheres of responsibility.

Areas of activity that for reasons of time were not included in the Budget Bill are taken up later, toward the end of the budget year, in the spring. Ensuing adjustments and amendments are submitted in the form of a Supplementary Budget Bill, and the earlier financial forecasts and national budget proposals are revised. A long-term budget, actually no more than a projection of measures already implemented at an earlier stage, is included in the Supplementary Bill.

During the spring session, the normal budget process gets under way in Parliament. The Budget Bill, with appended comments and/or proposed amendments from opposition members, together with any supplementary government proposals, passes through the mandatory committee stage. Only when the standing committees have concluded their deliberations and appended their own comments and proposals, is the bill debated and put to the vote before the full House. In the next, and final, stage of the budget process, the government drafts the separate spending regulations, which put the now statutory allocations formally at the disposal of each agency and regulate the way in which the funds are to be spent.

Routine or Rethinking?

What kind of questions are normally dealt with in the budget process? Historically the budget process emerges as little more than a complex routine for decisions already taken, and in which budget work consists of numerical adjustment rather than factual discussion (Tarschys & Eduards 1975; Amnå 1981; Jacobsson 1984; Lane & Back 1989). This is partly the consequence of the severe time constraints invariably associated with the budget process. As a consequence, a traditional budget process can not readily deal with evaluation as a basis for policy desicions.

Attempts have been made, however, to change the content of this process. These have been concentrated in two particular periods: first, the program budget experiment in the late sixties, and, second, the recently initiated three-year budget process. The following discussion will describe these two experiments and then discuss the question raised above, i.e. the feasibility of realizing any aspects of the evaluation concept within the framework of a budget process.

The Program Budget Trials

In 1967, a commission recommended the introduction of program budgeting into the Swedish civil administration (SOU 1967:11). A trial project was launched in 1968 aimed at introducing program budgeting concepts in a number of agencies, finally amounting to some thirty in all. A training program coordinated by the Ministry of Finance in collaboration with the Swedish National Audit Bureau and others was organized and carried out. Responsibility for its direction was delegated to the ministries involved, while each agency remained formally accountable for its activities within the program.

However, it was essential for the introduction of program budgeting to be accompanied by the provision of the instruments and aids necessary to implement it. At the Swedish National Audit Bureau, various activities grouped under the title of State Financial Management System (SEA) were already under way. Although the underlying SEA concepts derived from program budgeting principles, the experiences of the trial project were also taken into account as was the necessity of adapting PPBS to the Swedish context. As a result, SEA identified and brought together planning and budgeting, accounting and results analysis, auditing, and associated development and training.

The financial management department at the Swedish National Audit Bureau directed their efforts increasingly toward the production of publications on operational planning, results analysis and related subjects. Another product of the program budgeting philosophy, the state accounting system (System S), was also developed at this time. It was acknowledged that without good accounting systems the follow-up and evaluation of activities would be extremely difficult. It was further recognized that if agency activities were to become more effective the impulse to change must proceed from below, i.e., from agency level. The program budget concept of a direct linear progression from work effort (input) through production (output) to effects and goal fulfilment was not always self-evident. Nevertheless, the goal-means concept, despite its complexity, provided both a point of departure and a basic approach, which was to lead to improved planning on the part of government agencies.

In the early 1970s the Swedish National Audit Bureau carried out four evaluative studies of the trial projects (Riksrevisionsverket 1975). The studies revealed a generally favorable response to program budgeting, which it was felt tended to enhance awareness and encourage discussion of agency activities. Also noted was a general improvement in cost accounting over the intervening period. On the other hand, problems were still encountered in articulating precise goals and measuring performance and effects.

The trials indicated that the main objects of the agencies' concern were insufficient information, training inputs and inadequate support from central bodies. It was also felt that not enough people were involved at agency level. There was therefore a call for more concrete, agency-specific information and training inputs and less emphasis on general approaches to evaluation and program budgeting models. Finally, it was noted that there had been no appreciable change in the character or level of dialogue between agencies and their ministries.

In their subsequent response to these findings, the government and Parliament expressed approval of those conceptual approaches that were considered to have boosted cost consciousness in the government administration. They were more critical, however, of the principle of a goal-oriented appropriations structure - as opposed to the traditional system of allocating funds according to organizational or programmatic criteria - in view of the fact that agencies often pursued various, sometimes unrelated goals, or that the same goal might be shared by a number of different agencies. Nor were they especially interested in the idea of allowing agencies greater leeway in the tactical disposal of their resources - a central concept in program budgeting. It was felt that this freedom might give rise to conflict between agency activities and other objectives, such as government employment and wage policies (FiU 1977/78:1, pp 9-11).

Many factors contributed to the relatively poor results shown by the program budgeting trial. Some of the failings were at ministerial level. The agencies received no support from the ministries and politicians saw few advantages to the system, apart from some improvements in accounting and reporting. Other goals got in the way. More importantly, however, the requirements the agencies were expected to satisfy were far too general, lacking specific application to the capacities or the various kinds of activities pursued by particular agencies. Thus the initiative specified neither a particular client nor a focus.

A number of factors, however, have recently prompted Swedish government to show renewed and growing interest in evaluation (or results analysis which is a broader concept than the idea of evaluation and which we shall deal with below). One of these, and possibly the most decisive, is the changing economic climate in Sweden. Most people now agree that the public sector should not be allowed to grow any larger. The emerging interest in results analysis is the product - as in so many other instances - of necessity. In a period when resources are readily available, that is, the 1960s, there is little incentive to analyze results. The simple remedy - the panacea - for all defects or inadequacies in the public sector is to boost resource allocation. In a time of vigorous economic growth, ex-post evaluation appears to be an irrelevant, even superfluous activity; everyone can see the all-pervading effects of increased prosperity for themselves. However, changing economic circumstances have led to different perspectives, which have influenced the evolution of a three-year budget cycle in the Swedish system of government.

A Three-Year Budget Cycle

The principal features of the revised system are an extended planning perspective, a new form of appropriation, appropriate results analysis and improved understanding of the ministerial role as both orderer and client of results analysis. These are now discussed in turn.

The Extended Planning Perspective

Sweden, like most other countries, has until now always operated an annual budget cycle, with the usual unduly curtailed planning perspectives. Agencies, for example, never knew what resources would be available to them in subsequent financial years. In the past this did not pose a serious problem when it was the normal practice for authorities to base the following years' appropriations request on their budgeted outcome for previous years. Hence agencies were generally able to estimate their forthcoming resource requirements with a reasonable degree of accuracy. The new elements in the budget process do not concern or affect the actual disbursement of resources, which will in fact continue to be allocated on an annual basis. To spread resource allocation over a longer period would clearly place undue restraint on the government's freedom of action, that is, the freedom to adjust its policies in response to changing conditions. However, what the revised budget process does provide is a triennial budget structure. Through this, agencies will now know what allocations they will receive not one but three years ahead (barring unforeseen developments) and plan accordingly. However, a five percent saving will be spread over the same three-year period.

The aim of this new arrangement is for agencies to conduct their planning activities within the context of a three-year budget cycle. Under the revised process the customary annual budget request will be replaced by a variety of budget documents. The most important of these is an extended (in-depth) budget request, which includes a properly devised account not only of results attained over the immediately preceding five-year period but also a detailed plan of proposed results for the forthcoming three-year period. Agencies will be required to submit this request every third year. Some smaller agencies can be excluded from this rule, but at least every sixth year they have to submit a request. In the intervening years when agencies are not required to present in-depth budget requests, a simplified budget request will be submitted. For most agencies this will serve a limited purpose: it will enable them to rectify earlier decisions, provided the process is restricted to certain technical and financial adjustments and does not entail a reappraisal of the approved direction for the current three-year period. In addition, agencies must submit a performance-based follow-up report every year, that is, a report whose main purpose is to show what has been achieved during the year in terms of activities. These documents thus constitute the main elements in the revised budget process.

A further aim of the revised process, apart from promoting a result-oriented approach to budget negotiations, is to encourage the Cabinet Office and ministries to revise their own working practices. Under the present arrangement, all the work of preparing the state budget takes place during a short period in the autumn. This places a heavy burden on ministerial officials, and prevents them from giving detailed consideration to the activities of individual agencies. As a consequence, the main point of discussion is the allocation, that is, input, rather than output.

The revised process is designed around a three-year budget cycle. However, this does not mean that all agencies will submit their in-depth budget requests at the same time. This would defeat the whole idea of attempting to improve planning practices. Instead, one-third of the agencies will present their triennial requests each year.

There is a further possibility of influencing ministerial budget working practices. In the year prior to drawing up in-depth budgets, agencies will be issued with directives from their respective ministries including a request for information on any aspects of the agency's activities the ministries may want to know about. Agencies may be asked to submit this information in the spring of the following year (the same year in which the in-depth budget request is due) in the form of a special report concerning those matters requiring special examination. This arrangement will give agencies and ministry officials more time during the less busy spring period to consider the matters in question. This procedure will not, of course, lead to a reduction in the total budget work load. It simply spreads the tasks over a longer period.

The New Appropriations Structure

An additional feature, though not a consequence, of the revised planning process is the introduction of a new type, or form, of appropriation. Under the former system, agencies were obliged to spend the whole of their appropriation before the end of the fiscal year in which it was made. To put an end to a state of affairs that forced agencies into a flurry of last-minute spending as the year drew to a close, the government has now introduced blanket appropriations. In practice, this means that agencies will now be able to carry over surplus funds from the current budget to the next financial year. It also means that agencies will be free to exceed their current budget. Although carryover dispensations have been made in the past, these were normally restricted to certain types of allocation intended mainly for investment purposes. The new appropriations framework extends this dispensation to what can be described as administrative appropriations, covering the agency's running costs, including staff, premises, etc.

If an agency exceeds its current budget the deficit is made up for in the following year's appropriation. In practice agencies will not be allowed to go over their budgets by more than 3-5 percent. Although this may not seem a great deal in percentage terms, it can represent a sizeable sum given the types of costs covered by the appropriations.

The Role of the Ministries as Sponsors and Clients of Results Analysis

Perhaps the most significant differences between what is taking place today and the situation during the program budgeting reform period is that conditions then were not favorable for the new ideas. Objectives and approaches are actually less ambitious today than they were twenty years ago and, methodologically, there has also been some progress.

There is another difference. It is now realized that ministry civil servants are crucial to the success of this reform. The key role of the ministries lies in the precise statement of the kind of result analyses they wish the agencies to produce in connection with their in-depth budget requests. The linkage between results analysis and the success of the reform is thus extremely strong: results analysis is a precondition of the reform.

Yet, what is meant by saying that ministries should specify their demand for results analysis, and what indeed is results analysis? The objects measured in a results analysis are either the final performance levels achieved by agencies or the effects of these performance levels. To perform an analysis of these objects, we either carry out a follow-up or an evaluation (Sandahl 1986, p. 8; Sandahl 1991, p. 11).

In Figure 7.1 the boxes represent different types of results analysis. In Box I, Follow-up study of output, the primary task is the structuring of final output, e.g., the number of matters dealt with, of inspections carried out, reports written, etc., in relation to a given element such as costs. In a subsequent phase, these data are compared with earlier results or with some other variable factor. This kind of information is primarily intended as a general guide to the developmental trends and patterns of a specific activity.

However, merely to produce a series of figures indicating development trends for a given activity may not always be enough. Indeed, for certain types of activity, it may not even be possible. In Box III, Evaluation of Output, the attempt is to explain or evaluate the result arrived at in Box I. For example, an examination of the task flow (part of the production process) in an agency may reveal the obstacles or shortcomings likely to be responsible for a slowdown in processing time and, in this case, a drop in productivity. Another type of analysis consists of the evaluation of output as such. Research work sponsored by the Swedish Research Council is evaluated on a regular basis with the help of different expert groups. The primary aim of these assessments is to maintain a high standard in scientific research.

FIGURE 7.1 A Matrix of Results Analysis

	OBJECTS	
APPROACHES	**OUTPUT**	**EFFECTS/EVENTS**
FOLLOW-UP STUDY	I	II
EVALUATION	III	IV

Whether the analysis is of unit costs or a product of output quality assessment, results are being viewed from within the agency. On the right-hand side of the figure, results are considered from an external point of view. To follow up effects/events (Box II) means either registering events or following up indicators of effects without necessarily having established any causal connection. To take a hypothetical example, Customs and Excise may notice that a change in routine or output at border posts has resulted in a rise in the number of drug seizures. Obviously, the alteration in output as such may itself have been the factor responsible for the increased effectiveness of the activity. Statistical follow-up studies of the total number of drug seizures made by the customs and excise authorities or, to take another example, of occupational accident statistics and medical care data as conducted by the Occupational Safety and Health Board, are essential if the activities in question are to be placed within a wider perspective.

The fact that an agency's activities in a given sector coincide with a certain development trend within that sector could be an indication of a cause and effect relationship. On the other hand, there is no real case for attributing the effects "out there" to those particular activities rather than some other entirely unrelated cause. There are many other variable factors that might equally affect the incidence of occupational injuries, developments in the health care sector, the scale of drug smuggling, etc. Box IV, therefore, encompasses evaluations aimed at establishing positive links between performance and effects, or discovering why a given effect has or has not come about.

Which of these different types of results analysis should be used? Unfortunately there is no general, ready-made answer. Rather, the analysis must be determined by the kind of activity the agency is pursuing. If an agency is involved in the routine handling and processing of administrative matters, an activity that varies little from year to year, perhaps the most appropriate option might be the "inside" perspective; i.e., unit cost calculations or productivity measurements. On the other hand, if a program objective is to reduce the incidence of injuries incurred in a variety of workplaces, the object of interest would be the effects produced in the different companies in question rather than the agency's internal effectiveness.

At the same time it is by no means obvious how far an evaluative analysis should be taken. It may not be possible for example to distinguish the impact of a public campaign to reduce energy consumption from that of similar activities with the same objective coming from other quarters. Rather one may have to be content with measuring the response to the campaign and the effect in terms of increased public awareness of the problem without actually being able to measure the terminal variable, the desired change in energy consumption. Consequently, it may be necessary to consider how near or far from the original activity the evaluation is.

No matter how appropriate an analysis might be, however, much of the significance of its impact on the budget process lies with ministry officials. They have the power to request results analysis. They are also the clients. If ambitious agency officials get no acknowledgment for the time they put into preparing results analyses, they will soon grow tired of doing it. It must be borne in mind that ministerial civil servants need not be methods experts. Their role is "merely" to understand what they are requesting and to be able to interpret the results the agencies produce. However, any request for results analyses must be preceded by a dialogue with the agencies concerned so that unreasonable demands are not placed on them.

Performance Auditing

It has been argued that the relationship between evaluation and the budget process is stronger now than at any previous period. Is the same true for evaluation and performance auditing? We may begin by describing performance auditing.

The auditing of central government authorities in Sweden is the responsibility of the Swedish National Audit Bureau, an administrative body forming part of the central government administration. Sweden differs in this respect from many other countries, where the largest auditing authority is normally a parliamentary - as opposed to a governmental - body. The Swedish Parliament (Riksdagen) does in fact have an auditing body of its own - the Parliamentary Auditors - but this is a much smaller organization. So are problems created by having a government body and not an external one such as the parliamentary auditors engaged in auditing state agencies? Probably not. Since there are many agencies, a number of them large and very independent and not in the least allied with the government in the way they would be under a ministerial regime, criticism of agencies does not imply direct criticism of the government. Moreover, the Swedish National Audit Bureau is very independent in its mode of operation and guards this position with jealous pride.

The Swedish National Audit Bureau engages in two principal and in fact wholly distinct types of auditing: *financial auditing* and *performance auditing*. The former has long occupied a prominent place in the bureau's operational program. As mentioned earlier, the latter was first introduced during a reorganization of the Bureau in the 1960s. This was a time when financial management was strongly influenced by program budgeting concepts, with their emphasis on setting costs against performance and effects.

Performance auditing spans a broad area of responsibility. In principle, it embraces all government measures and regulations, all central government agencies and public enterprises (utilities) and a large number of state-owned companies and foundations. It was first regarded as an instrument for the periodic scrutiny of agency effectiveness. However, it soon became apparent that effectiveness was far too complex a matter to be analysed in this way. The large number of items to be audited and the countless possible perspectives and aspects to be considered made regular audits impracticable. Attention was directed instead to the central problems of effectiveness.

FIGURE 7.2: Operational Objectives of a Performance Audit

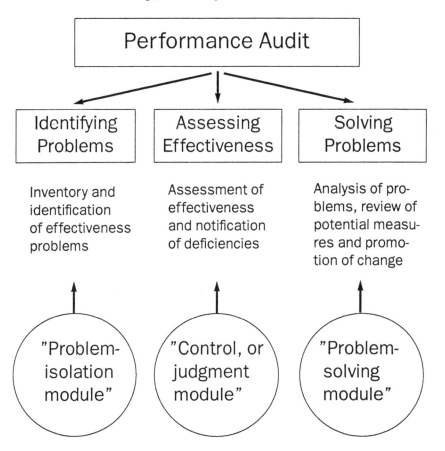

The operational objectives of a performance audit are described in Figure 7.2. Nowadays this type of auditing is concerned increasingly with providing solutions, as opposed to merely identifying or passing judg-

ment on the problems at issue. A survey of performance audits undertaken in recent years shows a steady rise in the number of central
government regulatory funding audits (aimed at determining the effects
of government grants to local authorities, private industry, etc.) and a
decline in function- and task-oriented audits of individual agencies or
organizations.

It should be noted that despite growing emphasis on a more interven-
tionist approach in recent years, it is not the business of performance
auditing to become actively involved in the implementation of any
proposed changes.

How Performance Auditing is Carried Out

With regard to its organization, performance audit units normally
work within prescribed areas, that is, with agencies whose activities all
fall within the specific ministerial sector assigned to the units involved.
The Financial Audit Program, too, is organized into audit units responsible for specific areas, though here the criteria for task allocation are
somewhat different.

As no performance audit unit can ever expect to cover all the agencies
or audit objects within its range, the problem of making the right choice
- of selecting relevant objects - is ever present. All performance audits
are self-initiated and thereby arguably independent in most respects, a
highly desirable and of course jealously guarded attribute. Some investigations are not, however, self-initiated; they are undertaken on government instructions (but are then called government assignments, not
audits).

The audit process itself has undergone considerable development in
recent years, with the emphasis on a more open and communicative
stance in relation to ministries and the audited authorities. Experience
has shown that a more interactive approach greatly contributes to an
audit's effectiveness despite the somewhat longer time span involved in
some cases. There is also an intention to coordinate auditing plans with
organizational and methodological reforms at ministerial level.

Before a report is published - and reports constitute a performance
audit's primary product - it is made available to the agency or agencies
concerned for their comments. The reception accorded to these comments will naturally depend on their quality. It is essential to rectify

instances of factual error so that the audited agency will have no pretext for minimizing the thrust of audit criticism. Nowadays, an audit is often concluded with a seminar at the agency concerned at which the results are presented. In this way both critical and constructive aspects can be combined.

Performance Auditing and Program Evaluation

Performance auditing is not an easy activity to define from the point of view of classifying the many different types of approaches that can be adopted. This is both a function of the activity's changing orientation in response to changing realities and of the personal views and preferences of staff members involved. The extent to which it is possible to insist on labeling issues is also a factor. Some people would undoubtedly classify everything connected with performance auditing under the heading of evaluation. Others would just as unhesitatingly regard some audits as evaluations and others - i.e., those mainly concerned with identifying problems as opposed to assessing the ways in which programs or activities actually work - as inquiries.

Unfortunately evaluation appears to have become a portmanteau concept, one which may be used to refer to virtually any type of official inquiry. There is thus a danger of adopting a concept devoid of all meaning. If program evaluation means a comprehensive and systematic ex-post analysis of the implementation or effects of a given set of measures, a good many audit reports could be appropriately classified under the heading of program evaluation.

There are, however, other audits of a different type: those concerned with organizational functions and the level of coordination achieved by different agencies working within the same sector. Admittedly, in many cases these could be regarded as ex-post evaluations, involving as they do an assessment of the agencies themselves, with no overt discussion of the way in which actual stipulated measures or programs work. Many of these audits have, as it were, a troubleshooting thrust. If evaluation is applied to all contexts such as these, that is, without regard to the objects under examination, once again it becomes a question of how the term is defined.

Regardless of the position adopted in relation to these definitional problems it is clear that performance auditing and program evaluation share the same ultimate objective, that of improving the quality of an activity. Here, too, however, a distinction may be made in that the former is carried out without regard to the audited agency's views as to what is most urgently in need of improvement. In the context of an evaluation, on the other hand, there is constant emphasis, in view of the application aspects, on the need for the affected party to participate actively from the outset.

The very existence of a difference between an externally applied performance audit and an evaluative analysis initiated by the authority itself is a reminder that in addition to its supportive role, the Swedish National Audit Bureau exercises a genuinely controlling function. However, one essential difference between the two approaches consists in the fact that, unlike an evaluation, a performance audit can never be regarded as complete upon the mere statement of problems uncovered. Performance audits are normally accompanied by proposals for improvements intended to enhance effectiveness.

Auditing and Budgeting

With regard to the extent to which information set out in audit reports is actually used, it is often difficult to determine whether or not the measures adopted by agencies are the result of an audit. This is because agencies or government frequently claim that they had previously thought of - and in some cases already begun implementing - the very proposals put forward in the audit report. The tendency to resist criticism is of course greater if shortcomings within an agency are ascertained by an external examining body than if the same defects are pointed out by an evaluator engaged by the agency.

The Swedish National Audit Bureau itself has no powers to force an authority to adopt the recommendations embodied in its audit reports. And of course there remains the perennial question of what constitutes utilization; i.e., are we talking about instrumental or conceptual utilization? What time scale should be applied and who are the users?

Many performance audit proposals undoubtedly lead directly to the implementation of appropriate measures. In many other cases, an audit report can lead to a government inquiry. Most proposals are dealt with in some way, for example, by their incorporation in government bills. This leads to some of the proposals made being incorporated in the budget process. But there is no direct link between the performance audit and the budget process, that is, as a continuous feature of the process. In this respect the audits may be regarded as on a par with any evaluation as such. The idea, however, is to try and adapt audits as they are carried out to the agency's in-depth budget requests. Thus it is beneficial if an audit can be processed in connection with other reviews by the ministry of the activities of the agency in question. Furthermore, a performance audit has other possibilities, including giving its views on the instructions issued by the ministry to its agencies before the presentation of the in-depth budget requests or scrutinizing the performance-based follow-up reports.

Yet, even if audits have a role in the new budget process, the principal task of performance auditing has been and will continue to be auditing performance independently of the various iterations of the budget process. The strength of performance auditing lies precisely in its ability to perform an audit at any time and in any area of activity. Thus, even if audits have a certain part to play in the extensive work of transformation being undertaken in renewing the budget process in Sweden, there are other factors that are considerably more decisive with respect to this process. This paper concludes, therefore, with a discussion of these factors to see what realistically may be expected of a budget process.

The Budget Process: Opportunities and Limitations

At various times the question has been put as to whether the budget process can go beyond the kind of incrementalism that results in small changes at the apex of the appropriations pyramid and no deeper questioning of the base. The budget process has also been described using the so-called garbage-can model, that is to say as a decision-making process most closely resembling a state of chaos (Cohen, March & Olsen 1976, p. 26 ff). Is there any real possibility of changing this process? What are the prerequisites in that case? Such a discussion starts from the assumption that the process must work at all levels if it is to work as a whole. This means that it must work within agencies, between agencies and ministries, within ministries and between Parliament and ministries. As yet it is too early to make any claims for the new budget process, since it has only been in use for a short time. Nonetheless it is still possible to discuss whether the prerequisites for success exist or not.

Within Agencies

It is the agencies that are responsible for carrying out the results analyses. One of the basic prerequisites for their achieving this is their access to relatively reliable briefing materials. These must comprise both statistics with respect to activities and cost accounts. The problem today is not the lack of either statistics on activities or cost accounts, but the lack of cost accounting in terms of results achieved. Quite often it is not possible to report the costs of different activities since the cost accounting model employed is not structured in this way.

However, this need not prove an insurmountable problem. In addition to the heavy emphasis laid on the necessity of having access to this fundamental information in the training seminars organized for all the agencies, a number of agencies have (through agency-specific directives) been allotted the task of creating a system of reporting and accounting in terms of results.

But there are other reasons for ongoing improvements that are taking place in accounting of this kind. The harsher economic climate in Sweden, where saving or rationalization is the order of the day, has generated increasing interest in this type of information. Charge financing and internal debiting within central government authorities has also become more commonplace. This brings with it the necessity of determining precise costs for any given performance.

A further reason is the competition with which the public sector is increasingly being faced. It is no longer axiomatic that all day-care centers or health-care institutions should be run under public management. A tendency toward a greater degree of delegation with proportionately greater budgetary responsibility is also increasing cost awareness.

Relations between Agencies and Ministries

The agencies' evaluations must have a client, namely the ministries, and the relationship between agencies and ministries must not be limited to altering the number of documents or their contents. From an agency's point of view, the budget process hitherto has been a question of demonstrating the inadequacy of the resources allotted to it, that is, trying to show that more resources would lead to better performance. Hence resource arguments, not performance criteria, have been the central feature of agency budget requests (Tarschys & Edwards 1975, p. 11 ff).

This has not previously been considered a serious problem. The Swedish model is predicated on the great confidence reposed in agencies. Guideline legislation in Sweden, that is the kind of laws that relate to a state of affairs rather than giving detailed instructions as to how this is to be achieved, have given agencies great freedom with respect to the exact formulation of regulations or official advice in their spheres of activity. The agencies have represented expert knowledge both in a professional sense and in the more practical sense of a repository of experience with regard to the actual operation of current legislation.

It is actually not an unreasonable division of labor to let the agencies take care of activities at the micro level while the ministries, on paper at least, are responsible for the smooth running of the whole. In international terms, Swedish ministries are small. The control exercised by ministries has emanated from organizational changes rather than by regulating the specific activities concerned (Jacobsson 1984, p. 143 ff) or requesting performance audits or results analysis.

It has been mentioned that budget information for ministerial civil servants is more comprehensive in the current initiative than during the program budgeting experiment. That may be so but it is still far from sufficient. The greatest shortcoming is in fact that there is no program of action in relation to the ways changes in the ministries should be brought about. It is up to each individual ministry to respond to these questions. The result is therefore completely dependent on the interest shown by each ministry.

It is the responsibility of the ministries to formulate the specific directives to each agency and thus take the first step. Many (but not all) agencies have received specific directives. For those without specific directives it is the general requirements that hold; that is, practically everything is to be evaluated. This is of course quite unrealistic. The purpose of the whole exercise is to engage in a dialogue with the agencies and in the course of this to have the objects of evaluation emerge both for the agencies concerned and for other bodies reporting in the same field. The concern of ministries for the "whole" must come into prominence here.

Even if as yet there has not been a great deal of movement at ministerial level there have nonetheless been positive signs of change.

Apart from the information efforts mentioned above, a number of ministries have gathered their agencies together to share experience and harmonize activities, which marks a departure from previous years. Another change involves the Ministry of Finance giving the aggregate budget responsibility to the specialist ministries, i.e., a framework within which the specialist ministries themselves are empowered to distribute the administrative appropriations between their agencies. The idea underlying this is that it will give the civil servants at the Ministry of Finance more time to reflect on questions of results analysis.

Changes at the Political Level

Are politicians any more interested in evaluations? It is difficult to formulate a clear answer to this question. It is often assumed that politicians have no deep interest in ex-post evaluations and a variety of factors are cited to explain this. First, Sweden possesses a highly developed parliamentary committee apparatus, which refers legislative proposals for review to virtually all affected parties. There is no obvious role for ex-post evaluations in such a consensus management model. The various parties concerned have already devoted a great deal of time and patient effort to arriving at a collectively satisfactory, often compromise, solution. This process involves protracted and often repeated discussion of a wide range of possible outcomes. It is scarcely surprising, therefore, that a further procedure involving yet another, "posthumous" assessment of the same decision should be contemplated with something less than avid enthusiasm.

Second, politicians deal in intentions rather than effects. They are primarily concerned with what is going to be accomplished rather than what exactly has been achieved, hardly an environment conducive to a productive discussion of an evaluative analysis.

Third, politicians are obliged to weigh in the balance a great deal of information from a large number of sources, of which this type of evaluation is only one example. On the other hand it is natural that some of the briefing information provided by agencies will consist of submissions that are not entirely impartial, and in such cases other material may be required to give a picture of what the agencies involved have actually achieved.

Moreover, the somewhat insidious propensity of ex-post evaluation for exposing shortcomings tends to generate a certain psychological resistance to its practice. It may also be the case that an evaluation requires a more precise formulation of policy goals than politicians would consider desirable. The intentions involved may be unclear, although they appear to be exact, and there may also be more goals implicit in the decisions than those stated explicitly in the relevant documents (Tarschys 1986).

The degree to which this is an accurate picture of members of Parliament and their lack of interest in evaluations remains to be investigated. But, whatever the case, in this respect Parliament remains the most ill-informed actor in the revised budget process. But does this mean that political representatives are uninterested in evaluation? The significance of the information that will be produced regularly by the agencies' results analyses should not be overestimated. There are many sources of information accessible to politicians. And it must be accepted that political decisions can be made regardless of how well or ill-founded the briefing material submitted by agencies or other interested bodies may be.

Thus, large-scale, revolutionary or innovative aspects often found in political life in general are seldom reflected in the budget process. But this does not mean the budget process should be discounted. A number of decisions taken by Parliament in Sweden do originate in the budget requests submitted by agencies. As this develops and Parliament is furnished with supporting information, so political representatives may come to ask more evaluative questions to a greater extent than previously.

The revised budget process in Sweden will not solve each and every financial problem or cope with the budget deficit. Indeed, no planning model will be able to solve this kind of problem of priorities. Rather the purpose of the revised budget process is to create better briefing materials, both for agencies in their internal business and for the government and Parliament. In the initial stages it is a question of trying to create a results analysis mentality within the public sector, of building up a reasonable method for cost accounting in terms of activities, and of evaluating the activities undertaken if this is feasible. If this can be done successfully then much has already been achieved.

Success?

What, then, are the prospects for the success of the revised budget process? First, one of the most compelling factors appears to be the altered economic situation. The political parties are all more or less in agreement that the public sector faces greater competition than hitherto, and agencies have an interest in developing internal and external debiting.

Second, a much enhanced program of information and training has been launched in agencies. There is a great interest in budgeting questions of this kind at all agency levels. However, a good deal of the basic information necessary for preparing good results analyses is not yet available. An effort to improve information has also been made at ministerial level, but here (as at the level of political representation) there are shortcomings that remain to be redressed.

Third, attitudes with respect to questions of results analysis are less rigid now and more realistic than they were at the time of the program budgeting experiment.

Fourth, the reform is predicated on the ability of the actors involved to subject themselves to a certain degree of restraint. That the government or Parliament may wish to introduce new or modified requirements during the three-year period is regarded by agencies as a perfectly acceptable and natural course of action. Conditions within the agency, the agency's ability to fulfill performance requirements and other factors connected with changes in the rest of the world are all reasons why changes might be expected during a normal three-year period. However, the budget reform is based on the premise that agencies know that "something extra" is required to alter (if nothing else) the prerequisites laid down at the start of the three-year period. This demands restraint from politicians. Thus a thorough understanding on the part of all those involved of the character and underlying premises of the new budget process is therefore essential if it is to succeed.

Finally, initial expectations must be kept at a reasonable level. The generation of unreasonably high expectation is often associated with large-scale reform. Here, too, the experience gained from the initiation of the program budgeting concept is relevant. Program budgeting was launched in a great hurry. From the start, the new budget process lacked clear practical concepts. The reform now being carried out is the result of a slow, arduous process of trial and error. Trials and studies have been undertaken in an attempt to devise forms suitable to the Swedish system of government administration and adapted to our working methods. From the first trials begun in the early 1980s to the point when the last agency completes its first three-year period in the summer of 1996, more than ten years will have passed.

Conclusion

One of the aims of this paper has been to elucidate whether there are connections between evaluation, performance auditing and the budget process, and if they exist, how they may be characterized. We have been able to ascertain that there are strong links between performance auditing and evaluation, weaker ones between auditing and the budget process and hitherto weak relationships between evaluation and the budget process. There are, however, plans to reinforce the latter relationships.

Is it reasonable to expect permanent elements of evaluation within a budget process? With regard to the Swedish experiment with a three-year budget framework, it is still too early to draw firm conclusions. There are, however, positive aspects to be seen, mainly at agency level, where there is a considerable will to incorporate evaluation or results analysis as permanent elements. The important question is whether this will also be the case at the ministerial or parliamentary levels. Moreover, heavy demands are also made on the service agencies whose task it is to give this process concrete shape. They will have to show, for instance, that it is possible to measure the activities in question. But it is not merely a matter of imparting a technique or even discussing what it may be reasonable to measure. It may in the end depend on political will to utilize the system in the interests of better public management.

References

Amnå, E. (1981). *Planhushållning i den offentliga sektorn?* Lund: Studentlitteratur.

Cohen, M.D., J.G. March and J.P. Olsen. (1976). "People, Problems, Solutions and the Ambiguity of Relevance," in J.G. March & J.P. Olsen eds., *Ambiguity and Choice in Organizations*. Oslo: Universitetsforlaget.

Derlien, H-U. (1990). "Genesis and Structure of Evaluation Efforts in Comparative Perspective," in R.C. Rist ed., *Program Evaluation and the Management of Government*. New Brunswick, N.J.: Transaction Publishers.

Finansutskottets Utlåtande (FiU) (1977/78:1).

Jacobsson, B. (1984). *Hur styrs förvaltningen?* Lund: Studentlitteratur.
Lane, J-E. and S. Back. (1989). *Den svenska statsbudgeten.* Stockholm: SNS förlag.
Riksrevisionsverket (1975). *Utvärdering av försöksverksamheten med programbudgetering.* Stockholm: Riksrevisionsverket.
Sandahl, R. (1986). *Offentlig styrning - en fråga om alternativ?* Stockholm: Riksrevisioneverket.
Sandahl, R. (1991). *Resultatanalys.* Stockholm: Riksrevisionsverket.
SOU (1967:11). *Programbudgetering.* Stockholm.
Tarschys, D. and M. Eduards. (1975). *Petita.* Stockholm: Liber.
Tarschys, D. (1986). "För döva öron? Politikern och utvärderaren," in I. Palmlund ed., *Utvärdering av offentlig politik.* Stockholm: Liber.

8

Muddling Through, Too:
Evaluative Auditing of Budgeting in Finland

Pertti Ahonen and Esa Tammelin

This chapter deals with the functions, institutions, processes and results of budgeting, auditing and evaluation in Finland, and emphasizes their intersections and integration. In pursuing its general objectives, the chapter advocates sensitivity toward the specific Finnish circumstances. Finnish government budgeting, auditing and evaluation are discussed applying concepts and typologies that have been found useful in Finland, unlike many imported typologies that have tended to commit a procrustean injustice toward the circumstances prevailing in the country. However, everything possible has been done in order to coincide with the general conceptual framework of the book.

Finland displays a unique combination of features, many of which exist elsewhere in the other developed Western countries but in different contexts and combinations. The legal system is of continental European origin even if Anglo-American innovations have been adopted and adapted as an overlay since the 1950s. The welfare state follows the Nordic model (Salminen 1991) and the economy has until recently been able to enjoy the stability provided by a substantial bilateral trade with the Soviet Union. Now, however, all the political and administrative heritage is threatened perhaps more than in any other Western country by truly adverse economic circumstances and political changes that are more uncertain than anything experienced since the 1940s.

The General Context of Finnish Government

In the Finnish political and administrative system, law and its literal intepretation have until recently been a crucial determinant of institutions, functions, and processes. Finland inherited its constitution and features of its law and public administration from Sweden, of which Finland formed a part until 1809, when it was taken over by Russia. Until Finland gained independence in 1917, the strong legalism it applied was a support to its constitutional, legal and financial autonomy against the imperial government of St. Petersburg.

The cornerstone of Finnish constitutional legislation, the Form of Government of 1919, established a system of governance that involved parliamentarism qualified with a strong presidency (Redslob 1918, Duverger 1986). Since the late 1980s, however, when reforms strengthened the legislature and weakened the presidency by shifting some powers from the latter to the State Council (i.e., ministers), there has been more parliamentary sovereignty.

Finland began its independence with a civil war. As a consequence a strict but precarious legalism was established to manage on the one hand white revanchism and chauvinist expansionism and on the other hand the suppressed demands of the popular social classes. There followed conflicts with the Soviet Union during World War II, with a consequent strict crisis administration from 1939 until the peace treaty of 1947, an economy designed to serve the huge Finnish war reparations to the Soviet Union until 1952, and rigidly regulated markets until the early 1960s. Finland's participation in the Marshall plan was ruled out in the 1940s, and partly as a result there were no significant efforts to develop national planning. In addition Finland did not turn to Keynesian demand management until the 1980s (Pekkarinen 1988), and incrementalism (Lindblom 1959, Wildavsky 1964) has characterized Finnish policy making.

In the twenty-five years after 1950, nearly 10 percent of Finland's population emigrated to Sweden, although by the 1980s the tide turned into net immigration to Finland. The emigration was caused by the overpopulation of small farms established through government policies aimed at social harmony after the world wars. Only during this period did an urban economy develop based on industries and services. This was part of a structural transformation, boosted by economic and social policies, that was the most rapid ever experienced by any of today's developed countries.

This transformation was facilitated by Finland's ability to turn the industrial capacity built for war compensation into export industries, including the supplementation of its established forest industries with substantial metal industries. Even though Finnish-Soviet bilateral trade usually made up only 15-20 percent of Finland's total foreign trade, it provided good export possibilities for industries such as shipbuilding and clothing at a time when these same industries were already declining in other developed countries. This bilateral trade also guaranteed a steady supply of Finland's main import from the Soviet Union, crude oil, during two consecutive oil crises.

Meanwhile, Finland progressed toward economic integration with the Western world. Initial treaties with the European Free Trade Association (EFTA) in 1961, the Organization for Economic Cooperation and Development (OECD) in 1968, and the European Economic Community (EEC) in 1973, were followed by efforts to establish common markets with the other Nordic countries and full membership of EFTA in 1986. However, despite phenomenal increases in productivity and a private sector protected from competition, the almost total disappearance of Finland's trade with the Soviet Union in 1991 and the extremely high level of industrial costs have pushed Finland into its worst peacetime economic crisis since the depression of the 1930s. There have been real threats to the survival of the commercial banks and the welfare state. At the same time, Finland is standing enthusiastically at the doorstep of the EEC, but geopolitical circumstances make the doorstep higher than for other Scandinavian applicants.

Functions, Institutions, and Processes of Budgeting, Auditing, and Evaluation in Finland

The Budgetary Roles of Parliament, the President, and the Government

Finland developed a unicameral Parliament elected by universal suffrage as early as 1906, but the government's reliance on parliamentary confidence followed only in 1919, when the new constitution expounded its doctrine of parliamentary sovereignty qualified by a strong executive.

The introduction of a parliamentary system made the slogan "no taxation without representation" a reality while the government also substituted a unitary budget for the many separate earmarked funds that had made up the budget until that time.

The new system of the government finances was in some ways progressive but in some respects it was also a step backward especially from the point of view of efficiency and effectiveness (Ahonen 1987). Contemporary Finnish discussion on government budgeting uses the pejorative term *cameralism* to signify the budgetary ideology that the country's central government consolidated in the 1920s. This concept refers to early continental European doctrines expounded since the 17th century for the frugal management of the government finances through minute attention to detail and the annual balancing of the budget in cash terms (Meier 1986, Heinig 1949, Senf 1977). Cameralism had such crucial consequences as budget surpluses, budgetary policies that were truly pro- as opposed to anti-cyclical, and large government net savings enabling the construction of new basic industries in the 1950s and the 1960s. In addition, it involved the necessity of constant devaluations of the Finnish markka particularly to boost exports, at the price, however, of higher inflation rates (Pekkarinen 1988).

Cameralism was supplementend by *constitutionalism*, which maintained that politics must be contained and bureaucracy controlled by detailed norms of legislation. This was reinforced by a constitution safeguarded by the qualified majorities needed to change it or to pass legislation that conflicted with it. Parliamentary sovereignty also remained qualified by the extreme cameralist detail of the budget, which prevented Parliament extending its budgetary powers into many matters of economic and social policy. The strict interpretation of the constitution on the separation between the legislative and the executive functions also kept the real initiative in budgetary appropriations in the hands of the executive.

The president of the republic exerts significant powers in foreign and defense policy, but in government budgeting his powers are those of a figurehead of the Council of State (*valtioneuvosto*). The latter body has a dual character. On the one hand, it comprises the Cabinet, that is, the eighteen or fewer political ministers, with the prime minister one among equals, appointed by the president but accountable to Parliament. On the other hand, the definition of State Council also comprises the ministries' (few) politically appointed officials who come and go with the cabinet ministers *and* the thousands of career officials.

The presidential rights to propose to Parliament the annual budget and its enabling legislation, as well to veto budgetary items, are in reality powers at the disposal of the Council of State. The council acts as the plenum of ministers, jealously guarding its powers and offering only limited delegation to each minister. The council relies on the efforts of career officials to prepare and implement the budget and combat parliamentary changes unwanted by the executive. Here, the senior officials of the Ministry of Finance are the principal actors, aided by certain agencies, independent (e.g., the State Audit Office) or less independent (e.g., the Treasury, *Valtiokonttori*, and the Economic Research Center, *VATT*), in the Ministry's branch of administration. The Ministry's senior officials are also usually the prime movers (through the Council of State to the president) in the use of the budgetary veto. Until 1987 the veto was unconditional, but since 1987 Parliament has been able to override it, originally after three months and since 1991 after two months.

Constitutional, Political, Cameral, and Management Functions of the Budget

Beside the *constitutional function* relating to parliamentary sovereignty and the division of powers, the budget has three other functions: the political, the cameral and the managerial. Consequently, Finnish understanding of national government budgeting relies on a terminology that differs somewhat from established Western notions of planning and control (see Chapter 1).

First, the budget has performed a *political function* since its introduction in the nineteenth century. As such it is an expression, tool and medium of the government's economic and social policies (Ahonen 1991). For example, the budget is the principal medium for the provision of public services. Nowadays the main responsibility for this lies with the municipalities, which are legally entitled to substantial central government grants for health care, social welfare, and education (though not higher education and research, which central government has chosen to run itself). But the budget is also a political tool for the promotion of infrastructural development of transportation, communication, defense and legal administration, structural economic support for chronically

ailing sectors (e.g., agriculture) and promising sectors (e.g., high technology) alike, and for anti-cyclical and stabilizing economic policies.
Moreover, it is a redistributive mechanism through grants to the poorest
municipalities, transfers to the least well-off citizens, nonprofit organizations and developing countries, and tax expenditures (which add a less
visible 50 percent to the visible annual total of the budget).

Until the early 1990s the *cameral function* of the Finnish budget was
particularly strong. In minor matters this function is still managed by the
Ministry of Finance, which is also the principal adviser on more significant items. The principal arena for most of the latter is the "financial
cabinet", i.e., the Financial Committee of the Council of State
(*valtioneuvoston raha-asiainvaliokunta*). This comprises the prime minister, the finance minister and a few other ministers, one of whom is the
so-called "revolving minister", i.e., from the ministry responsible for a
matter under consideration. The hardest cases are resolved by the Council
of State itself as the plenum or Cabinet of all the ministers headed by the
prime minister. The strength of the cameral function, managed by the
Ministry of Finance, explains at least in part the way that executive
auditing has been able to proceed toward evaluation instead of restricting
itself to fiscal and fiduciary questions. However, this strength also helps
to explain the relatively marginal status of auditing in general.

The cameral function has three elements, two of which will lose much
of their influence by the mid-1990s. First, there is the *ex-ante control*
over matters of economic importance and appropriations that have not
been not capped by Parliament and whose caps can be exceeded after a
decision by the Ministry of Finance (minor items) or the Financial
Committee of the Council of State (major items). The existing guidelines
presuppose economic evaluations at this stage, where needed, and these
are performed by the Ministry of Finance or its Economic Research
Center (VATT). Second, there is the *executive budget* (*erityismenoarvio*),
which adds binding and nonbinding items to the parliamentary budget,
thereby also defining in any fiscal year the system of government
accounts. In 1990 Parliament decided only one-third of the total budget
items, the remainder being determined at the execution stage. Third, there
is the centralized system of government *cash management*, where the
ministries must, on a monthly basis and with focus on the largest
appropriations, ensure that they are ready for the payment of their
expenditures during the budget year.

A recent reform has sought to substitute a *management function* for the cameral function of the budget. In 1988 the government initiated a system of "direction and control by results" (*tulosohjaus*), and to adjust the budgetary system (*tulosbudjetointi*, "budgeting for/by results") and the management of the agencies and offices (*tulosjohtaminen*, "management for/by results") to these demands (Schick 1989, Drucker 1982). The *tulos* reform has integrated government budgeting with the medium-term programming of government operations and finances (*toiminta- ja taloussuunnittelu*), making the coming fiscal year the first of the four programming years. It has also introduced the use of the programming results as the basis for annual budget frames for each ministry's branch of administration (these are decided on by the Cabinet as part of the annual guidelines for budget preparation) and pushed through a constitutional amendment allowing the Cabinet to go as far as to check its parliamentary confidence by an extraordinary report on economic policy rendered a few months prior to the submittal of the budget itself. The reform also requires explicit statements of agency objectives by respective ministries, a single two-year appropriation for the operating expenditures of each agency and ministry to replace the multiple (3-15) separate appropriations used prior to the reform, the substitution of a parliamentary limit to the staffing levels for the earlier detailed parliamentary decisions on each new post, and, finally, the introduction of new monitoring systems.

Other reforms have been launched to streamline the programming of government investments and to renovate the tax systems by widening the tax base of income tax, lowering marginal tax rates, curbing tax expenditures, developing turnover tax into a value-added tax, and increasing the employees' share of the social security taxes. There is also a streamlining of the systems of central government subsidies to the municipalities. This includes general revenue sharing and large block grants, which will be less exposed to welfare losses due to changing local preferences and offer fewer incentives for waste and inefficiency. The municipalities have recently adopted a new budget structure, based on "management by results" thinking. However, although the central government has no say on the structure of the municipal budget systems, these are influenced by the same general atmosphere as the central government systems.

These developments in Finland show evidence not only of a change of emphasis from control toward management, but also a turn away from

planning, which is in part being replaced by management. The explanation of this paradox is political disappointment in the many planning
systems established in the 1960s and 1970s, which became routine and
inflexible. Hence, the new budgetary system aims to provide political
executives with real opportunities to have their say in setting the objectives of the ministries, agencies, and offices. In this context, it is also
relevant that Finland is decreasing its emphasis on the established Scandinavian institutional model of the welfare state with the government
itself taking on a crucial direct role in providing for welfare (Salminen
1991). There is also an increasing emphasis on the regulatory model, best
known in the United States, where much of government intervention is
restricted to control and occasional interventions in the dealings of
business and nonprofit providers.

Auditing: First in Time but Not in Significance

The first Finnish audit agency was an executive one established in the
1820s with features of an audit court. The court functions, finally
inherited by today's State Audit Office (SAO), were last used in the 1950s
and abolished in the 1980s. The early audit agency never held a central
position, and once the primitive Parliament of those days started to
convene (from the 1860s) it soon reestablished the traditional rights to
monitor the executive's dealings with government finances.

Finland has preserved this fundamentally dualistic structure of government auditing (see Figure 8.1) in a way analogous to that in Sweden.
There are the Parliamentary Auditors (*valtiontilintarkastajat*), a body of
the Parliament, and there is the State Audit Office (SAO), an independent
agency subordinate to the Ministry of Finance. In addition there are
scattered bodies of internal auditing in the ministries and the agencies,
either auditing internal financial management of their host organization,
or auditing the users of the government subsidies awarded by the organization.

The cameralist ethos gradually declined at the SAO, which abandoned
its concentration on the audit of accounting books and vouchers and
started audits on site in the 1920s. In 1947 it received the statutory right
and obligation to expand its audits to government subsidies and government joint-stock companies and then in the early 1980s, after a series of
scandals in these companies, expanded significantly the coverage and

FIGURE 8.1 The System of Government Auditing in Finland

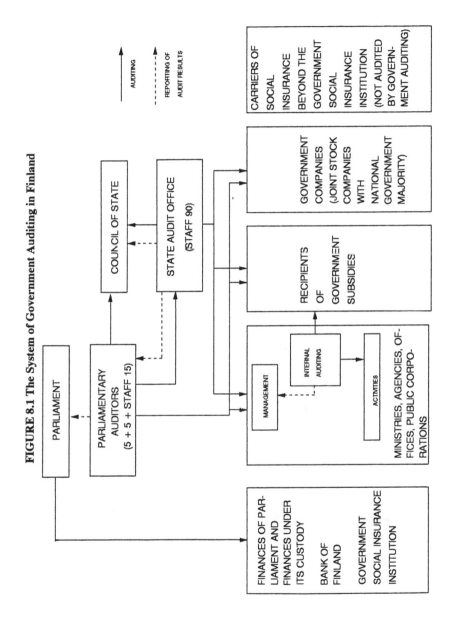

frequency of the company audits. In the 1970s the Parliamentary Auditors began to depend less on SAO reports and gradually increased their own staff numbers from two to fifteen. Later, in the 1980s they also received the right to audit the government companies and the subsidies.

The Parliamentary Auditors comprise five members and five reserve members reflecting the parliamentary strength of the political parties. This leads to an overrepresentation of the largest parties and often those parties that join to form the government in the Finnish multiparty system. Unlike parliamentary standing committees, not all of the members of the Parliamentary Auditors are MPs, even though most of them tend to be so, and most of the remaining members are at least ex-MPs. A de facto political mandate is also common among the senior staff members of the Parliamentary Auditors, but this need not discount their professional qualifications.

From 1992, the statutory term of the Parliamentary Auditors will coincide with the electoral period of Parliament rather than a single fiscal year. This is unlikely to affect the composition, because there are records of people having been reelected auditors more than twenty consecutive times. However, the gradual progress of reforms of the parliamentary auditing - increase of staff, extended audit powers, protracted term - add to the authority of the Parliamentary Auditors, probably making membership as desirable as that of a standing committee of average importance.

Even after the reform, the Parliamentary Auditors will continue to organize their work by each fiscal year and focus their auditing and evaluation on each fiscal year's budget. The Parliamentary Auditors are also unlikely to change their reporting habits - a single annual report to Parliament. Parliament will continue to consider the report, together with one rendered by the government on the management of the public finances, in first the Finance Committee and finally in plenary session. In the latter, Parliament will express its opinion on the government management of public finances during that given fiscal year. Finally, some three years after the end of the fiscal year in question, the government will submit to Parliament a report on the government's response to Parliament's requests.

The Parliamentary Auditors request and receive comprehensive written reports from their auditees, carry out site audits, and pursue independent investigations. Although they do not use them in their own reports, the Parliamentary Auditors also receive the audit reports of the SAO, and the two bodies coordinate their activities and even carry out joint projects. In practice there is little difference between the evaluative emphasis of the Parliamentary Auditors' work and that of the SAO.

The SAO remains one of the few truly independent "central agencies" (*keskusvirastot*), most of the rest having been slaughtered in various reforms of the late 1980s. It is not true therefore that the SAO is in practice subordinate to the Ministry of Finance despite its location in the ministry's branch of administration. The ministry does, however, have an influence on less visible matters such as the relatively scant resources of the SAO. Despite the fact that by force of logic a body of auditing and evaluation should not precommit itself to a budget process whose result the body will have to criticize, it is striking that the SAO's links with the crucial parts of the process are quite marginal. The SAO does not hesitate to criticize the financial management of the Ministry of Finance, but it does not often evaluate the ministry's policies; indeed it might not have the know-how to do so in the prevailing circumstances because other bodies evaluate the results of the fiscal policies. It is also remarkable that in the comprehensive budget reform launched in 1988 the SAO was a given a role only late and even then a marginal one. The expectation, arising from several proposals over more than twenty years, that the SAO be made another arm of Parliament and combined with the Parliamentary Auditors staff might have added to the SAO's marginality and its reluctance to define its role in budget reform. However, it is the very marginality of the SAO that offers a partial explanation of its positive progress toward conducting evaluation. It has needed to find for itself a valuable function and respond to international influences at a time when Finland is increasing its international links.

The SAO is coupled with the annual budget process, but this coupling is predominantly a technical one. The SAO has a statutory obligation to audit the annual accounts of the 110-fold basic units of government accounting, but the SAO need not do this annually. If it so chooses, it can audit the accounts of several years at the same time and comment on earlier and later years in its reports. Until at least 1994 the SAO will also audit compliance with the results of the cameral *ex ante* control of the budget execution and compliance with the executive budget.

In reality the SAO dedicates most of its audit effort to projects that are not organically tied to the budget cycle of any given year; it audits

organizations and parts of organizations including regional parts, functions, certain policy tools, programs, projects, and cooperation between
organizations and bodies established for the cooperation. However, the
resources used in all these cases usually stem from the budget of a certain
year or some other source of government revenue or income.

Evaluation Did Not Appear First in Auditing

Evaluation has existed in Finnish central government for a considerable time, even though the terms signifying evaluation, *arviointi* or
evaluaatio (*utvärdering* in Swedish), gained little ground before the
1980s. The first systematic evaluations known under that name were
pursued in the social and the welfare sectors in the 1970s, although the
tradition of evaluative social studies was established as early as at the
turn of the nineteenth and twentieth centuries in such fields as poverty,
land reform, social insurance, and alcohol studies (Ahonen 1991). The
thirty-odd sectorial planning systems established in the 1960s and the
1970s were also supposed to include some degree of evaluation of the
results accomplished at their monitoring stage, but the evaluations tended
to run into problems of output and outcome measurement, implementation and utilization. The government guidelines for the preparation of
proposed legislation, devised at the turn of the 1970s and the 1980s
(*hallituksen esitysten laadintaohjeet* - "HELO"), also introduced the
requirement that the expected impacts of laws should be made clear by
the ministries in question, but the scope of these evaluations has remained
minuscule.

The term "evaluation", *arviointi*, first appeared in the Ministry of
Finance's annual guidelines for budget preparation in the mid-1980s, and
was introduced in the new Budget Act in 1988 as something that ministries, agencies and offices must conduct as part of their monitoring
activities. The State Audit Office, SAO, really became interested in
evaluation in the early 1980s, but it had in effect performed evaluations
since the 1960s. The introduction of evaluation in government budgeting
has further emphasized the evaluative role of many of the audits by the
SAO. Since the 1970s the work of the Parliamentary Auditors has also
included increasing amounts of evaluation.

Evaluation at the Intersection of Budgeting and Auditing

An Overview of Evaluative Auditing in Finland

Since the Parliamentary Auditors' report is a verbal rather than a quantifying document it is hard to draw a distinction between evaluative and non-evaluative comments, evaluative and other audits, and evaluations and mere critical reviews. However, a certain degree of evaluation is present probably in almost any one of the numerous themes annually taken up by the auditors.

The audit plan of the State Audit Office (SAO) applies a systematic categorization of its projects. First, there is *operational auditing*, which has three parts: that of ministries, agencies and offices (in 1990 this constituted one-third of the audit effort), that of government subsidies, and that of government joint stock companies with an emphasis on monopolies and those in crisis. Second, there is the *financial auditing* annually of the basic accounting units of government.

Both direct and indirect operational auditing come close to a restricted form of *program evaluation*. The auditing of the government companies is also evaluative, there being separate company auditors including private sector certified public accountants required by the Act on Joint-Stock Companies to do the regularity audits. According to the SAO, its direct operational auditing assesses the adequacy and the consistency of the objectives of the activities being audited, the quality of planning and decision making, the monitoring of efficiency, economy and effectiveness, the quality of program organization and implementation, and the accomplishment of objectives. The indirect operational auditing investigates whether the objectives of the systems of government subsidies have been accomplished, i.e., the quality of the decisions to award subsidies, the accomplishment of the intended results, the extent of the reallocation of resources enabled by the systems of subsidies, and the quality of evaluation in the ministries, agencies and offices awarding the subsidies.

In 1990 annual financial auditing was still what its name suggests and was tied organically to the cameral control exerted by the Ministry of Finance. However, since 1991 this type of auditing also includes operational audits and evaluations. This is a response by the SAO to the comprehensive government budget reform focusing on the results accomplished by the ministries, agencies and offices. However, it remains uncertain if the reform will bring an end to a good deal of the work of the SAO (as many of the auditees see the situation), or instead offer what is no less than a new beginning (as the Office itself sees it).

In 1990, twenty-one of the fifty nine audit reports published by the SAO included evaluation at least to a substantial degree. However, if we remember the fact that the office has fewer than ninety employees and that the average size of its projects is only forty to fifty employee days, the evaluative scope of many of its audits is obviously limited.

Goal-Free Evaluation

Goal-free evaluation (Stufflebeam & Shinkfield 1988) is common in the reports of the Parliamentary Auditors, who often introduce explicit or implicit values or criteria and apply them to the object of the audit. The connection, albeit often a loose one, to government budgeting arises from the inclusion in the expenditures of the tasks being audited in the government budget. Three examples drawn from the Parliamentary Auditors' report for the fiscal year 1989 illustrate this. Applying the criterion of *reciprocity*, the auditors suggested that Finland might consider closing its embassies in countries without embassies in Finland, with the exception of certain developing countries. Applying the criterion of *earmarking*, the auditors suggested that the "off-budget" government fund subsidizing municipal and voluntary fire and rescue services should be preserved and not replaced with annual appropriations, which may come and go. The criterion of *self-sufficiency* was the basis for the auditors' suggestion that Finland preserve some merchant marine of her own without flagging it out.

For decades the SAO allowed its auditors to reconstruct what the objectives of the organization or function being audited would have been had they been stated explicitly. Other cases of goal-free evaluation have occurred where the raison d'être or the tasks of an organization have enabled inferences about what results the organization should accomplish. In 1990 the principal examples of goal-free evaluation were a case where *variety* was seen as a defensible value, supporting the multitude of services by the Government Accidents Insurance Agency, and a case where the value of *pragmatism* defended the supply of services from many overlapping government sources that sought to turn the unemployed into entrepreneurs.

Goal-free evaluation belongs to the type of strategies that seek to correct failures of rationality in the budgetary process. It inputs evaluative criteria where they have been absent and forces actors to be sensitive to the values involved in the tasks they pursue. However, there are the dangers of auditors' subjectivism and lack of systematic approach, both of which may lead to suboptimality in the implementation of the audit recommendations.

Evaluation of Administration, Organization, and Implementation

The Parliamentary Auditors' evaluations of administration, organization and implementation link to government budgeting through the notions of efficiency and economy, albeit quite loosely defined in comparison to economic evaluation proper. In their report for 1989 the Parliamentary Auditors reported overlaps, inconsistencies and lack of coordination in vocational training, and they required that the rationalization of the subsidies to light industries finally proceed.

The SAO routinely remarks on deficiencies in administration, organization and implementation. In 1990 it made several comments on inadequate division of labor between the authorities, inadequate control and implementation of projects and badly organized and old-fashioned procedures. Beside these comments, which resemble those frequently made by the Parliamentary Auditors, the SAO also expounded more focused criticisms that come closer to true evaluation. It maintained that extensive backlogs of applications at the Government Accidents Insurance Agency endanger the citizens' civil rights, that the Finnish government, as a principal, should change its agent if a project of development cooperation starts faltering, and that the agricultural exports policies structured in the present way have too many objectives, instruments and second-order consequences ever to be controlled efficiently.

Evaluation of Economic Efficiency

There is a long tradition of Finnish government auditors commenting on lack of economic efficiency no less fluently than on deficient administration, organization and implementation. In the former case there is a direct connection to budgeting through inefficiency wasting public expenditures and therefore putting taxpayers' money to suboptimal uses.

The Parliamentary Auditors' report for 1990 included a few simple comments on lack of timeliness, queues to be eliminated and lack of profitability in government enterprises. The report also included a few elaborate comments evidently based on evaluation, requiring an efficient allocation of jobs in public health according to regional need and higher hospital productivity, and the continuation of deregulation to curb the remaining inefficient monopolies and other restrictions to market competition.

Economic efficiency is the principal focus of evaluations in the audits by the SAO: in 1990 several of the projects by the SAO disclosed where the most efficient policy instrument (e.g., tax vs. fee, tax exemption vs. subsidy) had been unduly abandoned, where cost coverage, cost recovery and allocation of costs according to the purpose in question had not been attained, where costs had not been minimized by minimizing seasonal fluctuations of an activity, where government subsidies had been an inefficiency incentive, and where the principles of budgeting and subsidization had been too inflexible. The more elaborate the evaluation of efficiency, the less there is to criticize in it, but only on one condition; efficiency enables doing things right only in an economic sense, but it is no corrective to not doing the right things, that is, acting ineffectively.

Evaluation of Effectiveness

The fact that in Finland Parliament does not accept detailed objectives of government planning leaves the Parliamentary Auditors very little room for systematic effectiveness evaluation. There is also a lot of truth in the general OECD conclusion that in Finland there "are no separate formal procedures for program . . . analysis and review" (1987, p. 89).

In 1990 there were quite a few effectiveness evaluations in the audit reports of the SAO. However, most of these did not deal with the accomplishment of objectives (which may not have existed at all) but with second-order consequences. The major cases were the adverse consequences of focusing too many pensions toward young instead of old farmers voluntarily giving up agriculture, the neglect of proclaimed stabilization objectives in agricultural export policies and related inefficiency through automatic overcompensation of costs to the alimentary industries, and the fading of basic income support as a refuge of the last resort, as a result of the abandonment of a means test. Although the analysis of second-order consequences is evidently a sign of advanced evaluation, Finnish practice has chronically concentrated unduly on agricultural policies in the thriving industrial and service society of Finland (Ahonen 1983).

Evaluation of Evaluation

The Parliamentary Auditors often make remarks that can be categorized as "evaluation of evaluation", be the linkages to budgeting close or distant. Here, the evaluation typically includes statements that what amounts to general economic rationality should be increased (in the very Weberian (1985) sense of calculability, such as by increasing planning and monitoring). The auditors' report for 1989 includes suggestions that the Council of State devise a national program of energy supply and submit it to the Parliament, that the Ministry of Social Affairs and Health devise a master plan and a monitoring system for the municipal social welfare services subsidized by the central government, and that an evaluation system be established for the Finnish policies of immigration.

The SAO has occasionally evaluated evaluations, such as cost-benefit analyses. The SAO also frequently evaluates systems of internal auditing and other systems of internal control and information systems. In 1990 it also reported among its findings that an "off-budget" fund should include a comprehensive annual profit and loss account, that all the effects of certain reforms should be accounted for, and that unified guidelines, principles and evaluation systems should be introduced in quite a few of the audited cases. So far so good, but will there ever be an end to requests that the supply of information be increased in order to support certain decision makers?

The Impact of the Evaluative Auditing of Budgeting

Not every evaluation made in the course of the work of the Parliamentary Auditors leads to a written statement in their report, and not every evaluative project by the SAO leads to a report or a statement in a report. There may be evaluations and projects whose intended or final results are not, in the first place, statements written and published in reports. There are cases where the auditor's curiosity is satisfied by observations that correctives are already being taken by the auditee. There are cases where the mere evaluative attention by the auditor is enough. There are cases where oral statements are the important ones to the extent that even if a report might be prepared, it might include but a minority of the relevant points.

The significance of the auditing and evaluation by the Parliamentary Auditors and the SAO arises from similar structural and historical reasons, which are, however, hard to study empirically. The mere existence of auditing and its regular interventions is a structural incentive to the auditees to act according to the criteria maintained by the audit body and the rules, norms and values grounding the auditing and the activity being audited. Both the Parliamentary Auditors and the SAO emphasize that their audit work is continuous, and both of the two bodies implement postaudits and reaudits. An important part of the significance of the auditing by the Parliamentary Auditors and the SAO also stems from the positive publicity that their reports usually receive (Diederich et al. 1990).

Summary and Conclusions: Evaluative Auditing Still Decoupled from Budgeting

In Finland, national government budgeting is understood in terms of four functions. There is the constitutional function, slowly changing in the course of constitutional reforms that strengthen parliamentary sovereignty and the powers of the Cabinet and weaken the presidency, and there is the crucial political function where the budget works as a principal tool of the social and economic policies. There is also the cameral function of using the budget as a tool for detailed control over budget implementation, but this is being replaced by an increasingly important management function aimed at greater effectiveness in ministries, agencies, offices and public enterprises.

The Parliamentary Auditors focus on tasks related to the political function of the budget, and the State Audit Office (SAO) has independently striven for a role related to the management function as opposed to the cameral function - to which some ill-willed auditees, admittedly, still connect it. Much of the evaluation pursued by the Parliamentary Auditors can be categorized as goal-free evaluation or evaluation of administrative efficiency, whereas the SAO's evaluative audits focus on economic efficiency and adverse second-order consequences. The rarity of articulate program objectives means that effectiveness evaluation as evaluation of goal-achievement is not a common element of Finnish government auditing.

Government auditing by Finland's two supreme audit institutions, the Parliamentary Auditors and the SAO, can be criticized on grounds of formal rationality. The Parliamentary Auditors may still be too dependent on their auditees in their requests for information. Further, however much this relatively small audit body honestly strives toward independence, its reports are untimely and cumbersome and its evaluations, although comprehensive, tend not to be very operational and therefore little use to the government. The SAO, in turn, is dependent de jure on only one of its auditees but an important one, the Ministry of Finance. The implementation process of the SAO's recommendations is often hazy due to the rarity of effectiveness auditing of explicitly stated policy objectives and many of the evaluative audits lack operationality. The SAO divides its scant audit resources among so many audit projects that diseconomies of scale arise and it still focuses much of its evaluative audit in areas where it has proven expertise.

One might have expected that Finland's comprehensive budget reform started in 1988 would have automatically increased the SAO's role as the principal expert in the evaluation of the results, which the ministries have started specifying for themselves and the agencies, offices and public enterprises in their branch of administration. However, despite the fact that close interaction between the ministries, the Ministry of Finance and the SAO would have been logical, the situation has turned into a conflict over an increased or decreased role for the SAO. Here, it is conceivable that existing organizational constraints for interaction in the existence of a legislative and an executive audit body, and the expectation that the combination of the two bodies might one day overcome the persistent political inertia, have undermined belief in the SAO's current capabilities and brought about unwillingness to utilize the valuable knowledge it has been accumulating for years in its operational auditing.

Further reasons for the awkward interaction and the continuing disintegration in Finnish budgeting, auditing and evaluation can be also traced to the different career backgrounds of the staffs of the Parliamentary Auditors, SAO and Ministry of Finance and differences of skill, data bases, and information networks at the disposal of the three different types of staffs.

The central problem in developing Finnish evaluative government auditing, including in budgeting, boils down to the integration of the two supreme audit bodies. Finland needs government auditing, which is both organizationally independent enough from influences harmful for its objectivity, and which has the technical skills, the authority and the adequate resources for the successful pursuit of the tasks. From the legal point of view the accomplishment of such auditing is only a technical problem, but the true obstacles are political ones. At the present moment it is hard to foresee where the political momentum for the reform so often suggested will be found. An interesting picture of the situation is painted in a working group report of February 1991, where the representative of the Ministry of Finance favored the status quo, the representative of the Parliamentary Auditors' Office wished to make an end to the State Audit Office's (SAO) dependence on the ministry without ruling out the combination of the SAO and the Parliamentary Auditors' Office, and the SAO's own representative held that the SAO might be made an executive agency linked directly to the Council of State, thus resembling the attorney general. Where is the political Solomon needed for the required Solomonic judgment?

We wish to thank Tauno Ylinen, Ministry of Finance; Marja Heikkinen, earlier of the Ministry of Finance, later of the Ministry of Transportation and Communications; Seppo Kivelä, the Treasury; Kalevi Mattila, the Parliamentary Auditors; Paula Tiihonen, the Secretariat of the Standing Committees of Parliament; Markku Temmes, Development Center of Government Administration; Raimo Ikonen, the Ministry of Social Affairs and Health; Pekka Väänänen, the Ministry of Commerce and Industry; Mauri Saikko and Arto Seppovaara, the State Audit Office; Pentti Meklin, University of Tampere; Timo Östring, the Ministry of Finance; Veijo Kauppinen, the Ministry of Commerce and Industry; and Teuvo Mäkelä and Jarmo E.J. Laine, the Parliamentary Auditors' Office.

References

Ahonen, P. (1983). *Public Policy Evaluation as Discourse*. Helsinki: The Finnish Political Science Association
Ahonen, P. (1987) *Public Enterprises, Administrative Theory, and Financial Adminis-tration.* [with an English Summary of that name]. Abo: Åbo Akademi University Press.
Ahonen, P. (1991). "Political Economy as a Perspective in Finnish Research on Public Administration, Politics, and Policy," in P. Ahonen ed., *Political Economy of Finnish Public Administration*. Finnpublishers, forthcoming.
Diederich, N., G. Cadel, H. Dettmar & I. Haag (1990). *Die diskreten Kontrolleure: Eine Wirkungsanalyse des Bundesrechnungshofs*. Schriften des Zentralinstituts für

sozialwissenschaftliche Forschung der Freien Universität Berlin, Bd. 59, Oplanden: Westdeutscher Verlag.

Drucker, P. (1982). *Managing for Results*. London: Heinemann.

Duverger, M. (1986). *Les régimes sémi-presidentielles*. Paris: Presses universitaires de France.

Heinig, K. (1949). *Das Budget*, 1, *Die Budgetkontrolle*. Tubingen: J.C.B. Mohr (Paul Siebeck).

Lindblom, C.E. (1959). "The Science of 'Muddling Through'" *Public Administration Review*, 19, 79–88.

Meier, H. (1986). *Die ältere deutsche Staats- und Verwaltungslehre*. Munich: Deutsche Taschenbuch Verlag.

OECD (1987). *The Control and Management of Public Expenditure*. Paris: OECD.

Pekkarinen, J. (1988). *Keynesianism and the Scandinavian Models of Economic Growth*. New York: United Nations, WIDER (World Institute of Economic Research).

Redslob, R. (1918). *Die parlamentarische Regierung in ihrer wahren und ihrer unechten form: Eine vergleichende Studie über die Verfassungen von England, Belgien, Ungarn, Schweden und Frankreich*. Tubingen: J.C.B. Mohr (Paul Siebeck).

Salminen, A. (1991). *Organized Welfare: The Case of Finland's Welfare Bureaucracy, A Nordic Comparison*. New York: Peter Lang.

Schick, A. (1989). "Budgeting for Results: Recent Developments in Five Industrialized Countries," *Public Administration Review*, 50/1, 26–34.

Senf, P. (1977). "Kurzfristige Finanzplanung," in F. Neumark, ed., *Handbuch der Finanzwissenschaft*. Bd. 1, 371–425. Tubingen: J.C.B. Mohr (Paul Siebeck).

Stufflebeam, D. L. & A.J. Shinkfield (1988). *Systematic Evaluation*. Kluwer-Nijhoff.

Weber, M. (1985). *Wirtschaft und Gesellschaft: Grundriss der verstehenden Soziologie*. Tubingen: J.C.B. Mohr (Paul Siebeck).

Wildavsky, A. (1964). *The Politics of the Budgetary Process*. Boston: Little Brown.

9

Horses to the Water:
Budgeting, Auditing, and Evaluation in
Seven Governments

Andrew Gray and Bill Jenkins

> *You can lead a horse to the water but you cannot*
> *make him drink.*
>
> —Old English Proverb

It is sometimes said of the United Kingdom and the United States of America that these countries share everything except a common language! From the chapters above it appears that a similar comment can be made of the practitioners of budgeting, auditing and evaluation both within and across national contexts. It may be too simplistic to argue that budgeting, auditing and evaluation represent separate professional *cultures* but there appears to be extensive evidence that while budgeting, auditing and evaluation often share linguistic concepts such as accountability, efficiency and effectiveness, the interpretation of these terms varies considerably.

The reasons for this state of affairs clearly differ within context. In some cases the history of political and administrative development means that budgeting, auditing and evaluation have emerged and developed along separate tracks (e.g. the case of Germany outlined in Ch. 4). In others a response to a changing external economic environment has led to a particular dominating perspective, as in recent U.K. and U.S. experience where economizing and financial control have resulted not only in a particular orientation on budgeting and auditing but also a subsequent redefinition of what is understood as evaluation.

185

The last point suggests that any assessment of the development of and links (or absence of links) between budgeting, auditing and evaluation must recognize what might be termed the *political economy* of the resource allocation process, namely that it is the political community which ultimately controls resources. Thus, the fate of audit and evaluation can be linked to the extent that they impinge on political priorities as reflected in the budgetary system. In brief, any examination of the integration or disintegration of budgeting, auditing and evaluation must recognize that all these activities are influenced by the politics of finance and by the political actors centrally concerned with this.

It is against this backdrop that our concluding chapter describes and examines the variations in historical development and experience revealed by previous chapters. In particular, we seek to identify the most striking variations in budgeting, auditing and evaluation and ask whether their present functions and patterns of integration are the product of differing strategies within the professional communities involved, or whether the explanation lies in wider differences in political and administrative structures.

As a consequence the tone of this chapter will be largely empirical and theoretical. However, we also seek to help those responsible for managing such systems to understand some of the problems they face and to deal with them in a practical way by focusing on the structures and processes they can influence. The tone will also be normative in the sense that all the authors, committed to the logic of budgeting, auditing and evaluation in government and its contribution to public management, seek ways to help the effective integration and performance of budgeting, auditing and evaluation.

This chapter will therefore first describe the functions that budgeting, auditing and evaluation serve in differing national contexts; second, examine the patterns of their integration; and third, identify the preconditions for their successful integration. How far such an integration is or will be possible is a subject for our concluding comments since, as is noted in the proverb at the head of this chapter, while horses can be brought to the water they cannot usually be made to drink.

The Functions of Budgeting, Auditing, and Evaluation

In chapter 1 we outlined our interest in the *functional* importance of budgeting, auditing and evaluation in different political systems, and noted the concern of many governments over the last thirty years with the control of public expenditure and the planning of policy. We hypothesized that budgeting, auditing and evaluation would be used in different ways to strengthen financial and political control in particular and contribute to planning and learning and economic accountability. These hypotheses were based in turn on assumptions of governments' perceived needs for political system cohesion and economic growth, goals that appeared common to the countries portrayed. However, we can now turn from theorizing to a more concrete analysis based on the evidence set out in the previous chapters.

The Functions of Budgeting

It is perhaps taking matters too far to agree with Wildavsky that "the purposes of budgets are as varied as the purposes of men" (Wildavsky 1964, p. 4), but there is a strong consensus in the chapter that not only do budgets serve a variety of purposes in political systems irrespective of institutions, parties and histories, but also that the budgetary process and the budget itself have been designed to serve primarily *a political function*. In particular budgeting appears to be a process for making political choices. It proceeds on the basis of political rationality rather than economic rationality, and for political actors, control over key stages of the budgetary process is perceived as a vital lever both for building and sustaining political support. Only in Sweden are there clear differences since, in this case, political choices are separated from budgeting by a process of consensus building that takes place prior to budgeting.

The politics of the budgetary process is therefore of paramount importance. However, it would be an error to neglect the fact that within the political economy of budgetary behavior *financial* functions also figure significantly. In all the countries represented above this function is normally overseen by a finance ministry or treasury that is itself often part of a core-executive structure (Rhodes & Dunleavy 1990). Moreover, the chapters describe how budgets frequently begin as mechanisms of financial control and move to instruments of *planning*. However, for many countries this move has faded, if not failed, and an emphasis on budgeting as a planning instrument has now given way, in the 1980s, to expenditure *control* and mechanisms of restraint. Examples of this come from Canada, the United Kingdom and, to a lesser extent, the United

States where more right-wing governments have concentrated on holding
down public expenditure and reduced planning horizons. Such moves
are common to other countries such as Finland. Indeed the only exception
to this trend appears to have been Sweden, where a three-year planning
cycle has been developed and into which a savings regime has been built.

However, planning and control also have *administrative* and *managerial* functions. Thus budgets are seen as authorizers of actions (e.g.,
Germany and Finland, countries with strong administrative and legalistic
traditions), and controllers of operations (Germany and Spain provide
evidence of the importance of management within and across government departments). The Spanish case is of particular importance here
since it illustrates a country attempting to move from a legalistic to a
managerial system of control within an emerging democratic structure.
This contrasts sharply with the German case, where systems are well
established and operate within firmly delineated traditions.

Finally, the *constitutional* functions of budgeting should not be overlooked. It is possible that legislatures have little influence over the
budgetary process other than nodding through choices made by the
executive. This would be true in a strong party system such as the United
Kingdom but would certainly not hold in the United States. Here and
elsewhere budgets can have a constitutionally enshrined role as mechanisms to check executives and facilitate accountability.

The Functions of Auditing

If budgets are at the heart of the political process, audit often appears
to be on the fringe. Few political actors become excited about the audit
process unless things are seen to be going wrong or their own favored
activities are attacked. In most countries, audit is the weapon for the
committed proponent of probity and accountability to harry the executive
or the departments of state.

The functions of audit also appear to vary sharply with the type of
audit being conducted and the location of audit activity. Chapter 1 pointed
out the differences between internal and external audit as well as the
expansion of audit functions from traditional compliance work to the
more rarefied heights of value for money and comprehensive audit. We
also noted the differences between internal auditors, who are often
employees of government departments or linked to treasuries, and exter-

nal audit bodies, which are the arms of legislative accountability (e.g., the General Accounting Office (GAO) in the United States and the Parliamentary Auditors in Finland).

While auditing functions are closely related to constitutional principles of accountability there are a variety of audit structures and a variety of audit practices. Thus in cases such as Sweden and Finland parliamentary and governmental auditing are separated while in the other countries they are combined. Moreover, not all countries have moved beyond the simple practices of *regularity* or *certificating* functions to the more challenging (from the audit viewpoint) and threatening (from the political viewpoint) *performance audit*.

Regularity audits, of course, relate to the extent to which expenditures and actions implied are authorized. This is the traditional function in countries as diverse as the United States, United Kingdom, Canada, Spain, Finland, and Germany. In contrast, performance audits deal with the extent to which the expenditure and implied actions have maximized the outputs from the inputs used, or minimized the inputs for stipulated outputs (efficiency), or maximized the desired products or impacts of programs (effectiveness). Whatever this type of auditing is called (value for money, efficiency and effectiveness auditing, or comprehensive auditing), its function is to hold activities and programs to account not only for the extent to which their spending and actions were authorized but whether they were appropriate in a managerial sense. This is clearly seen as the function of national or supreme audit offices in such countries as the United States, the United Kingdom and Sweden. However, in most countries, in theoretical terms at least, this type of audit activity stops short of policy questioning. If it does so question, then audit is fundamentally a political activity challenging policy choices and budgetary allocations.

The Functions of Evaluation

Evaluation is less well established as a regular activity in the political systems studied here than either budgeting or auditing. However, there have often been reformers who have hoped to rationalize budgetary processes by institutionalizing evaluation as a regular part of the expenditure process, as in the widespread experiments with planning programming and budgeting systems (PPBS) in the United States and elsewhere.

Moreover, the shift from regularity to performance auditing begins to blur the auditing-evaluation boundary, questioning whether auditors are different from evaluators and whether audit can take on an evaluatory role and mission.

These trends, the attempt at reforming the budgetary process and the development of audit activities, can be linked with the emergence (or failure to emerge) of evaluation in the countries studied. Hence, in the cases observed it appears that evaluation develops from two sources: ex-post internal audit and ex-ante assessment of options. In the first instance countries such as Canada demonstrate how internal audit can, in certain circumstances, develop a program function as internal evaluation. In the second instance Spanish experience shows attempts to develop an evaluative function via techniques such as cost-benefit analysis, which have been used to assess alternative capital projects. In both these instances evaluation performs what is essentially a *program* management function, i.e., evaluation has been developed to assist the management of programs and resources rather than to facilitate accountability. This is best shown structurally in Sweden where evaluations (either ex-post or ex-ante) involve the participation of the agency in question while auditing, at least traditionally, does not.

But what of the role of evaluation? As a newcomer, compared to the historically well-established activities of budgeting and auditing, it sometimes struggles to establish clearly whom (or what) it is supposed to serve. It could have been developed to support the budget function but in practice this is not what has happened. Instead evaluation serves different masters (e.g., the Legislature in the United States and deputy ministers in the Canadian case) and provides a range of products from providing advice on the termination and revision of major policies and programs to information on the management of programs and service delivery mechanisms. As such evaluation has the potential to be multi-functional but its actual use is primarily as a management rather than a policy instrument. Its weak relationship with budgeting systems may thus be unsurprising.

Budgeting, Auditing, and Evaluation: The Functions Assessed

The above discussion indicates that budgeting, auditing and evaluation can each serve a variety of functions within political systems, and these functions may vary further with time and circumstances. But are the functions really distinct? Are they discrete or overlapping? Do they have anything in common or are their rationalities and methodology different? And does any of this really matter?

Such questions *are* important as their answers have implications for the appropriateness of the structures designed to serve budegting, auditing and evaluation, and the patterns of integration that are desirable and feasible. Not least such questions reveal the importance of understanding the nature and evolution of political systems and the way that arrangements for budgeting, auditing and evaluation evolve in differing political and economic contexts.

Thus a comparison of the different national experiences reveals both functional similarities and differences. The budgetary system for example has, in almost every case, been designed to serve the control and planning functions of political systems both in terms of *economic* and *political* control. Such systems, however, require "feedback" in order to correct errors, develop and learn. Auditing and evaluation, where they have been developed, are designed to provide at least some sort of feedback to the budgetary system.

However, this picture hides a number of subtle differences that indicate how political history and political development influence whether budgeting, auditing and evaluation run together or are separate. For example, some constitutions clearly provide for or oblige a separation of function for the activities in question. This is true for the United States where it appears to emerge from the historically important separation of powers that underpins the U.S. constitution. In Germany the separation is provided for by law, even to the extent of a separation of the revenue and expenditure sides of budgeting, while in the United Kingdom it is based on custom and practice. But the United States also demonstrates an interesting variation arising in custom and practice between auditing and evaluation in that the activities of the General Accounting Office had tended to weaken the distinction between auditing and evaluation, giving audit a greater evaluative capacity (a development much less made in United Kingdom and Germany).

But how far can auditing and evaluation provide a regular and integrated feedback function into the budgetary process? The evidence from the different national experiences indicates that even where the need for this function is recognized its realisation is infrequent. Further, in some political systems the position is made impossible by the historical rationalities that pervade state activities. An example of the former is Canada. Here, as Segsworth demonstrates (Ch. 5), there has been much lip service paid to the necessity to design a system where budgeting is informed by auditing and evaluation, but little success in achieving this in practice. This he attributes to the lack of "maturity" in the system, i.e., the rhetoric of the reformers and system designers is rarely matched by the reality of implementation in terms of effective changes that draw together the activities of budgeting, auditing and evaluation (see also Spain, Ch. 6).

In other countries however, not even the rhetoric of change can be detected and systems seem to proceed changeless down separate tracks. This is particularly the case in Germany and also to some extent in Finland. Here, as these differing accounts show, there is a powerful legal rationality that pervades the development and practice of government. This approach, where law and traditional rule-based perspectives are powerful and all embracing, not only keeps the activities of budgeting, auditing and evaluation separate but also affects the way these activities are conceptualized and practised. In such a climate managerial rationality has a particular interpretation, i.e., that which complies to law and tradition, a view developed and sustained by state organizations staffed predominently by jurists or individuals who have received legal training. As such these systems differ sharply from those in which reform perspectives seek to link budgeting, auditing and evaluation in such a way that techniques to assess policy effectiveness are incorporated into budgeting and auditing procedures.

Structures are also important in explaining the different functions that budgeting, auditing and evaluation serve. For example, in Sweden a traditional separateness between policy-oriented ministries and execution-oriented agencies sets up distinctive operational forms of budgeting, auditing and evaluation. However, it is not just the structures and processes that are functionally different here but also the type of questions that are asked and answered. This observation holds a more general sense for many of the other countries studied. Budgeting raises questions about priorities and political muscle, auditing the *how* questions of expenditure while evaluation asks *why* services or goods were provided in a particular way or at all. These questions do not always fit well together since they reflect tensions and differences within political systems and administrative organizations. It is perhaps for this reason that they have often developed separately and at a pace different from each other. Yet while separation is a feature of many systems, overlaps are also notable and considerable. In Germany, for example, there is a function for auditing within budgeting (i.e., concomitant auditing as described in Ch. 4) while in Canada the auditor general is involved in the format of estimates. Further, in the United States, the United Kingom and especially Sweden, there is a considerable mutuality of function in auditing and evaluation through the activities of supreme audit bodies (GAO, NAO, RRV). In Finland too, the parliamentary auditors have ventured, albeit with limited resources, into VFM evaluations although the success of this venture remains to be determined (Ch. 8).

These overlapping functions perhaps reveal that there may be, in many of the systems studied, more feedback into the budgetary process from auditing and evalution than would immediately seem to be the case on first analysis. Further, not only may there be a common thrust in feedback provision but there may also be shared benefit in a competitive tension between these activities. However, whether this leads on to assist in integrating the activities of budgeting, auditing and evaluation is a different matter.

Patterns of Integration

A tentative conclusion that can be drawn from the above discussion is that while budgeting, auditing and evaluation contribute to a general planning and control function, each in particular ways asks different and specific questions regarding both the supply and delivery of goods and services. In a classic sense while sharing certain common goals within political and administrative organizations, they are also separate activities, generally staffed by separate groups who deal with particular niches of the political and economic environment. Such a differentiation is wholly functional in the sense that it enables a political system to cope more effectively with the multiple demands of a changing environment. However, it also leads to a world in which the differentiated parts of political systems engage in administrative politics (Gray & Jenkins 1985).

In terms of the successful management of the state it appears important to compensate for this differentiation by integrating the answers to the questions posed by budgeting, auditing and evaluation. But what does one mean by integration in this context? Structures and procedures may well appear to be institutionalized to provide it but these do not mean that it exists. In the analysis that follows we identify four types of integration that appeared important to members of the IIAS Working Group.

Logical Integration

In theoretical terms the concept of *logical integration* reflects the extent to which the products of one process are consistent with those of the others. In our specific sphere of interest budgets, audits and evaluations are all distinct products of unique processes and reflect particular ideologies and rationalities.

It can be argued that any political system seeking to control its environment and plan its survival and growth would also seek to develop arrangements where budgeting, auditing and evaluation have a logical coherence. However, the chapters above contain little to suggest that this hypothesis is confirmed in reality. Rather, different national experiences indicate that political logic is dominant. The extent to which integration takes place is thus determined by this. This is not to deny, however, the evidence of some logical integration. Derlien (Ch. 4) suggests that in the German case arrangements have some political logic while Sandahl's account of Swedish experience (Ch. 7) indicates that there at least are mechanisms for dealing with political choice prior to, rather than by means of, the budgetary process. In most national systems, however, there seems to be little evidence of the presence of any coherent system linking political and financial management. Perhaps this is attributable in part to two decades in which macroeconomic management has often been driven by doctrine rather than any coherent conception of policy development linked to planned implementation strategies. For example, recent British, American and Canadian governments of the Right influenced by market-based ideas and a dislike of the public sector, have developed a particular concept of budgeting that audit is required to serve. The role of evaluation in all this has often been doubtful, with little logical integration between such evaluations that have been done and the budgeting and auditing processes.

Governments are not the only causes of failures to achieve logical integration. Frequently administrative institutions with their own partic-

ular interests ensure that the products of budgeting, auditing and evaluation are conceptualized in particular ways and kept as separate activities.
This is clear in the United Kingdom where there are inconsistent interests
between major players in these processes, in Finland where the fading
traditions of cameralism are incompatible with those of management,
and Spain where the dominant role of legalism has shaped development.

Organizational Integration

We define *organizational integration* as the ways that the structures
and processes of government bring together budgeting, auditing and
evaluation in a schematic order. This involves setting out the functions
and their institutions in an interlocking structure of responsibilities and
with networks of processual interrelationships. Such an arrangement
would allow the processes to contribute to and draw on each other to
produce a synergy in the management of government. The idealism of
such a system does not need to be overemphasized. It assumes not only
a deliberate strategy of organizational design but a concern with machinery of government questions that go to the heart of the political
process itself, i.e., the link between administrative *and* political forms in
the policy process. Such a fundamental approach is rare in recent political
history. Rather governments, for example in the United Kingdom and the
United States, have engaged in administrative tampering while leaving
political forms intact. This has rarely contributed to effective policy
making.

Evidence from the country chapters supports such conclusions. No
country has a clear scheme for the organizational integration of budgeting, auditing and evaluation, and few more for the simple integration of
budgeting and auditing. There is some evidence from German experience
that budgeting and auditing can be organized on a consistent basis but
the particular circumstances operating here results in evaluation remaining separate from these arrangements.

There is perhaps more evidence of organizational integration between
budgeting and evaluation particularly as this involves supreme audit
institutions. This is the case with regard to the General Accounting Office
in the United States and tha National Audit Office in the United Kingdom.
Elsewhere, results analysis in Sweden promises the strongest organizational integration of auditing and evaluation but, as in Finland where

political integration is characterized by conflict, in reality there is an important institutional division between the parliamentary audit of government and the governmental audit of operating agencies. In such circumstances organizational integration appears difficult if not impossible to achieve in practice.

What appears to exist in organizational terms is a series of bipolar links between the major activities in question that reflect the political and administrative histories of particular countries. Hence while auditing is structurally distinct from budgeting and evaluation in Canada, this can facilitate links between the two latter processes. In the United Kingdom, where arrangements are clearly different, there is a potential for closer organizational links between budgeting and evaluation, merging as a result of recent administrative reforms such as the Financial Management Initiative (FMI) and the creation of executive agencies. However, since budgeting remains in the hands of the Executive and the Treasury and evaluation is conceptualized in a narrow, cost-minimizing fashion, the value of these links has yet to be realized. In Spain, too, there are potential links between budgeting and auditing, budgeting and evaluation and auditing and evaluation. But again, possibly due to a centralist inheritance and a strong tradition of legalism, their operational significance remains weak, at least for the time being.

Informational Integration

Informational integration is shared data, information and communication systems between budgeting, auditing and evaluation. On the surface this requirement might seem to be a strictly technical one which, in an age of more sophisticated technology, improved statistics and data sets should be amenable to solutions. However, such a position would neglect the extent to which information is a currency in political life and that different approaches to the assembly, storage and use of information and data reflect different cultures and subcultures within political and administrative systems.

Unsurprisingly, therefore, the picture that emerges from the chapters is one of almost uniformly low integration. There are clear efforts to improve systems, particularly in the area of the management of government activities involving the development of performance indicators and management information systems. However, in terms of the evolution of a *common* framework that would facilitate the communication of budgeters, auditors and evaluators, there is little evidence of progress. On the positive side it might be argued that in Sweden the information bases of results analysis are used in budgeting while in Germany there is some information sharing between budgeting and auditing although, as Derlien reports, this excludes evaluation (Ch. 4). However, in the other countries described, informational integration is low if not nonexistent. Rather, as in the Tower of Babel, budget makers, auditors and evaluators develop sophisticated languages that serve their own purposes and interests and lead to products that are either ignored or disparaged by other parties.

Social Integration

Social integration is the homogeneity of culture, background, skill and experience of the personnel involved in budgeting, auditing and evaluation. Our hypothesis here is that such homogenity is necessary to service other aspects of integration, i.e., in an era where human resource management has finally been seen as important, and the active design of organizational cultures or even a common culture is crucial for political development.

The chapters show some evidence of shared backgrounds but never across all three processes. British experience offers a good example of this. With regard to the United Kingdom civil service, the social class and generalist homogeneity of the British administrative class is legendary and insofar as this relates to the development of budgeting and program evaluation within the major departments of state this contributes to common outlooks and shared norms. However, these generalists are increasingly distinct from the specialists in audit institutions in the United Kingdom (a development that itself follows some way behind the evolution of the General Accounting Office, in the United States). For the central administrators, budgeting and evaluation follow political ends but do not question them. This leads to tensions between administrators and external auditors. It also leads to particular conceptualizations of evaluation as this is performed *within* the administrative departments, and a failure to develop evaluation as a separate and valued activity.

In all this the United Kingdom is very unlike the United States, Canada and some other European countries. In these cases evaluation has professionalized in a more distinct sense both inside and outside government. This is reflected in the presence of designated "evaluators" within departments and within supreme audit institutions, and the emergence of professional societies that link academics and practitioners (e.g., the American Evaluation Association and the Canadian Evaluation Society). Perhaps as a consequence there is a collegiality in these countries that facilitates links between audit institutions and departments of state. There is also something of a shared socialization process and a common culture of evaluation.

Continental European countries reflect different patterns of social integration in which the influence of legal rationality and legal training seems clear. In Germany and, to a lesser extent Spain, for example, there appear to be close ties between budget-makers and auditors, most of whom share a legal background. This integration clearly has both functional and dysfunctional aspects, not least the exclusion of evaluation from these processes. Whether such a situation could be changed either by training or the infusion of different personnel remains an open question. Training on the job is clearly potentially important in promoting social integration and indeed is used in Sweden for personnel involved in all aspects of results analysis. However, even here the effectiveness of this development remains to be assessed.

Integration Assessed: Maturity in Political Systems

In an ideal and possibly utopian world, the separate dimensions of integration (logical, organizational, informational and social) would knit into a coherent whole. Further, a political system with a concern for developing and learning would install processes to ensure not only that these functions were developed separately but also that mechanisms were introduced to ensure their integration. Such a perspective comes close to Schick's model of a mature budgeting system discussed in Chapter 1. This was based on a developmental notion of integration by which the separate elements of budgetary systems evolved to become institutionalized adaptive systems. As was noted, this particular view of the world can be questioned. However, the discussion in this chapter allows us to suggest an alternative view of what a "mature" system of budgeting, auditing and evaluation might be. In this sense it is one where there are high levels of logical, organizational, informational and social integration.

As must be clear, this ideal type of system can only emerge if there is a move toward a common culture of political and administrative organizations or at least a set of cultures with sufficient communalities to permit cooperation between the budgeting, auditing and evaluation communities and an interchange of their products. However, the chapters above indicate that no country is mature is this sense or even moving toward such maturity.

In his earlier discussion of the evolution of program evaluation in a number of countries, Derlien has distinguished the phases of development into what he terms first and second wave countries (Derlien 1990). This classification identifies the first wave countries as the United States, Sweden, Canada and the Federal Republic of Germany, whose interest in policy evaluation can be traced back to the 1960s. These were followed by a second wave of countries, in particular the United Kingdom, Norway, Denmark, France and the Netherlands.

It is not our purpose to comment or question this classification here. Rather it is of interest to note that to some extent Derlien's "first wave" countries show perhaps the least immaturity in terms of integration. However, even in Sweden, which has a more coherent design than most countries for budgeting, auditing and evaluation, integration is limited and this is the case even *in* a deliberately constructed functional system. Indeed, from the Swedish example emerges a paradox echoed by other countries: that as a system of government institutionalizes budgeting, auditing and evaluation, it establishes barriers to their integration. The internal organization of government thus tends to differentiate into groups and organizations concerned with particular activities (e.g., budgeting) or across different activities (e.g., budgeting and auditing). Hence, as is clear from different national experiences, institutions develop their own cultures and communities and in turn their own interests that reflect the traditions of different parts of governments and the distinctive technologies and skills demanded by the differentiated functions. Consequently, the values of accountants, economists and program managers (quite apart from the politicians) come to have different institutionalized existences that do not always serve the holistic planning and control functions of budgeting, auditing and evaluation in consistent ways.

In part much of this is the product of piecemeal reforms or of the development of activities that Derlien, citing German experience, has identified as a "two-track" pattern. However, even when comprehensive development is sought, it might be argued that the improvement of budgeting, auditing and evaluation will always have an opportunity cost as long as these activities retain a separate organizational and institutional existence. Thus, a strengthening of the parts will frequently if not always be at some cost to the whole.

Preconditions for Effective Integration

It has always been tempting for politicians and administrative reformers to search for simple panaceas or technical fixes for perceived ills. Such an approach leads to fads, fashions and disillusionment. For example, two decades ago the rhetoric of rational planning was ushered in to solve the problems of budgeting - clear goals, option appraisal and assessment, and systematic evaluation would resolve the problems of policy choice and policy failure. Now this rhetoric has been replaced by the language of management accounting, operational management and markets. Cost control is a primary aim, and delegated budgets and systems of rewards and penalties are fashionable, while competition and markets within public sector activities are seen as the route to instant salvation.

The difficulties with approaches such as these is that they become ends in themselves rather than a means to an end. Indeed, in many instances they have the stamp of theology, set out as acts of faith to be questioned or denied only with peril. Such a stance, however, neglects the difficulties of designing change in political and administrative systems, of recognizing the heterogeneity of political and administrative activities and the organizational forces that develop over time. Hence, change is less the panacea or the quick fix than an engineered approach tailored to meet appropriate circumstances. As such both design and implementation are important. Change must not only be designed to fit particular sets of circumstances but its implementation must be feasible.

It is these arguments that lead us to explore how, if at all, budgeting, auditing and evaluation might be integrated within political systems that display different characteristics and, further, how the functions these processes serve can be realized effectively. From the experiences in different countries already set out we would argue that for such goals to be realized, a number of preconditions must be met or at least coped with.

These preconditions we will term technical, organizational, political and constitutional.

Technical Preconditions

As has already been indicated, it is too facile to assume that the simple availability of data and personnel will allow functions to be achieved in political systems. However, their absence means that great ideas frequently evaporate with some speed. For budgeting, auditing and evaluation to be performed and for their integration to be effective there seems to be little doubt that a need exists for purpose-designed structures and processes, user-led data, information and communication systems, and personnel with the requisite skills and orientations. A simple example of this need may be drawn from the world of government audit. Here, traditionally, routines demanded secure and often unchanging information systems and were operated by staff in a fashion that had changed little over decades. In contrast, the modern state audit office operates in a less rigid environment, calls on more sophisticated information systems, and utilizes a variety of differing professional skills to complete its assignments.

So what evidence is there of deliberate technical system design to facilitate the integration of budgeting, auditing and evaluation? From the countries studied here, only in Sweden is there much sign of efforts to purpose-design systems. At least there is some evidence of attempts to strengthen the results analysis process through the training of staff and the development of information systems. Elsewhere, however, information system weaknesses are widely cited. Both Spain and Finland, for example, suffer from a lack of appropriate systems and information. These examples may simply reflect the difficulties of countries trying to move a long way in a short time. However, even in more entrenched regimes, internal management information systems have only rarely been adequate to support changes to financial and budgetary systems, and even where they are developed they have been subject to political interference and abuse (for example, for the United Kingdom, see Gray & Jenkins 1991).

Systems on their own, however, are of little use without the presence of skilled staff to employ, understand and develop them. The demand for skills is not uniform throughout budgeting, auditing and evaluation.

However, it might also be argued that a low demand for skills can be interpreted as a sign of "immaturity" or at least of of political and administrative neglect of particular spheres of activity. Hence in the United States the status of evaluation is greater than in many other countries, perhaps because of a move into government generally (certainly in the pre-Reagan era) of economists, statisticians and operational researchers. This is reflected in the community of analysts in Washington who move in and out of budgeting, evaluation and, at least, in the General Accounting Office (GAO), the strong methodological underpinning of evaluative work.

In all this, however, one cannot neglect the nature of labor markets nor the fact that in many governments the ability to recruit professional skills (e.g., in accountancy) is limited by the salary differentials between public and private sectors. This may explain why in Germany it is difficult to obtain cost and management accountants to work on evaluations.

Organizational Preconditions

Earlier discussions suggested that the structural and processual integration of budgeting, auditing and evaluation is generally weak. This weakness, however, is not uniform across all the countries surveyed. In Sweden, for example, there is some attempt to process audits in connection with other reviews. However, the normal pattern observed in the countries examined is one of organizational fragmentation. This may have contributed significantly to past failures of budgetary reform and may limit changes that are currently taking place. Thus organizational fragmentation can be identified as one of the causes of the demise of planning, programming and budgeting (PPB) in the United States and of the Policy and Expenditure Management System (PEMS) in Canada. Similar problems have also occured in the United Kingdom, not least in relation to the more recent Financial Management Initiative (FMI). Thus while the FMI brought the prospect of processual links closer within departments, the continuing separation of procedures for expenditure planning from those for program control works against any significant and effective integration.

Similar organizational fragmentation is also identified in Germany, especially in the way budgeting and auditing are structurally and processually distinct from evaluation. From elsewhere emerges evidence that there are few incentives within political and administrative structures for organizations to integrate their procedures. For example in Canada, the way that savings are recouped by the center offers no inducement for departments or other agencies to integrate their systems or recoup savings, and in Spain the absence of consideration of rewards and punishments has contributed to various dysfunctions of budgeting, auditing and evaluation. These and other factors have had serious effects on other Spanish developments and have contributed to the difficulties encountered by the Spanish system in enhancing its "learning capacity" (Ch. 6).

Political Preconditions

Even if data sets were available, skilled staff in place and organizations designed to further the causes of budgeting, auditing and evaluation, would these activities come together effectively and succeed in changing the routines and norms of political and administrative life? To answer these questions demands some knowledge of power distribution within political systems and of the politics of organizational life, factors often either hidden from view or ignored.

For most program managers in administrative departments, budgeting, auditing and evaluation are at best necessary evils and, at worst, subversive threats to their programs if not themselves. Such managers are prepared to learn the rules of the budgetary game and the skills required for its playing but even here their posture is often essentially defensive. With regard to auditing and evaluation such a stance is similar but much more so unless a political interest or organizational advantage is seen to result from these activities. Such an interest can be brought about, as in budgeting, by predicating resources on participation, or by law (as in the case of audit) or by political authority being imposed (as appears to be the case of evaluations in the United States). However in many, if not most, systems examined there is really no systematic will to integrate because of the complexity and internal differentiation of the system. In particular the interests of managers, auditors, parliamentarians and ministers are differentiated. Although alliances can be forged, they tend to dissolve from issue to issue. Hence budgeting, auditing and evaluation take place within a shifting kaleidoscope of factional interests.

Away from organizational politics there is also no doubt of the importance of politics in the wider sense. Hence the history of the General Accounting Office demonstrates not only the distinct drives of bureaucrats and politicians but also the influence of Congress in advancing the office's cause. In this instance congressional politicians have a political interest (e.g., the furthering of their own political careers) in supporting the GAO and the integration of its activities. In contrast, countries such as Spain show that weak political support for integration has a clear demotivating effect on the budgeting, auditing and evaluating systems.

In terms of changing and integrating systems the importance of political will cannot be overestimated, since it is this more than anything else that can overcome organizational inertia at the lower levels of government. Thus Segsworth suggests that in Canada the changes that took place in 1988 were designed to impose a political solution on a recalcitrant (and essentially differentiated) system. In Britain, too, political support was important in imposing management reforms ranging from efficiency scrutinies, the FMI and the more recent creation of executive agencies. However, it is also worth noting that such changes promoted a particular type of integration in which objectives were not questioned, audit specified in a particular way and evaluation restrained. Consequently, while it might be argued that supreme political authority may be necessary to forge the integration of budgeting, auditing and evaluation, the paradox of this prescription is that the result is an integration that leaves the machinery of government intact.

Constitutional Preconditions

All of the governments discussed within this book operate within constitutional conventions whether written or unwritten. For the integration of budgeting, auditing and evaluation such factors are important, not least in countries with a legalistic or similar tradition. For example in Finland, the cameral tradition enshrined in the independence of constitutional and legal codes appears to have acted as an impediment to integration. The German and Spanish systems have displayed similar tendencies and difficulties. However, there is also evidence that such systems are not immutable where there is an appropriate political will.

Preconditions: Necessary or Sufficient?

The development of an integrated system of budgeting, auditing and evaluation appears to involve both policy formation and implementation. There needs to be a firm policy in political and administrative systems that these activities need to be developed and linked and for strategies to be designed to implement this. However, as any survey of the literature on policy making and implementation would demonstrate, this is no easy task, especially where goals are unclear and the world is populated by organisations and groups with varying priorities and interests.

Therefore, the discussion above should not be seen as a guide to the successful integration of budgeting, auditing and evaluation but rather as a map of constraints that have to be recognized and overcome. As Hood (1976) has pointed out, perfect implementation is rarely possible, and rather than seek it one should design policy initiatives with an eye toward the constraints their implementation faces. In the case of budgeting, auditing and evaluation these constraints (technical, organizational, political and constitutional) are also interlinked and influenced by specific contexts. Indeed the histories of budgeting, auditing and evaluation often reveal as much interesting information on the nature of the political system in which they are embedded as on the activities themselves.

However, while the country chapters set out different histories and different experiences, certain common factors stand out. First, in most if not all of the countries considered here, the major thrusts both to develop budgeting, auditing and evaluation and to link these activities has occurred during times of changing economic circumstances. In the 1960s and most of the 1970s these countries saw one or more of the following: an increase in spending on public programs, a rise in the number of central and local agencies implementing these programs and an increased separation between the funders and providers of these services. These are what Mathiasen (Ch. 2) suggests makes ideal conditions for the rise of the evaluative effort. In some cases this effort clearly followed; in others, however, while moves have been made to develop budgeting or to extend the role of audit, results have not matched ambitions, i.e., structures have not been able to adapt to changing pressures.

The 1980s, however, brought with them different pressures from the 1970s. During this period countries have witnessed a relative recession in their economies. The reaction to this has often been a shift of political priorities from the public to the private sector. This has also been accompanied by a change both in budgetary language and focus. Where once the budget makers focused on output and volumes of services they now focus on cost control and restraint. To this end the role of audit has also been enhanced and, here and there, forms of evaluation developed. Hence certain (if limited) integrative advances can be traced back to external economic pressures on political systems.

Such integration, however, varies according to the type of system being studied, not least in relation to its political history and culture. In Germany the separation of evaluation can be traced back to the domination of legalistic influences in the budgetary and auditing processes, while in the United Kingdom the presence of a strong executive system, which (during the 1980s) sought to advance New Right-type policies regarding the management of the state, clearly shaped developments in budgeting and auditing. The importance of political and administrative cultures can therefore not be underestimated. Budgeting, auditing and evaluation have rarely been developed or integrated according to economic logic but rather according to the logic of political systems. Yet this should not be surprising since what is functional in economic terms is often dysfunctional in political ones, that is, initiatives for change are assessed and advanced to the extent that they serve political ends whether these be the ideological ends of the center of government or the institutional ends that preserve the power of the core executive structure.

This last argument also supports our final point. In discussing the preconditions for the successful integration of budgeting, auditing and evaluation we have drawn attention to the importance of political influence in ensuring the implementation of change. Thus, however well the technical, organizational and constitutional preconditions may be met, they remain relatively spurious and ineffective if they lack political clout. In both the United States and the United Kingdom real change has followed high level interest and pressure on departmental and administrative systems. In brief, if reform is not on the *political* agenda its progress is likely to be patchy and its survival problematic.

Political clout, however, is likely to be used to promote changes compatible with rather than challenging to, the dominant political norms. Types of politics lead to types of implementation and types of budgeting, auditing and evaluation systems reflect the political cultures from which they emerge. This may be particularly the case in a strong central executive system with strong parties (e.g., in the United Kingdom) rather than a system with weak parties and a strong constitutional separation of powers (as in the United States). Such examples suggest that the advance of budgeting, auditing and evaluation is really a matter of constitutional reform and serious reshaping of the machinery of government arrangements rather than of advancing economic and managerial rationality within present systems.

Coda

In the assessment of private and public sector organizations it has been fashionable for some years to chart the criteria for excellence and success. This often follows the part of Peters and Waterman and their path-breaking volume, *In Search of Excellence* (1982). However, it is also often noted that many of the "excellent" companies of the early 1980s have now fallen on hard times and that Peters' message to managers has more recently focused on how to deal with chaos (1989)!

We mention these developments both as an encouragement and as a warning: an encouragement to seek evidence of success in administrative behaviour and a warning (already noted above) to beware of easy panaceas. We might also add that, in current times, the management of chaos and uncertainty might be as important for governments and public sector agencies as for private sector organizations.

The collected evidence in this volume reflects this absence of a panacea for would-be budgetary reformers. What we have found is less evidence of common and coherent strategies between functions, and patterns of integration of budgeting, auditing and evaluation than systems that reflect the differentiated traditions and political cultures of the countries themselves. In these terms success and excellence are relative concepts specific to particular circumstances and sets of conditions. Future improvements are also subject to compatibility with current constraints unless systems undergo more fundamental changes.

A second point that also arises from the analysis of different experiences is that even if it is possible to develop a coherent framework of functions for budgeting, auditing and evaluation to meet the technical, organizational and constitutional preconditions described, it is not possible to forge effective integration if external economic and specifically political forces are hostile. Accommodating such forces will have identifiable costs, while ignoring them also has its dangers. Effective change requires a supporting pattern of incentives. Integrating budgeting, auditing and evaluation might lead to the better management of the state, more informed choices or efficient feedback mechanisms that sustain, support and prevent future mistakes. Yet such products are not of themselves self-evidently *politically* advantageous; rather, this needs to be demonstrated. As the proverb at the head of this chapter notes, you can lead a horse to the water but you cannot make it drink . . . unless it is dying of thirst. Rather, the animal must be induced to indulge and this is more a process of skillful persuasion than threats. Hence the task for reformers may be to sharpen their marketing skills and sell their products. Failing this, the ability of governments to deal effectively with the chaos they face may be strictly limited.

References

Derlien, H-U. (1990). "Genesis and Structure of Evaluation Efforts in Comparative Perspective," Ch. 9. in R.C. Rist ed, *Program Evaluation and the Management of Government*. New Brunswick, N.J.: Transaction Publishers.

Gray, A.G. and W.I. Jenkins. (1985). *Administrative Politics in British Government*. Brighton: Harvester-Wheatsheaf.

Gray, A.G. and W.I. Jenkins with A.C. Flynn and B.A. Rutherford. (1991). "The Management of Change in Whitehall: the Experience of the FMI," *Public Administration*, 69/1, 41–60.

Hood, C. (1976). *The Limits of Administration*. London: J. Wiley.

Peters, T.J. and R.H. Waterman. (1982). *In Search of Excellence*. New York: Harper and Row.

Peters, T. (1989). *Thriving on Chaos*. London: Pan Books.

Rhodes, R.A.W. and P. Dunleavy. (1990). "Core Executive Studies in Britain," *Public Administration*, 68/1, 3–28.

Wildavsky, A. (1964). *The Politics of the Budgetary Process*. Boston: Little Brown.

Glossary

BOE	Spain's Official Journal of the State
BRH	Bundesrechnungshof; Federal Court of Audit (Germany)
BYOPs	Budget-year operational plans (Canada)
C & AG	Comptroller & Auditor General (UK)
CEA	Council of Economic Advisers (USA)
CIP	Committee for Public Investment (Spain)
DGB	Directorate-General for the Budget (Spain)
DOE	Department of the Environment (UK)
DTI	Department of Trade and Industry (UK)
EDA	Economic Development Administration (USA)
EEC	European Economic Community
EFTA	European Free Trade Association
FMI	Financial Management Initiative (UK)
FRG	Federal Republic of Germany
GAO	General Accounting Office (USA)
GIS	General Inspectorate of Services (Spain)
ID	Interventores Delegados: delegated auditors (Spain)
IGAE	Intervención General de la Administración del Estado: General Audit Office (Spain)
IIAS	International Institute for Administrative Sciences
IMAA	Increased Ministerial Authority and Accountability (Canada)
INTOSAI	International Organisation of Supreme Audit Institutions
IOS	Inspecciones Operativas de Servicios: audit of stadard operating procedures (Spain)
MBO	Management by Objectives
MEF	Ministry for the Economy and Finance (Spain)
MOUs	Memoranda of understanding
MYOPs	Multiyear operational plans (Canada)
NAO	National Audit Office (UK)
NHS	National Health Service (UK)

OCG	Office of the Comptroller General (Canada)
OECD	Organisation for Economic Cooperation and Development
OMB	Office of Management and Budget (USA)
OPMS	Operational Performance Measurement System (Canada)
PAC	Committee of Public Accounts (UK)
PAR	Programme Analysis and Review (UK)
PEMS	Policy and Expenditure Management System (Canada)
PES	Public Expenditure Survey (UK)
PPB	Planning, Programming and Budgeting
PPBS	Planning, Programming and Budgeting System
QUAGO	Quasi Autonomous Government Agency
QUANGO	Quasi Autonomous Non-Government Agency
RRV	Riksrevisionsverket: The National Audit Bureau (Sweden)
SAO	State Audit Office (Finland)
SEA	State Financial Management System (Sweden)
SOU	Swedish Civil Administration
UAB	Universidades Autónamas Barcelona (Spain)
VAT	Value Added Tax
VATT	Economic Research Centre (Finland)
VFM	Value-for-money
ZBB	Zero-based budgeting

Contributors

PERTTI AHONEN is professor of public administration/financial administration at the University of Tampere, Finland. He was with the Finnish State Audit Office from 1977 to 1985. With a Ph.D. in political science and a master's in business administration (accounting and fnance), his research focuses on public policy and politics, policy evaluation, public enterprises, and technology and industrial policies. He has published widely in books and journals in Finland and abroad. He is the vice-president of the Finnish Association for Administrative Studies.

HANS-ULRICH DERLIEN is professor of administrative science at the University of Bamberg, Germany. His research interest is in the political aspects of local and national government in general and policy evaluation and the administrative elite in particular. He has published widely in German and English including providing the comparative and concluding chapter in the IIAS Study Group's first volume, *Program Evaluation and the Management of Government* (1989). He has been working with the group since its inception.

ANDREW GRAY is reader in public accountability and management, Board of Studies in Accounting, University of Kent at Canterbury, UK. His books and articles on the political and accounting aspects of public management include *Administrative Politics in British Government* with Bill Jenkins, with whom he also directs the Public Sector Management Unit at the university. He has carried out teaching, research and consulting assignments for a variety of public organizations in ten countries.

BILL JENKINS is reader in public policy and management, Board of Social and Public Policy, University of Kent at Canterbury, UK. His founding status on the study group reflects his research interests in a wide range of aspects of public management in central and local government. His publications include *Policy Analysis* as well as numerous books and articles written with Andrew Gray. He has been a member of a health authority, acted as a consultant for a range of government bodies, and is now associate editor of the journal *Public Administration*.

DAVID MATHIASEN is the special assistant to the assistant controller general of the United States. He concentrates on budget and public management issues. He has held several senior posts in the U.S. Office of Management and Budget, the National Economic Commission, and has worked for the U.S. Agency for International Development in Turkey, India, Pakistan and the United States. He holds degrees from Oberlin College and the Woodrow Wilson School of Public and International Affairs of Princeton University and has been a lecturer and Becton Fellow at the School of Organization and

Management of Yale University. He is a fellow of the National Academy of Public Administration.

ROLF SANDAHL is the audit director, Financial Management Department, Swedish National Audit Bureau. Since gaining his Ph.D. in 1983 from the University of Uppsala he has maintained an interest in writing in the field, including "Bostadspolitiska styrmedel" ("Instruments of Swedish Housing Policy") (1983, "Offentlig styrning-en fraga om alternativ?" ("Instruments of Public Policy - a Question of Alternatives?") (1986), and "Resultatanalys" ("Results Analysis") (1991).

BOB SEGSWORTH is associate professor of political science and coordinator of the Diploma Programme in Public Administration at Laurentian University. Another founding member of the IIAS Group, his research interests include evaluation policy and Canadian public administration. He has published a number of articles in the *Canadian Journal of Program Evaluation, Canadian Public Administration*, the *International Review of Administrative Sciences*, and *Public Policy and Administrative Sciences*.

ESA TAMMELIN is head of the Planning Division in the State Audit Office of Finland. He is responsible for the office's annual planning and the development work of different audit methods. During the last few years his special interest has been in improving the methods used in the SAO's performance auditing area.

EDUARDO ZAPICO GONI is currently head of the Public Management Unit at the European Institute of Public Administration (EIPA). He gained degrees from the University Complutense of Madrid and the University of New York (MPA) before working on a doctoral thesis on public budgeting reform in Spain. He worked as a finance inspector in the Ministry for Economy and Finance in Madrid. He also taught and carried out research at the National Institute of Public Administration in Spain. His fields of interest and publications are public budgeting, financial management and comparative public management.

Index